M000101808

LOVE BOTH
KEEP BOTH

PASSPORT TO PEACE, PROSPERITY
AND STRENGTHENED DIPLOMACY.

LOVE BOTH
KEEP BOTH

PASSPORT TO PEACE, PROSPERITY
AND STRENGTHENED DIPLOMACY.

KEN REIMAN

Indigo River Publishing

Copyright © 2019 by **Ken Reiman**

All rights reserved. No portion of this publication may be reproduced, stored in a retrieval system, or transmitted by any means—electronic, mechanical, photocopying, recording, or any other—except for brief quotations in printed reviews, without the prior written permission of the publisher.

Indigo River Publishing
3 West Garden Street, Ste. 718
Pensacola, FL 32502
www.indigoriverpublishing.com

Editors: Deborah DeNicola and Joshua Owens
Cover Design: Robin Vuchnich

Ordering Information:
Quantity sales: Special discounts are available on quantity purchases by corporations, associations, and others. For details, contact the publisher at the address above.

Orders by US trade bookstores and wholesalers: Please contact the publisher at the address above.

Printed in the United States of America

Library of Congress Control Number: 2019941852

ISBN: 978-1-950906-05-5

First Edition

With Indigo River Publishing, you can always expect great books, strong voices, and meaningful messages. Most importantly, you'll always find . . . words worth reading.

CONTENTS

NOTE OF THANKS

This book is in honor of those who came before and those who follow our footsteps to advance the cause of social justice and equal opportunity regardless of race, religion, gender, or dual nationality. To the Jesuit Fathers that taught me the importance of social justice and remaining true to one's principles, I am grateful. To the Poor Sisters of St. Joseph who opened your home and your hearts to us when my family was evacuated out of Burkina Faso, thank you. This is also dedicated to my sons, John Francis Reiman and Max Joseph Reiman: may you fight for your heritage and make your ancestors proud. Finally, to my American and Japanese grandmothers, my dual saints, may your love transform the world and make it more welcoming and tolerant of others. Thank you for inspiring me. There are countless other people from my editor to mentors and friends who made this book dream into a reality. Thank you to everyone who helped me along the way. Lastly, my wife Eriko deserves the greatest thank you for her patience and unending support, looking after our family and our two beautiful boys while I was working on this book.

DISCLAIMER

The views expressed in this manuscript are strictly those of the author and do not necessarily represent the views of the U.S. Department of State or any official or office in the U.S. government. Most of the names used are of real people; however, the names of *some* individuals and modified identifying features of others, as well as some places, have been slightly altered in order to preserve their anonymity. The goal in all cases was to protect these people's privacy without damaging the integrity of this true story.

Preface

When we speak of minorities, we often speak in terms of broad generalities. We group people together as Blacks, Latinos, Native Americans, Asians, and other ethnic categories without delving deeper into the various subgroups and sub-identities found within each minority group. These days, more and more individuals consider themselves "hybrid" – a combination of two or more ethnic groups. And we often do not have an honest conversation or dialogue on race either in the United States or Japan.

Whatever term we use to describe people of mixed heritage, all of us are in some form "mixed." Just as cultures blend and styles change, human beings commingle and reproduce among people of different backgrounds – historic, ethnic, religious, and other distinctions. The sense of either acceptance or alienation an individual may feel within mainstream society depends upon his or her unique experience and the life events and people one encounters along the way.

There is even a danger in stereotyping Caucasians as there is no monolithic identity. Irish, Polish, Russian, Italian, and other European individuals who immigrated to the United States from Europe have their own unique history, tradition, and experiences. So do U.S. citizens of Vietnamese, Taiwanese, Chinese, and Korean ancestry. I can only speak from my own experiences as a Japanese American, but some people from different ethnic backgrounds might draw parallels from my own experience while others may gain greater insight into the complexities involved in juggling dual identities, especially in governments that all too often recognize only one.

There will be critics of dual or triple nationality, individuals who narrowly argue for only one passport. I count them among my friends. I do not judge their mono-nationality, so why should they judge my dual nationality? Jealousy? Feelings of unfairness? Are dual nationals in their minds prone to criminality or disloyalty to one country or another? I would argue the opposite. Dual nationals are an asset. One can be fully American and fully Japanese. Why can I not represent the beauty of both people? The world is not simply composed of governments but people who, like me, have a love and respect for more than one heritage. For me, my dual U.S. and Japanese nationality is part of who I am. Born with both, I believe strongly that neither government should ask me to refuse one or choose one. *I choose to have both.*

Mixed children are common and continue to increase as individuals from various continents join hands in holy matrimony. Their experience will shape future generations. Society will need to adjust and governments will need to accommodate to the demands of a new political clientele – the "mixed generation" whose loyalties are to various competing interests that are not mutually exclusive and go beyond the boundaries of one particular nation-state. One can be a loyal American and a loyal Japanese. When will nation-states and their respective intelligence branches and governmental departments learn to nurture that dual identity to the advantage of all—as opposed to attempting to own exclusive ownership rights to an individual's entire being by forcing him to choose one nationality? Forcing one choice is counterproductive. It's also unhealthy.

I am telling my story for four simple reasons: first, to allow my soul to feel liberated from restrictions placed on my "duality" by society and government. I elect to fight against prejudicial statements such as, "Your mother is Japanese so we doubt your loyalty to nation and country" as incorporated all too frequently into government policies in the hiring, recruitment, and assignments process. The same discriminatory rhetoric is heard among many Japanese who have often let me know in not too subtle a manner that, "You're an American so you can never understand the unique Japanese spirit nor be one of us." I oppose such rhetoric, statements or policies that are meant to demean, demoralize, and defeat the spirit into believing that one can only be either Japanese or American, but never both at the same time.

Secondly, I want to bring the Japanese-American story to the forefront of ethnographic discourse. We often hear of Japanese-Americans taken prisoner and stripped of their property and livelihoods during World War II in internment camps, but we do not have much literature or ethnographic accounts since then. Sure, we have some fictitious stories involving Japanese American families, but no TV sitcoms or major best sellers involving the Japanese-American experience in America outside of the internment camp narrative. Robert Kiyosaki's *Rich Dad, Poor Dad* is a case in point. His book gained national attention not for insights into the Japanese-American community, but for his tips on how to become wealthy. In other words, a book on and about a Japanese American's experience written by a Japanese American is long overdue.

Thirdly, my intention is to bring forth the prejudices present on both sides of the Pacific divide—in Japan and in the U.S. Unlike the Chinese-American experience, Japanese seldom welcome with open arms Japanese that have either left the islands, are not fluent Japanese language speakers, or do not "look" Japanese. I have the advantage of speaking the language fluently, but the disadvantage of not "looking" one hundred percent Japanese. I will always be viewed as a foreigner because of my appearance. No amount of fluency in the Japanese language or knowledge of Japan and its people or history will change that fact. The economic cost is that Japan will not be able to take advantage of highly talented individuals who choose to stay abroad and contribute to the development of other economies, not because they do not want to contribute to Japan's social and economic advancement, but because they do not feel welcome in a society that places a premium on race, ethnicity, language, and national identity.

From an opposite angle, most Americans will continue to view me in terms of sushi, karate, Hondas, and Pearl Harbor. Many Americans associate my Japanese heritage as somehow related to the Japanese government's attack on Pearl Harbor. I still distinctly recall my fourth grade classmates in Tempe, Arizona staring at me and asking why my family attacked Pearl Harbor during a history class on World War II. All I can remember is that I felt guilty for committing some terrible crime when neither my family nor I had any involvement in World War II. At that age, I didn't understand why I was somehow seen as part of the enemy.

I grew to understand that the media plays a significant role in portraying people of certain ethnic groups, or races, as behaving in a certain way, even defining them by spreading stereotypes that most of us can live without. The Japanese media is in no way exempt from such patterns of behavior (see *A Public Betrayed* by Adam Gamble and Takesato Watanabe), but its reports on the United States and its citizenry tend to be far more extensive than the amount of time the U.S. media spends reporting on Japan. Of all the time I spent in Japan, I never had a Japanese person point at me for dropping atomic bombs on Hiroshima and Nagasaki.

And fourth, I write this personal story to encourage the next generation of Japanese Americans to examine their roots and take pride in their unique heritage against the backdrop of a society and political structure that still does not know how to fully embrace "duality." There is nothing wrong about wanting a win-win situation for two different countries and cultures at the same time. Governments can benefit from maximizing the talents of dual national citizens. Just remember, you are not less American or less Japanese because one society or group wants you to conform to only their particular set of norms or regulations. You have a choice. Embrace both your American and Japanese heritage because ultimately, you are an Ambassador to both nations– even if neither knows how to fully embrace you.

My name is Ken Reiman. I am a Japanese American. This is my unique story and value proposition to forever alter U.S.-Japan relations, and ultimately, create more open, tolerant societies on both sides of the Pacific divide. *LOVE BOTH KEEP BOTH* is ultimately all about human dignity and love—applicable to each and every one of us regardless of race, nationality or heritage. When we embrace our diversity, we embrace humanity. When we embrace humanity, we honor God's creation.

Introduction

There is no country called "half." Most of us are born in one country and hold only one passport and nationality. Yet statistics reveal that dual nationality is soaring in both the United States and Japan with actual unreported numbers two or three times higher. Parents are opting to give the gift of both nationalities to their children, and why not? The U.S. and Japan represent two of the three largest and most powerful economies in the world with combined annual wealth of $24 trillion. With dual nationality come benefits beyond economic, what I call *cultural capital*. The gift of two cultures, two languages, and two identities. Why settle for one if you can keep two?

Growing up bilingual, bicultural, and biracial as a youngster in the streets of Tokyo and deserts of Arizona, I knew my parents were giving me a gift that I did not quite fully understand. My parents were by no means rich, famous, or powerful. My mother came to the United States as an immigrant. My father cleaned hospital instruments for a living and was raised by a single mother in New York. What they lacked in resources, however, was compensated for by hard work, love, and education. They instilled in me a love for both countries, invested in language lessons for me, and made sure what opposition they faced in their interracial marriage would not prevent me from loving both sets of people and cultures.

My parents raised me to appreciate my duality, but they could not protect me from prejudices faced outside the home. I faced bullying and discrimination growing up in Japan for being the "white, foreign, American" who was viewed as "half" Japanese but never accepted as fully Japanese. I remember one particular experience when I was walking home from school on a bright, sunny afternoon, and I saw a group of kids that I knew from down the street playing a game. As I approached them to participate, one of the kids looked me directly in the eyes and told me I wasn't welcome. At the time, this experience rocked my world. In contrast, in the U.S., I was just as American as the kid sitting next to me, who happened to be Muslim and from Bangladesh. While being half Japanese didn't necessarily make me unique in the U.S., I certainly felt that way when all eyes turned to me during discussions of Pearl Harbor.

As I grew older, I started to realize that what I considered natural seemed "foreign" to others, and I found great meaning in translating two vastly different cultural sets of values to others. At first, it was difficult for me to understand why others would harbor any animosity toward the other country. These were two countries rich in history and culture, two countries I loved dearly, two countries that have much to offer each other and the world. United, these two countries can accomplish so much. Divided both suffer. *LOVE BOTH KEEP BOTH* offers a simple lesson: be who you are and accept both heritages at all costs. Doing so is only human. I learned this lesson the hard way and do not want others to make the same mistakes I did. Embrace both. Do not let fear or pressure or intimidation strip you of your dual dignity and rights.

You would assume that of all the federal agencies, the Department of State, which champions mutual understanding and advancing human rights, would also champion the dignity of dual nationals. Far from it. The Department of State's Foreign Affairs Manual (FAM) has a provision in 3 FAM 2424.5 on Dual Nationality which does not permit its employees to be assigned in states in which they are nationals without renouncing their non-U.S. nationality. This provision is dated December 11, 2017, three days after the U.S. entered World War II by declaring war on Japan 75 years prior. It's time to champion peace and let dual nationals live in peace too.

My dream, since day one entering the U.S. Foreign Service

in 2002, was to serve in Japan to advance U.S.-Japan relations as a diplomat; my desire was to go beyond World War II animosities and the tragedies of the Japanese internment camps to create a more positive narrative on the U.S.-Japan relationship. After all, I had spent my entire life learning Japanese and studying Japanese culture with hopes of becoming a bridge to two societies. It was also the reason the Department of State recruited me. Throughout this period my dual nationality was never a secret. Upon entering the Foreign Service I received an immediate letter notifying me that I would be precluded from serving in Japan. I was led to believe that I could serve in Japan at some point after that initial preclusion was lifted. I just needed to prove my loyalty, I was told by others, and serve in other countries and get known to the Japan policy decision-makers. I accomplished all of that over 16 years, only to be told once again, based on newer FAM guidelines that only through renunciation could my dream be made possible.

Imagine having your dream shattered over and over again, applying for Japan positions, lobbying to be sent, meeting the right people, going to Human Resources, and having your family members renounce their ties to Japan too. After five years, and tours in Taiwan and Nigeria, I was finally able to have my preclusion to Japan lifted in 2007. But that did not lead to an assignment in Japan. Time and time again, my dream was denied on account of my background, the very background that would make me an effective representative of the United States in Japan. Each rejection was way more painful than the last.

Fluent in Japanese and knowledgeable of Japanese culture, the U.S. taxpayer would also save money in that the U.S. government would not need to provide years of language and cultural training. I already possess both. The reason the State Department recruited me was to bring diversity within the ranks of the diplomatic corps. If the State Department cannot effectively utilize the talents and skills of dual nationals, other organizations will. The Japanese government also does not accept dual nationality. It is time for both governments to reconsider their policies toward dual nationals for the sake of creating a more humane and robust U.S.-Japan alliance.

Preventing dual national diplomats with fluency in both countries' languages and culture from serving in their country of origin is not only harmful to the employee eager to serve, but a wasted diplomatic resource in a time when U.S.-Japan relations matter most. The future of Asia hinges upon a solid relationship and partnership between the U.S. and Japan. This is not possible if both governments discard their greatest asset: dual nationals eager to utilize their background to advance that partnership. With the nuclear threat of North Korea ever present, China's growing military assertiveness, and Russia's subversion of democracy, we need a strong U.S.-Japan alliance now more than ever.

Fear and ignorance breed prejudice and hatred. Those elements, unfortunately, seep into government policy. You would think two governments would welcome dual nationality if they viewed dual nationals as assets rather than liabilities as other non-governmental and private sector organizations do. This book presents a real life human face to a dual national diplomat's dilemma to live in a world that only understands one or the other. I decided to live my life according to my terms and accept who I am even in the face of prejudice and discrimination. I found that the organization that claimed to preach diversity, did not live up to those ideals when it came to dual nationals. But like any challenge and obstacle in life, raising awareness is the first step in changing people's hearts and minds. I remain hopeful that in writing this book, others will benefit from the sacrifices I made and that it will help pave the way for other dual nationals – Japanese-Americans and others alike.

As I was struggling to reconcile my dual national identities and embrace my diversity, I looked for answers in books. But I could find no memoirs on the topic of dual nationality and diplomacy, let alone a current book about a dual national U.S. diplomat's journey for inspiration and guidance. I could find no book that calls on governments and the general public to allow dual nationals to love and keep both nationalities without renouncing either nationality. In response, I decided I should write a memoir to help others and inspire the growing population of dual nationals to embrace their extraordinary background to transform the world for the better.

Dual nationality is part of the diversity I bring and giving up one or the other is akin to giving up half of who I am. Two of the most powerful economies and richest countries in the world can surely come together to change legislation to protect and promote dual nationality among its citizenry. We do not ask people to choose between loving one's father or one's mother. Let's not ask dual nationals to make that same choice either. If I have to choose, I choose both.

Championing diversity and dual national rights among government institutions that do not appreciate the human and health costs involved in such a decision is not easy, but denying yourself acceptance of who you are comes at an exponentially greater cost. Try as I may, I could not abandon either country because I refuse to give up on either one. I believe in America and I believe in Japan. I cannot give up loving both. Keeping both nationalities is my way of declaring my love for both people and societies. It is not a government decision; it is a people decision. A decision straight from the heart. I was a dual national at birth, not by choice. As an adult, I made the choice to keep both and to love both.

Through it all, I have overcome prejudice with love and continue to champion a duality that I believe comes from God. I believe my mission in life is to carry two crosses – one American and one Japanese. This story is uniquely mine, but it could very well apply to you. Somewhere in your DNA, you probably have a mix of cultures and identities too. It just may not be as pronounced if you were never afforded the opportunity to view yourself as multifaceted nor given the educational gift of learning your heritage and culture. Whatever crosses you bear, bear them all. Accept all of who you are, as God intended you to be. Be fully yourself; be fully alive. This book shows us how to do so and inspires readers never to give up on themselves and their dreams. We are all part of a duality continuum that starts with Adam and Eve. With many people now able to check their DNA and personal genome, we are proving the spiritual tenet that we are all one human family.

Chapter One

"I want to lead an important life. I want to do it because I was born a human being."

~Eiji Yoshikawa

I made it into the U.S. Foreign Service as a diplomat to represent the country that provided my family and me so many opportunities. I made it to a pinnacle of success even greater than I might have ever imagined, prepared to use my bilingual/bicultural background to serve America the best way I knew how – as a U.S. diplomat in Japan where I could advance U.S.-Japan relations. This was my dream since day 1 in entering the diplomatic corps. Surely, 22 years of investing in Japanese language and culture and my dual background would be viewed as an asset or so I believed. There's no way dual nationality could prevent my dreams from coming true. After all, the U.S. and Japan are the closest of allies. But not close enough, as I learned, to allow dual nationals to love both. I had countless lessons to learn about navigating the diplomatic terrain but had no dual national mentors to show me the way.

A handbook on how to balance dual identities growing up in Tempe and Fountain Hills, Arizona does not exist. Born to Etsuko

Reiman, a Japanese citizen, and Carl Reiman, a United States citizen, I never thought twice of bilingualism or biculturalism. As far as I was concerned, these were mere academic terms that my mother used in her own research and writing on bilingual education as a Professor of Asian Languages and Literature at Arizona State University. Little did I know at the time about the sacrifices my parents made in raising me to speak and understand a language and culture so different from my place of birth, Iowa City, Iowa.

No Japanese American schools or language institutes existed in Tempe, Arizona to train a child in English and Japanese. So my mother took on the task of speaking Japanese to me at home, and hiring Japanese graduate students to tutor me in writing Japanese. She took me with her to Japan every summer to live with my Japanese grandmother (my grandfather had long passed away) and attend public schools in Japan when the American schools entered summer vacation. My father had the unenviable task of staying in the United States working and taking care of the house for three months while mother and son stayed in Japan.

In Japan, my mother would conduct research on *Kokuji*—distinct Japanese characters created by the Japanese that are not found in Chinese characters—while I attended school like any ordinary Japanese citizen. I wore my school uniform and carried my *kaban* or school backpack on my shoulders equipped with textbooks, notebooks, and school supplies. For three months I was a Japanese student studying in an all-Japanese school. Naturally, as the only non-Japanese and light skinned kid in the class, students would often stare and be very curious about me. But we played together, ate lunch together, studied together, and did all the things young Japanese school kids typically do during the summer, watch animation, participate in *matsuri* or festivals, play baseball, eat watermelon, and do summer homework.

While all my school friends in the United States enjoyed summer vacation, mine was spent attending summer school in Japan where summer vacation was only one month. In addition, we were assigned homework we needed to complete during our "vacation." A lasting influence on me during this period was the impact of my Japanese grandmother who daily made me breakfast. She was the first person I saw when I returned from school, and the first to warmly welcome me home with one of her homemade Japanese meals I still miss to this day. Through living with her, I learned that the Japanese language consisted of various polite niceties and sayings that one would use according to rank, stature, age or gender of the individual you were speaking with.

It was an excellent introduction to the complex Japanese communication system of *sonkeigo* (praising your guest) and *kenjyogo* (humbling yourself and achievements to raise your partner's stature). I also realized that men and women were taught to speak Japanese differently and end their sentences in a masculine or feminine sentence structure as defined by Japanese social and gender norms. Indirect and subtle forms of communication replaced the often comparatively direct and straightforward form of communication I was accustomed to in the United States or when speaking English.

My Japanese grandmother was also the first to comfort me when kids at school bullied me for not conforming to Japanese standards. I could never understand why I was not accepted because in my mind, I spoke Japanese, had a Japanese mother and grandmother, and was every bit as Japanese as the next kid. The only difference was that my father happened to be a Caucasian American. In addition, since I was young, my mother had applied for Japanese citizenship for me in case something happened to my father and she needed to raise me in Japan. I had a Japanese passport and yet I could never understand why I could not pass as Japanese.

As years passed, I understood that it was not common for an American or half-white kid to attend Japanese public school nor was it common for one to speak Japanese. I was an oddity. I would often cry to my grandmother asking why I was bullied. My grandmother and mother decided to have me transferred to a different public primary school. Things improved. My life changed when I entered secondary school in Bunkyo Ward in Tokyo during the summers of 7th, 8th, and 9th grades.

In the United States, my American grandmother would often notice that my facial expressions and hand gestures would change automatically when I had to change from speaking English to Japanese. I can only describe it as an automatic light switch that turns on and off based on whether I am speaking English or Japanese or depending upon the audience. I do this unconsciously, and have witnessed other bilingual and bicultural children do the same. My parallel ties to both cultures go as far back as my early childhood when my American grandmother would read me "Mother Goose" stories, while my mother would read traditional Japanese children's stories like *Momotaro* or Peach Boy.

At home, we spoke both English and Japanese. We ate pasta, apple pie, and celebrated American traditions such as Thanksgiving while at the same time enjoying Japanese food and eating *mochi* or rice cakes on New Year's Day. We used chopsticks as well as forks, spoons, and knives. We listened to Japanese and American songs. We drank beer and *sake* (well, only when my father allowed me to take sips secretly from his cup while my mother wasn't looking). I was fortunate to have two grandmothers (both sets of grandfathers had passed away earlier) and two parents from different sides of the Pacific and blessed to attend schools in the U.S. and Japan, the birthplace of my dual identity. I was proud of my unique upbringing. I was taught to love and respect everything Japanese and American about me. Little did I know of the future burdens that dual nationality and identity would entail.

Because I identified myself as being outside of mainstream white America, I gravitated towards people of color. One of my childhood friends, and still one of my best friends, is a Nigerian-American. My other friends also tended to be Korean-American, Chinese-American, with some multiethnic or multilingual background, or foreign.

My Japanese identity made me feel like an outsider and a foreigner, separate from my American classmates. Although I had no difficulty interacting with all of my classmates, I felt the strongest bonds to minority students. I sensed that we shared a common experience in a society dominated by a predominantly white majority.

We were always taught to study harder and work harder to achieve success in life because we did not have the same luxuries of time and capital as our wealthier white friends – at least that was the mentality I had growing up. I can truthfully say that I've always felt welcome in the African-American community. And the Nigerian, Ghanaian and Burkinabe people welcomed me with open arms during my Foreign Service postings overseas and in DC. Embracing others allows them to embrace you. I now have a West African community that I can call on along with an East Asian one. Connect the diplomatic dots and your world just gets that much richer! You've created your own continental shift.

As time went by and I joined the predominately white male Foreign Service, I realized that my own biases and definitions of "whiteness" or "color" became murky and I learned that we deceive ourselves with silly classifications based on race that never hold water. The Irish-American and Polish-American and Italian-American have a unique duality too. I adjusted my lens to include all people because that is the only way we learn about ourselves and grow in our common humanity.

I cannot deny my white background just as I cannot eliminate my Japanese heritage. I live with both. What amazes me is that the Voters Right Act of 1965 signed by President Lyndon Johnson granting blacks the right to vote and eliminating discriminatory prerequisites for voting such as literacy tests has to be renewed every so often by Congress for blacks to vote. This is one of the most ridiculous and absurd policies. African Americans or blacks in the United States who hold U.S. citizenship should be able to vote without the President of the United States or Congress having to renew this Act. There should be no questions asked and no bills signed. White Americans don't need Congress or the U.S. President to renew an act every 15 years to allow whites to vote, why should blacks? This is a form of duality that we all need to question regarding what purpose it serves and who it benefits. Segregation and prolonged separation helps no one. It simply breeds further distrust, suspicion, division and discrimination. How can we combine the best of both worlds? Dual nationals and supporters of dual nationality can provide that answer: empathy toward others starts at home.

∞∞∞

Education and Exposure
Create a Dual Environment for Success
Let Your Diversity Shine Through

Fitting in is not fitting in if you are not wearing the right shoe size. An ideal job is not an ideal job unless the culture and people feel right. When you carry two cultures or identities that are dramatically different from one another, even at times opposed to each other, the first step is to recognize and acknowledge those differences within yourself. Exposing yourself to other cultures to help illuminate your way forward allows you to grow and translate your values cross-culturally. My effectiveness as a Foreign Service Officer depended upon increasing my awareness and cultural sensitivity toward others who do not share my background in order to create common bonds. Those bonds led to business opportunities that have expanded my circle of friends beyond government and academia. The more diversity you have, the easier it is for you to connect with an array of people, expanding and enriching your life—spiritually, professionally, and financially further. Diversity keeps humanity moving forward, leads to innovation, and is the only diplomatic solution for peace. By affirming dual nationality, we are affirming humanity.

In a world of division and hate, we need at minimum a double dose of understanding and love. Dual nationals double our chance for peace if we create an environment that allows their diversity to shine through too.

Two is Always Better than One

I encourage you to think about two people you love. This may be your parents, foster parents, grandparents or other close family figures. If you did not grow up knowing both your biological parents, think of a coach or teacher or another individual that played that role for you. Write down in one sentence what you positively learned, inherited, gained from the two most important people in your life. Meditate on how they educated and exposed you to greater truths beyond yourself. Read aloud your sentence and affirm your values and connection to them. Below are my own examples:

1. I am the son of Etsuko Reiman, an immigrant mother who taught me that Japan has much to offer the world.

2. I am the son of Carl Reiman, an American father who taught me that it's ok to seek truth in different religious traditions.

Now, expand that list to include other people who shaped your worldview and had a profound, transformational impact on your life.

3. I am the grandson of Kuniko Obata, a Japanese Buddhist grandmother who led me to Christ.

4. I am the friend of Mohamed Albusaidi, an Omani Muslim who taught me that the Arab World and Muslims are my brothers and sisters too.

Connecting Your Diplomatic Dots

This exercise allows you to connect the dots of diversity in your life. Imagine losing any one of those dots. You lose a crucial connection between you, the world, and all the diversity of ideas, people, and resources that could help you and your family succeed for generations to come. Spend a moment to remember these figures who made you into the person you are today. Now read your sentences again in gratitude to reaffirm who you are and thank those people who cared enough about you to invest in you. When you do this, two things happen. First, you realize that you are not alone. Someone is always there along with you on your journey. Second, you recognize that you can always learn something from someone completely different than you. Be open to further education and exploration.

When we connect our diplomatic dots that's when we can make the impossible, possible, and envision the best of both worlds as opposed to thinking in terms of a clash of civilizations in which no side wins. Love does not dominate but cultivates. If we sow the seeds of hatred by denying dual nationals their right to be who they are, reject the diversity inherent in their dual nationality, prevent them from loving both people and countries, and label those who chose both as disloyal and unpatriotic, we lose a part of our humanity.

There is a way for individuals to be loyal to both. If I can be loyal to the State of Arizona (where I was raised), the State of Iowa (where I was born), the State of Virginia (where I own a home), and the United States of America (whose interests I defend as a diplomat), there is no contradiction. No one is asking me to renounce one state over another, so why ask dual nationals to renounce one nation over another? Some would argue that in the case of the United States and Japan, Japan's entire existence is dependent upon the U.S. military and nuclear shield; that Japan is more like a 51st state of the United States. I do not prescribe to that view, but I do believe the U.S.-Japan alliance is unique enough and robust enough to allow dual nationals to be viewed as invaluable assets to the future success of both nations.

How we imagine the world shapes how we live in it. Peace in the Middle East is possible when humans embrace their common humanity and create a dual environment for success that cultivates trust versus fear. We then can move on to create a model for multilateral success. But first we need to start with two partners and two allies and two concrete action plans for accepting dual nationals as valued assets. Why not start with the U.S. and Japan, East and West, to demonstrate our global leadership and renewed sense of commitment to each other's success? Two is always better than one. If General Motors and Honda can partner on next-generational fuel-cell technologies to create economies of scale and drive down costs to benefit consumers, there should be no reason why the U.S. and Japan can't partner at the governmental level to create an economy of dual nationality and reduce costs for taxpayers on both sides of the Pacific.

When we acknowledge duality, we acknowledge diversity. When we acknowledge diversity we acknowledge divinity. The first letter "d" in duality represents, after all, the same letter found in the beginning of the Latin word for God – *Deus* – the source of all inspiration and diversity. Our duality can and should be turned into a gift of the most divine kind when both nations keep their diplomatic agendas in line with God's mind. Becoming the number one and number three largest economies in the world means nothing if both ignore the source from which their wealth derives. If we cannot see God in each other, then we cannot see God at all.

For those more scientifically inclined, $E=MC^2$ is an equation most of us have learned from the Nobel laureate Albert Einstein, a holder of triple nationality. Einstein held German, Swiss, and U.S. citizenship. He also was fervently against racism and discrimination and was a champion of diversity and civil rights. Imagine the loss to science and humanity if Einstein was asked to renounce his citizenship and serve only one nation. He adamantly demanded to be allowed to keep his Swiss nationality as a condition to work at the Prussian Academy of Sciences where he laid further groundwork to the field of quantum physics. Had he been denied the opportunity to retain his Swiss and U.S. citizenships, he very well could have lost his life in a German concentration camp or been forced to develop a nuclear weapons program for Nazi Germany against the United States. Either scenario paints a gruesome picture. If governments had prevented Einstein from retaining his dual nationality and demanded renunciation, a great mind like Einstein's would have forever been lost along with his countless scientific achievements.

The Polish Saint Maximilian Kolbe is reportedly known for sharing his own equation that is much less known to the world: $w=W$. The lower case w representing our will and the capital W representing God's Will. When our will is aligned with God's Will, anything and everything becomes possible. There's nothing wrong with a little divine intervention. On many occasions I have turned to God for assistance before, during, and after a diplomatic crisis. He answers the call of those He loves. Perhaps if we loved God more we would learn how to love each other more.

We can learn many lessons from religious figures whether Catholic, Buddhist, Jewish, Muslim, atheist or everything in-between. I regret that diplomats, I have found, chase after another kind of wealth rooted in status, titles, power, and promotions that ultimately never lead to peace of mind. An hour of mandatory meditation or prayer for diplomats who are often operating in high-paced, high stress environments is one way to keep diplomatic minds sane. Good diet and exercise are needed to keep the heart healthy and the mind alert. Daily rituals or routines have also proven to help lower stress levels and provide the self-regulation needed for all of us to lead and manage our hectic lives.

DIPLOMACY AND DEUS

Know any other individuals who remind you of a dual nature, fundamental to our own understanding and belief in him or her? I can. I look to Jesus. For the Catholic, the Church teaches us that Jesus was both fully divine and human. In other words, he was both God and man. Do any of us dare to ask Jesus to choose to only be one or the other? Had he not carried both crosses I wouldn't be here writing this memoir today. If God himself asked you to accept his duality would you deny Him? I know I wouldn't. Better to let God be God and dual nationals be dual nationals. Now let's move back to what we can do to understand the diversity of duality and promote that within ourselves and others. Here's how:

YOUR OWN PERSONAL GAME PLAN
~3 SIMPLE STEPS TO PUT DUALITY IN ACTION~

1. *Write Down Your 1-Sentence Diversity Affirmation Statements. People who loved you enough to invest in you will inspire you to honor yourself and them by becoming fully yourself.* I wasn't born alone. Instead, it was because of two people, my father and mother, who gave birth to me that led to my entry into this world. My duality and yours started at birth.

2. *Read Aloud Your Unique Diversity Statements and reaffirm the gift of duality you received from your father and mother with gratitude.* Your father and mother each gave you something unique. By reading aloud your unique diversity statement, you connect past with present and shape your future.

When you write down and vocalize (#1 and #2) your internal thoughts into simple sentences like above to read aloud, you create positive energy that fuels your sense of confidence. You become more comfortable accepting all of who you are and appreciate why you are who you are today out of a greater understanding of the role others played in enriching your life. Duality can then evolve to create a positive domino effect.

3. *Expand your exercise to include an additional sentence immediately after the first to identify what else you learned from the persons you listed. Here you are educating and exploring further your duality and adding one positive brick after another to build your diversity core where you feel right at home.*

Spend some time writing and have fun doing so. This is not an exam, nor something you need to share with others. But write what speaks to you. Find a quiet place with no distractions. Give yourself silence. And if you cannot immediately come up with material, that's perfectly fine. You need to be in the right state of mind to write, read, and reflect.

Here are my own examples below.

1. I am the son of Etsuko Reiman, an immigrant mother who taught me that Japan has much to offer the world.

   She taught me that Japanese women can accomplish anything.

2. I am the son of Carl Reiman, an American father who taught me that it's ok to seek truth in different religious traditions.

He taught me that being white doesn't mean you're always right.

3. I am the grandson of Kuniko Obata, a Japanese Buddhist grandmother who led me to accept Christ.

She taught me that you do not need a high school degree to have a PhD of the heart.

4. I am the friend of Mohamed Albusaidi, an Omani Muslim who taught me that the Arab World and Muslims are my brothers and sisters too.

He taught me that regular prayer and avoiding alcohol helps the heart and the soul find greater peace.

Feel free to write more and add to your list if you want to go even deeper. But the goal is quality, not quantity. Keep your list, carry it around, laminate it, place a version on your mobile or laptop if you like. But it is your diversity list, and you've just demonstrated how duality is fundamental to who you are, how two is better than one, how accepting both creates a positive multiplier effect, and learned to connect your past with your present to positively shape your brighter future. And you're not alone. You can think of Einstein or Jesus or anyone else whose duality truly changed the world. Your duality is a gift from your parents, make the most of it and do not let anyone take a double dose of joy from your treasure box or ask you to forego one for another. Any organization or person who asks you to do so, does not value God, your health, your heritage, or your parents.

Chapter Two

Educational Differences: Sushi Bentos and PBJ Sandwiches

Studying hard is a rite of passage for any young Japanese child hoping to gain acceptance into a renowned school and later a top company. Japanese students from the time of elementary school to high school are forced to study in a competitive atmosphere and go to cram schools just to prepare them for entrance examinations into the top schools. Parents spend a lot of money for cram schools to give their children a chance in society. School children learn to respect upperclassmen and elders, while learning that education is the only way to ensure a bright future. The pressure on Japanese students from society and their families is intense. In fact, one argument cited for Japan's high suicide rate among youth is the exceptionally competitive entrance examination system. Japan has the highest suicide rate of any developed country. Every year there are cases of Japanese youth committing suicide after failing a school entrance examination. There are even Buddhist amulets on sale with prayers for students to pass entrance exams sold in temples across the country.

Surveys reveal that compared to American students, Japanese students on average test higher on math and science exams. But American students do not have to pass competitive entrance examinations to get into good public schools. American primary, secondary, and high school students also do not need to go to cram schools after school to prepare for test taking. Having attended public and private schools both in the U.S. and Japan, my experience has been that American student life is less regimented than Japanese student life. Unless attending a private school, most American students did not need to wear uniforms. In Japan, students wear school uniforms from primary school onwards until they reach college or university where there is no uniform dress code.

Attending schools in the summer in Japan, I also wore a uniform, school cap, and Japanese style school backpack used in Japanese elementary school. At the middle school I attended again I wore a school uniform but we were not required to wear hats or carry backpacks. In high school, the uniform we wore in terms of school color and style also changed. In general, anyone who has lived in Japan or gone through the Japanese educational system can instantly spot by looking at the uniform worn if the student is a primary, secondary, or high school student. No such dress code exists in the U.S. in our public school system although there are private schools in the U.S. that enforce a uniform dress code.

When we gathered for Physical Education (PE) class all of us wore uniform PE clothes and the same type of sports shoes. In the U.S., each student wore whatever pair of sports shoes he or she liked. In Japan this was not the case. You would not wear your Air Jordan shoes to PE class. In many ways, the Japanese education system's emphasis on uniformity, regimented schedule, and grouping students into smaller groups where you would eat together and share school chores reminded me of the military. In elementary school, for example,

I remember every week one student would lead other students in his or her neighborhood to go to another student's home, round up other students, and then march as a group to the elementary school. During announcements from the school principal, all students would go to the outside school field, stand to attention and line up in perfect rows based on height to listen to the Principal's remarks. Seniority, rank, and uniformity were all instilled in me at an early age through attending Japanese schools in the summer. In contrast, American schools emphasize individuality as opposed to group harmony. In Japan, the focus is on group first and individual second.

REGIMENTED LIFE: JAPANESE PRIMARY SCHOOL

Japanese education begins with six years of elementary school. Elementary students are conspicuously cute wearing yellow hats with different logos according to each individual school and carrying yellow backpacks. While there are private elementary schools, the majority of students attend public schools. At school, the students will learn calligraphy, art, moral education, as well as the required math, science, social studies and Japanese. I remember even having to take a class on cooking and sewing in a home economics class. I wish I took that course more seriously now as to this day I'm neither good at sewing nor cooking Japanese food. My wife, thank God was a better student in home economics class than I was. Love you honey!

The homeroom teacher assigned to a specific class teaches all of these subjects and is responsible for each student. There are no honors programs or advanced placement classes, so everyone learns the same material at the same pace. However, as stated earlier, many elementary school students attend cram schools. These schools are meant to prepare students for the tough entrance examinations for middle school, high school, and college. Most students attend cram schools around third or fourth grade while some start as early as kindergarten. Yes, Japanese mothers do take their children's education very seriously. For extracurricular activities, many elementary school students take swimming lessons, sports lessons, and music lessons. When I was attending elementary school in Japan, I remember students attending *soroban* or abacus school to learn calculations as an extracurricular activity, but that is no longer popular among Japanese parents these days as the computer and modern technology have made *soroban* learning obsolete.

A typical school day in primary school begins with the sounds of the school bells ringing alerting students to the 8:30am start time. Before class, students place their walking shoes in the designated shoe lockers and change into school shoes. When the teacher enters the classroom, one designated student for that day shouts the commands, "*kilitsu, kiyotsuke, rei*" which means stand up, attention, bow. Elementary school students also receive chores and cleaning duties at school as well. Students are divided into groups with one student selected as the group leader. Each week the various groups are assigned different tasks. These tasks range from cleaning the homeroom, scrubbing the halls, washing the stairs, sweeping the floors, or serving lunch to classmates. The reason behind performing chores like cleaning is to teach students how to work in community, serve the community, and take responsibility for contributing towards that community life. Students required to clean their environment are less likely to mess it up as one teacher of mine liked to remind me. In fact, it goes deeper than that. The tradition of cleaning in schools is a form of moral training originating from monastic Buddhism and it teaches students responsibility.

GRADES AND LUNCHES

Other differences between American elementary schools and Japanese public elementary schools are report cards and lunch periods.

Japanese elementary students receive their report cards at the end of each trimester. The grading scale does not consist of A's and B's. Rather, students are graded by number scales ranging from 1 to 5, 5 being the highest and 1 being the lowest. The lunch periods are also different. In Japan, I distinctly remember students assembling into their designated groups by moving their desks together to face each other. Usually this was done in groups of four or more. Unlike in the U.S. where students eat lunch outside the classroom, in Japan, lunch is served in the classroom and each student eats the same lunch. No one is bringing lunches from home. A designated group from the class serves lunch to the rest of the class. That group is dressed in white hats and white aprons and is responsible for rationing out the food equally among students to ensure that there is no shortage of food. The homeroom teacher joins the students, but eats at his or her own large desk.

I remember we were expected to finish the food we were served. Sometimes, I didn't like to eat the food, particularly *shiitake* mushrooms which I had no taste for as a kid. I preferred my grandmother's cooking, but all of us had to follow the rules. After all, even the teacher had to eat what we were eating, so I figured we better shut up and eat. I don't remember the food as particularly bad. But I do remember that while we were expected to finish what was on our plate, we could leave over half a piece of bread. During days where we were served *shiitake* mushrooms or other foods I didn't like, I would stuff the food I didn't like inside the half piece of bread that I could throw away without getting into trouble. Ingenuity at a young age! The teacher and other classmates may have known what I was doing, but they never scolded me. As far as they were concerned, my actions did not go against established rules of eating nor did they disrupt school harmony.

The Only White Kid

After school, students usually went home in packs to eat afternoon snacks. When I attended Tanaka Elementary School in Taito Ward in Minowa in the summers, I remember the only time we were allowed to bring *bentos* or lunch boxes from home was during the annual school sports festival with parents and family members in attendance cheering the students on during sports competitions. The pattern my friends and I in Japanese elementary school followed was to either go to cram school, play baseball, or play Nintendo games at friend's houses after school. Although we had to go to school on Saturdays for half-day lessons and received lots of homework during summer vacation, I remember those school days with fondness. There were times when I thought it was unfair that after studying in the U.S. for nine months I could not have a summer vacation and hang out like my American friends. Instead I would have to do more schoolwork, and wear Japanese uniforms, and keep studying. But in hindsight those days and experiences shaped me to become the person I am today. I wouldn't trade those experiences for the world. I had a head start on the benefits of duality and multiculturalism.

My experience as the lone white foreign kid in an all Japanese elementary school did pique my classmates' interest in America. They would ask me why the U.S. dropped atomic bombs on Japan. I don't know how I responded to that question at the time, but I probably changed the topic to something I did know like baseball. I collected baseball cards growing up in Arizona and did the same when I was attending school in Japan. In Japan, you would not buy baseball cards in packs or at a sports store. Instead, baseball cards of Japanese baseball stars were found inside snacks like potato chips for kids. That's where I'd find the cards to add to my Japanese baseball card collection. I still have cards of sports stars like Kiyohara of the Seibu Lions, Hara of the Tokyo Giants and Randy Bass of the Hanshin Tigers. Unlike in the U.S., we didn't collect cards to buy and sell or trade, but kept them as reminders of players we admired. We didn't place any monetary value on the sports cards because there weren't any baseball card stores or shops that engaged in buying and trading such cards at the time.

I lived in the neighborhood with my grandmother, had Japanese citizenship, spoke Japanese and yet my situation was unique in that I was only attending Japanese public school in the summer. Somehow my mother convinced Tanaka Elementary School and other Japanese schools to allow me to enroll only in the summers when I returned to Japan on the basis that I held Japanese citizenship no matter how "foreign" I appeared, and therefore was entitled to receive an education just like everyone else. In addition, my grandparents were tax-paying members of society and contributed to the local economy of the neighborhood where they lived. I remember that my grandfather's portrait was displayed prominently with other individuals in the school where photos were kept honoring past presidents of the Japanese PTA or Parent Teachers Association. I always felt pride seeing his photo displayed there.

While my mother and grandmother did everything they could to make my summer school experience enjoyable, they couldn't prevent some of the trouble that did occur. As the outsider and foreigner, I did encounter bullying such as name-calling, being excluded from group activities, and being kicked, punched on the shoulder, flicked on the forehead, or goosed. When I say bullying, I'm not referring to bullying involving only one or two people, but larger groups. One day, I remember trying to avoid being the target of jokes or teasing or physical foul play but the teasing would not stop. The group of male classmates whom I tried to fit in with decided to target me as the foreigner, call me a foreigner, and test how I would respond. I turned around and swung at one of them. While the altercation did not lead to bloody noses or injuries, increasingly I had to fight to defend myself when I could no longer ignore the name-calling, isolation, and cold looks followed by statements: "foreigner, go home."

It got to a point where my mother had to enroll me in another elementary school for the summers of my fifth and sixth grades. I can't even remember the school I transferred to, but I do remember feeling confused and sad that I had to experience bullying at Tanaka Elementary school during third and fourth grades. In my mind, I was just as Japanese as they were so I couldn't understand why I had to be treated any different. I was too young to realize that the American part of me got in the way of them accepting that I was truly Japanese. It is ironic that later on in life (joining the U.S. Foreign Service) I would have to battle a different dilemma, the Japanese part of me getting in the way of Americans accepting that I was truly American.

Bullying is quite a common phenomenon in Japan and is a rising social problem. Bullying and not drug use or petty crime is cited as the biggest problem that occurs in Japanese elementary and middle schools. There are cases reported in the media almost every year where some students committed suicide on account of prolonged periods of bullying.

LIFE IN JAPANESE MIDDLE SCHOOL

Japanese middle schools like high schools are three years each as opposed to two years in the U.S. for middle school and four years for high school. Japanese middle school students are conspicuous because they all wear black uniforms with gold buttons as opposed to the yellow uniforms they wore during elementary school. They are also required to always carry a handkerchief and pocket-sized tissue boxes with them. I remember my homeroom teacher periodically checking to make sure I had those two items available. Just like at Tanaka Elementary School, we ate lunch at our desks, were assigned cleaning duties, and were part of designated groups.

I attended middle school at Number 9 Bunkyo Middle School located in Bunkyo Ward. We don't have school buses in Japan. Instead, every day I would ride the regular city bus from Minowa in Taito Ward to Hakusan Ue in Bunkyo Ward. From that Hakusan Ue station I would walk to school, avoiding the black crows that liked to harass me en route to and from middle school. I made friends and had some good teachers. Like in elementary school, we were assigned homeroom teachers. However, one noticeable difference was that unlike in elementary school, the homeroom teacher in middle school did not teach all of the subjects. Different teachers taught individual subjects to us in mathematics, Japanese, science and so forth. For the first time, students could join in school sports or clubs and it is in middle school when students, for the first time, are required to take English as a second language.

Regarding social interactions, I noticed that in middle school, for the first time, boys and girls were separated when taking classes in physical education and home economics. Girls chat with girls and boys with other boys. Unlike in the U.S., I remember there was hardly any dating craze in middle school. The students were very shy about even discussing the topic of dating. There were no school dances or pep rallies. However, boys and girls did go on school field trips together and we would have opportunities to mingle during sports festivals. But, you could definitely see an attempt to separate boys and girls with certain classes segregated based on gender.

At Bunkyo Middle School again I was the only white foreigner. We did have one Korean exchange student but that was it. He and I got along well, but I do recall him being teased more because he had an accent when speaking Japanese. I certainly encountered people that liked to tease me as well, but it was my ability to play basketball that won the admiration of my peers. I was able to make more friends simply because I excelled on the basketball court (more so than I did inside the classroom). Another element that helped my cause was that all of a sudden I noticed my Japanese classmates treating me as a "star" simply because I was an American and they liked to watch American movies. I certainly found it funny because I'm not particularly tall and handsome, nor did I have any acting skills. And, I don't think I even closely resembled any American actor at the time. But none of that mattered. The American brand label made me gain instant stardom even though I certainly didn't deserve that extra "special" treatment.

It was also in Japanese middle school that I began to notice non-white foreigners receiving a harder time gaining acceptance as *gaijin*, the term for foreigner in Japanese. At the supermarkets I noticed individuals with Chinese or Korean backgrounds not receiving the same cordial treatment. Some of that may be attributed to the fact that many spoke Japanese with an accent or did not speak the language fluently. Nonetheless, it was in middle school that I began to realize that Japanese people definitely show favoritism towards foreigners with European or American backgrounds (particularly those that are white) than those with a non-Japanese Asian ethnic mix. Many Japanese classmates at the time, associated American or European with being white. The MTV boom was also hitting Japan at the time so there was an assumption among my Japanese classmates that black people were "hip," "cool," "and groovy," and could play basketball. It is amazing how lack of exposure and media images leave people with false impressions. There was a boom among some Japanese girls (mostly in their twenties) to tan themselves as dark as possible to become "black" because in their minds, being black was fashionable.

EARTHQUAKE DRILLS AND MUSIC CLASS

Unlike my experience at McKemy Middle School in Tempe, Arizona, in Japan I participated in mandatory earthquake drills and took music class. Also we never used the computer to type up assignments or reports in Japanese. Rather, we would hand-write our reports to present to our teachers. We had pillows placed on our chairs for use during earthquake drills. We were instructed to place the pillow on our heads and duck underneath our desks during emergencies such as earthquakes. Tokyo definitely does have more earthquakes than Arizona and Japan is known for earthquakes. So it certainly makes sense that school children are taught how to prepare for such an occurrence. But as a seventh or eighth grader, I always felt silly having to use a pillow as a protective helmet, especially since I never had to participate in earthquake drills during school in the U.S.

We were also required to take music class in Japan. We learned to play the flute and harmonica as well as how to sing. Every school has its school song. The same was the case for Tanaka Elementary School. We would not have to say the "pledge of allegiance" like in American schools, but we were expected to know the Japanese national anthem. We were also required individually to go up to the front of the class and sing a designated song. There was no "show and tell" time as in American schools. Again, the focus is on the group as opposed to demonstrating your own individuality or special talent. There is a famous proverb in Japanese that says "the nail that sticks out gets pounded." That philosophy is still prevalent today throughout Japanese schools, businesses, and society.

More Differences in Middle School

There is no yearbook club as is typically the case in American schools, nor do Japanese schools have mascots. There are no school buses. Students must find their own way of transportation by either taking a city bus or train. There are also no vending machines or snack bars on the school premises in Japanese elementary or middle schools. Students are not allowed to buy snacks after school until they have returned home and changed clothes. When you are wearing the school uniform, you are representing the school, and hence are expected to follow school rules and guidelines outside of school. In theory, that is taught. In practice, many of us bought snacks, comic books, and so forth on our way home from school without changing clothes.

One major difference between Japanese and American schools is that in Japan we were all taught to bow and greet our classmates and teachers. As soon as we entered the school compound we were expected to say "good morning" or "good afternoon" in Japanese to our seniors, classmates, and faculty. I remember someone from the school would always be waiting in the front entrance gate checking that students are not late for school, are not bringing prohibited foreign objects like cigarettes, and are carrying a handkerchief and pocket-size box of tissues. I hated having to carry those two items because I never had to do so while attending middle school at McKemy Junior High, but when attending Japanese middle school one must do as the other students do.

Japanese middle school students have to face reality much sooner than their American middle school counterparts. Passing the entrance examinations in order to enter high school is taken as a life or death matter. Without a high school diploma, there is not much one can do to make a sufficient living in Japan. Students are faced with the reality that only higher education affords one to live a decent life because no future exists beyond middle school if students are unable to enter high school. In middle school, Japanese students for the first time take semester and final exams. Attending middle school is mandatory in Japan and home schooling is not an option.

In contrast, in the U.S. it is only in high school when students worry about final exams and passing the SAT in order to continue receiving formal education. Japanese middle school students, on the other hand, spend time after school attending cram schools and often do not go to sleep until late at night. As a Japanese middle school student I remember seeing the lights of a cram school still burning brightly at 11pm at night in front of a cram school located near my grandmother's home. I understood for these students and their parents passing entrance exams to get into good high schools was a serious issue and I sympathized. I also felt lucky that my educational future didn't depend upon passing an exam. American students don't know how lucky they are in that respect.

JAPANESE HIGH SCHOOL

High schools in Japan consist of three years of education with most Japanese attending public schools. The majority of Japanese students enroll in general education course programs, but there are vocational schools specializing in business, industrial arts, agriculture, homemaking and other fields. This is a time when students learn to respect and obey their *senpai* or seniors while making lifelong friendships with peers. As in the middle school and elementary school years, there is a dress code enforced prohibiting students to wear hats like baseball caps to school or to wear jewelry. Vehicles are also not allowed on campus for high school students. The schools inspect both the uniforms and general appearance of both boys and girls, but tend to place more emphasis on the girls. At least when I was enrolled in Japanese high school, I remember inspectors paid special attention to skirt length, hair length, and hair color. Again, what counts is the group and representing the organization. Schools do not tolerate students veering off course. Students are expected to assume the responsibility of representing the school just as later in life they will represent a firm, a family or a corporation.

Although 24 years have passed since I last attended Japanese high school, one thing that has not changed is that the seniors still run the show. When talking to a senior, one must speak in a polite manner, bow, and run any errands demanded. A first year high school student is lowest on the food chain. The second year high school students control the lives of the freshman and the third year high school students oversee the second and first year students. Any break in protocol is not tolerated. If a second year student goes up against a third year student the entire third year student class will back the third year student. There is power in numbers. That's what keeps the order intact. In the U.S., seniors do have to earn respect. In Japan, the title of senior and mere fact that one is older entitles that person to respect. Juniors that do not show proper respect should expect trouble from their seniors including the very real possibility of being beat up.

REITAKU HIGH SCHOOL AND DORM LIFE

Some high schools have dorms and the private Japanese high school I attended did. Reitaku High School in Chiba, Japan had a beautiful campus with trees and greenery. It had its own golf course and even horse stall. I attended Reitaku during the summers of 93, 94, and 95. Again, I was the only American and the only foreigner attending an all-Japanese school. I joined the basketball club and practiced basketball with the school team. Through my mother's connections to the school, I was fortunate enough to receive scholarships during the summer to attend high school there. I would love to return some day to teach students there. My former English teacher at Reitaku is now the school principal.

Reitaku was unique in that students, both boys and girls, came from all across Japan to study and live there. Boys and girls had their own separate dorms. Although I commuted via train from my grandmother's house to attend high school there, most of my classmates lived in the dorms. The seniors ran the dorms and were responsible for keeping order. They made my underclassmen classmates clean, buy groceries, and even provide entertainment. Seniors held nightly meetings inside the dorm to ensure everything was operating smoothly. Some even asked juniors to sing or dance in front of the group for entertainment. It also wasn't uncommon to hear of seniors forcing junior members to stay awake until 1 or 2am to keep them company while they were studying for college entrance examinations.

Seniors are entitled in the dorms to blast music they want to listen to and have the authority to choose where they would like to sleep. Dorms have one large communal public bath which is shared by students living in the dorm. Seniors enter the bath with authority while junior members shiver outside hoping that a senior in a bad mood won't take out his frustrations on junior members. My classmates told me that the seniors were not shy about exposing their bodies proudly in the public bath. I suppose after living two years in the dorms the seniors feel comfortable exposing their goods. In comparison, underclassmen tended to cover their private parts with a towel hoping that seniors wouldn't pick on them. As one can see, being an underclassmen has its demerits. But, everyone has to go through the process of learning how to obey the seniors.

Dorms at Reitaku separated the boys from the girls. The girls' dorm had much stricter rules than the boys'. The same rules for obeying seniors applied just as much to the girls as the boys. Girls that failed to bow and appropriately greet upperclassmen girls received a tongue lashing and punishment. That punishment could entail more house chores or silent treatment. In addition, no males, not even fathers or brothers, were allowed to enter the girl's dormitory. As far as deciphering whether one was a first, second, or third year student, all one had to do was look at the color of the school slippers he or she was wearing. If you noticed someone was wearing upperclassmen slippers you'd best bow and show deference.

Daily Schedule, Exchanges and Speeches

The high school day began around 8:30am and ended around 3:30pm. First and second year students at Reitaku followed a structured academic schedule while third year students usually divided into two separates tracks of science or humanities. Like any other Japanese high school, there were no honors, international baccalaureate, or advance placement courses. English was a required course and Japanese students did not have many elective courses to choose from. Many students also joined after-school clubs such as tea ceremony, *kendo* (Japanese form of sword fighting), *kyudo* (archery), rugby, baseball and so on. You did not have a student involved in several clubs at the same time. Unlike the U.S. where different sports are played based on the season allowing one to join the basketball, football, and baseball teams in the same school year, the opposite is true in Japan. If a student picks a sport in Japan and joins the team, he or she will be involved in that sport for the entire school year. During lunchtime we could not eat off campus, but we did have a school cafeteria where we went to eat and every school day ended with cleaning.

I recall my days at Reitaku fondly. The seniors never gave me a hard time, rather they embraced me as an "upperclassmen" probably because I could help them with their English. Again, as the only American kid on campus, I was treated like a celebrity. Upperclassmen would ask me about the U.S. and try to teach me many things about Japan. I am very grateful for the experience and actually cried during my last summer high school experience in Japan. I knew even back then that what I had experienced was special.

Every summer I would have to prepare a speech, bow, and introduce myself not only to my homeroom class and teaching staff, but also to the entire faculty and student body of over 600 people in a large auditorium. I dreaded having to make a speech. Nonetheless, every year I had to do so during the summers. *Aisatsu* or greetings are an essential part of Japanese society. As a foreigner, I learned to bow and greet each and every person I met on campus just like my *sempai*. That was the Reitaku influence. I credit my ability to speak in front of large audiences to my experiences at Reitaku.

COLLEGE IN JAPAN

With a 99% literacy rate and minuscule number of high school dropouts, Japanese schools have succeeded in ensuring that everyone has a basic education at least until high school. Unlike problems faced in the U.S. over high school dropout rates, such problems are unheard of in Japan. Nor do you hear of problems with guns or gangs. In comparing kindergarten through 12th grade education in both countries, I have to say that Japan has the edge. However, when comparing college and graduate school education in terms of rigor and quality, I would say the U.S. has the comparative advantage. That is not to say that Japan does not have leading professors and academics involved in world class research, but most Japanese students don't place nearly as much energy into their studies as during their K through 12 years. Their minds are focused on other pursuits, partying, connecting with members of the opposite sex, working part-time, and generally trying to enjoy life before the rigors of working for a company begin. Third and fourth year Japanese students hardly attend class as they prepare for job hunting and interviews. It is commonly said that getting into colleges or universities in Japan is difficult, but graduating is easy. Once on campus, college students no longer have dress codes and can gamble, smoke, and drink should they choose to do so.

Other differences include not having as many extracurricular activities and flexibility in fields of study. In the U.S., it is common to witness students changing majors two or three times. However, that is uncommon in Japan. During high school, students decide their future field of study (medical school, engineering, humanities, etc.). Unlike in American universities, Japanese college students cannot change their original course of study, for instance, change from studying architecture to business. In addition, transferring between colleges is just as rare as switching majors.

Another difference between the U.S. and Japan in terms of college education is that the top ranked universities in Japan are considered public schools (Tokyo University and Kyoto University for example) both of which have harder entrance examinations to pass. However, in the U.S., private schools like Harvard and Stanford tend to lead the pack. In addition, entry requirements into college differ significantly between the U.S. and Japan. In Japan, entrance into a public university depends on passing a test score. For private universities, the same rules generally apply although exceptions are made in terms of the type of exam, or if one even has to take an exam for students who study abroad, are talented athletes, artists, or media stars. In certain cases, like for Keio University, students who attended Keio elementary school through high school are allowed admission without having to pass an entrance examination.

In stark contrast, considerations that affect the decision process for American students applying to universities in the U.S. include scores on the standard SAT, high school grade point averages (GPAs), references, extracurricular activities, foreign languages, work experience, and usually, writing sample such as an essay. Universities are not primarily basing decisions to accept or reject candidates on test scores. In the U.S., a student with an average SAT score but high GPA and stellar talents can very well be accepted to an Ivy League school. In contrast, Japanese universities take a more "all-or-nothing" approach. You either pass the exam or you don't. As a result, if a Japanese student really wants to get into a particular school and program (for example, medical school at Kyoto University), he or she may take the test two or three more times. Tests are held only once a year so if a candidate fails, he has to wait one full year before being able to retest. That means spending an entire year or two (if one fails to pass again) preparing for an entrance examination.

Japan's Global Influence Depends on Educational Reform

In order for Japan to increase its global influence several things need to happen. First, the Japanese education system needs reform to educate citizens on what it means to be Japanese. That entails a thorough study of history as well as an education that emphasizes debates and public speaking. Too often, Japanese children are not taught the fundamentals of Japanese history in such a manner that creates confidence and pride in being Japanese. Moreover, these children are not taught to defend their culture or country in public debate. They need to receive an education that provides them the tools to effectively serve as Ambassadors of Japan and represent their country with dignity and pride. You cannot promote Japan if you yourself are not comfortable being Japanese. The only way to appreciate the beauty of Japan is through an understanding of its rich history. The second step is being able to explain that to a foreign audience.

Much is talked about regarding the poor level of English language ability and education in Japan. Unlike Singapore, Japan has failed to promote a bilingual education policy to prepare Japanese citizens to effectively communicate to non-Japanese. The problem lies again in the education system and this is where reform is needed. One may argue that Japanese children are learning English as early as kindergarten. Yet, the English they are learning is meant for the middle school, high school, and college entrance examinations which predominantly test an applicant's memorization ability and reading ability instead of speaking, listening, and writing. Too few Japanese have attained a level of English proficiency needed to effectively communicate to an American or English speaking audience.

In terms of U.S.-Japan relations, the Japanese government performs poorly in advocating on behalf of Japan. The reason is simple. Their government officials, including the so-called "best and brightest" bureaucrats based in the Japanese Embassy in Washington, DC do not understand Washington and what it takes to influence the political process. My time in Congress affirmed this. While the Koreans, Chinese, and Taiwanese would frequently brief congressional members and staff, and hence be able to push legislation and agreements forward in their countries' favor, the Japanese did not do this to their own detriment. Japanese diplomats would complain and seem confused that Congress would not support some of their agenda items when they themselves had not cultivated the personal relationships needed to gain Member support.

The Japanese diplomats think that just because the U.S. and Japan are allies that somehow their demands will be automatically met. I'm afraid that is not the case. Too often the diplomats sent do not understand how Congress works and hence are unable to shape the political process or serve effectively on behalf of the Japanese people. The Koreans and Chinese have been aggressive and can often be found engaging Members of Congress and their staff. They get it. Shockingly, the Japanese Embassy assumed that just by placing an ad in one of the frequently distributed Hill newspapers that outreach was fulfilled and that they would get their way. I'm afraid you need more than a newspaper ad to influence the U.S. Congress. You need a sustained, persistent, and consistent effort to lobby Congress. The Japanese have failed and hence trail others in this category.

Another aspect of the Japanese government's failure in promoting Japanese culture abroad, and particularly in the U.S., is in the realm of media. There is not one Japanese language channel that Americans can watch to study Japanese or hear Japanese news in Japanese on standard cable. In contrast, the Chinese government promotes its agenda and Mandarin language study through several TV channels on standard cable without extra charge. The Koreans also have a number of channels that not only the Korean-American community can access without additional charge through basic cable, but also non-Koreans can enjoy. The NHK channel in English lacks substance and quality. Moreover, the one Japanese language NHK world premium channel available requires individuals to pay 3,000 yen or $26 or more a month (at the current exchange rate of 113 yen per one U.S. dollar) for a subscription. This is no way to promote Japanese language, language study, or culture. Even the Vietnamese communities have more Vietnamese language channels accessible to audiences in the DC/VA/MD area than do the Japanese.

Japan is losing its battle in lobbying Congress, as well as in media and social outreach. That is why more Americans are supporting and appreciating non-Japanese Asian cultures and political agendas because the other Asian communities are doing a much better job promoting and marketing themselves. You cannot promote greater tourism and investment in Japan if you are unable to gain the interest of the citizens of your biggest trade and security partner, i.e. the U.S., to visit Japan and study Japanese. The battle to capture hearts and minds is waged daily through TV, Internet, radio, and social media. Japan isn't even in the ballgame because it is not using this medium aggressively to promote and market Japanese interests, culture, language, and business.

There is a language barrier and I understand that it is not easy to learn English or French or Spanish or German for many Japanese citizens. But that is no excuse for not incorporating a greater and more robust language education agenda. Japan's global influence and survival depends not only upon promoting the Japanese language, but also learning to speak foreign languages at a near native fluency level. Too often, messages are lost in translation and nuances and sentiments are not captured forcefully through use of translators.

At the same time, foreigners are playing an increasingly key role in spreading Japanese culture. Bento booms in France, raising of Japanese carp in Belgium, origami displays in Switzerland, the building of a Japanese garden in Monaco, bonsai museum and university in Italy, Japanese style green tea in Germany, futons with

Japanese characters in Spain, and animation and *manga* throughout Europe, Japanese culture is spreading throughout the world. In the United States, there are Japanese tea gardens, flower arrangement, and *bonsai* booms. In Phoenix, Arizona you have a Japanese tea society while Japanese tea gatherings, flower arrangement, and bonsai continue to spark interest in New York. What is encouraging is that many of these recent initiatives throughout Europe and the U.S. are the result of foreigners finding beauty in Japanese culture and history, and deciding to promote this heritage in their own respective countries of origin. Here, dual nationals play another important role as carriers of culture.

∞∞∞

EDUCATION AND EXPOSURE
WHAT DIFFERENT FOREIGN SCHOOL SYSTEMS CAN TEACH ONE ANOTHER

Exposure to another system of education allows you to appreciate different methods of learning. There is a lot of information both Americans and Japanese can learn from each other in the realm of education. We both love our kids. We both value education. We both believe that education is the key to innovation, upward mobility, and survival in an increasingly technologically advanced world. Here are some key takeaways:

- The Japanese public school system of collective ownership and assigning chores on a rotating, equitable basis for each student is a great way to instill class pride and a sense of collective responsibility. The message is clear: This is your school, take care of it!

- The U.S. public school system's emphasis on teaching students how to think as opposed to what to think creates a more relaxed environment for learning. The message is clear: You are not just memorization machines, but have other unique gifts to offer.

- A combination of memorization with emphasis on creativity and coming up with one's own answers creates a dual learning environment for success.

Japanese students can benefit from a learning environment that does not put excessive emphasis on examinations to the detriment of other aspects of growth and development. No, they are worth much more in God's eyes than machines expected to spout out a memorized answer. There should be no need for a dual track system of education where students need to go to school after school in cram schools just for an entrance examination. That type of pressure can be deadly on children who do not want to let their families down, especially in a culture with a very heavy emphasis on shame like in Japan. Kids need to be able to be kids and failure in an exam is not failure in life. In addition, no child should have to take three years off just to study for an entrance examination to enter a particular field of study at the college level.

U.S. public schools, on the other hand, can be deadly in that not a year goes by when we do not tragically hear of a shooting, stabbing, or other violent activity claiming the lives of innocent students, teachers, and other victims. There is no place for guns in schools. The Japanese parent does not have to worry about his or her son being shot one day at school. Schools should be safe havens for children. The U.S. can learn from Japan in this regard. Japan forbids the possession of firearms and swords and only under certain provisions can civilians own them. If they do, they must go through rigorous testing and inspection on an annual basis. There are no second amendment or constitutional requirements regarding the civilian right to bear arms. In fact, the opposite is true in Japan where gun control laws begin with the premise that no person should possess firearms. Revisions to gun control laws make it harder, not easier to own guns with harsher punishments for violation. The result: one of the lowest gun-related homicide rates in the world. People in Japan do not own nor care to possess firearms, creating a much safer society and learning environment.

Interestingly enough, the emphasis on cleanliness and taking care of one's school environment has given Japan international media attention, including in the Middle East. In Saudi Arabia, the media showcased Japan's emphasis on students cleaning and taking care of their schools as a model for Saudi Arabia to mimic. On the world stage, we read of Japan garnering positive international acclaim during the 2018 World Cup in Russia, how their fans showed respect and responsibility by cleaning up after attending soccer games. The habits we pick up as kids carry into adulthood. If you have to clean your school, you are less likely to trash it. The Japanese education system and emphasis on respect for one another and the environment translate into more than simple health dividends, but life lessons that can benefit America too.

Chapter Three

AN IMMIGRANT MOTHER: LOVE OF A
JAPANESE GRANDMOTHER SUSTAINS ME

As the only Japanese American attending a private Jesuit high school in Phoenix, Arizona, I remember my high school days with fondness. The Jesuit fathers and teachers at the school instilled in us a desire for social justice and community service. They poured their hearts into teaching us how to become good students and men for Christ. The all-boys private high school provided me an opportunity to discover my identity and question religion. Up until that time I was an atheist. I believed in the love that my Japanese grandmother showed me in Japan and thought whatever religious faith she held would be the one I would follow. Her faith was in Buddhism.

My grandmother was a model of living faith. She would perform the ancestral worship rituals every day at home in front of a portrait of my deceased grandfather, burn incense, and pray. She would also go to a cemetery located in Hamamatsu to clean his gravestone, pull out the weeds surrounding his tomb, and chant Buddhist sutras. Naturally, I would follow her lead when I lived with her in Japan. Some of my Christian friends would tell me that she was damned or that I would not go to heaven if I did not put my faith in Christ. My grandmother was not a Christian. I refused to believe she would be damned if she did not convert. I never met a more loving and caring person in my life. If the Christian heaven was not for her, I told myself it is not for me either. Through the seminars, religious classes, friendships with priests, and school retreats at Brophy, I became a theist. But I was still undecided about which religion to call my own. Later I would become a Christian, but my high school years were a time for me to question many aspects of my life.

One aspect was my identity. For some reason, the summers in Japan, my education in Japan, and my unique cultural background made me think that I represented Japan and so with that burden of responsibility on my shoulders (which I placed on myself) I convinced myself that I needed to perform well in school. I had all A's and always pushed myself to be at the top of my class. I graduated with honors and at the top 3% of my graduating class. But behind my belief was my mistaken thought that I was representing my "Japanese family" which included all Japanese people.

I had placed faith in Japanese nationalism. I did not realize it then, but in essence nationalism had become my religion. I thought that what separated me from the rest of my classmates was my Japanese heritage and that I would dishonor my Japanese family's name, particularly my dead grandfather's name, if I did not perform at the top of my class. My grandmother had instilled in me a belief that I was never to conduct any acts that would bring shame to the family name. I truly believed in my ethnic identity and felt I was representing the country of Japan while studying as an American citizen at Brophy. I later came to realize the falsehood in putting faith in nationalism and the danger in doing so.

Nations are arbitrarily carved upon a map and one becomes a citizen often by default. You are born in a country and become a citizen or immigrate to another country and get naturalized. But the process is often random and very political. There just so happens to be a country named the "Federal Republic of Nigeria" or "Republic of Oman" but that is a man-made phenomenon and temporary. You deceive yourself if you put faith in borders and limit your willingness to expand your purview outside the territory that your passport claims is your native soil. In today's world of Internet and global communications, we're able to transcend the borders of nation-states quite easily. But governments still have a vested interest in making you believe that you belong to the particular area carved out on the map over which they have governing authority. From a governing perspective, it makes sense for the authorities to promote nationalism in order to create citizens loyal to nation and state. Otherwise, it would be difficult to send soldiers to die in the battlefields of Baghdad or Kabul without making them believe they are fighting for an important cause. The distinction between nationalism and patriotism often appears blurry. These terms are often used interchangeably based on who is using them and what political agenda he or she may have in mind. Nationalism is a reality, but one that hopefully will not be used by governments to spur war propaganda and misery.

What had served as my philosophical and spiritual foundation in high school crumbled after discovering that many of my Japanese relatives never really accepted me as one of their own. I came to realize that I was only deceiving myself in thinking that my half-Japanese ancestry made me a member of the Japanese club. Time and time again, I would be reminded that 50% Japanese just doesn't make the cut. But, I did not imagine that my own Japanese uncles and aunts would hold a bias towards me. To understand why requires me to share my mother's story.

AN IMMIGRANT MOTHER

My mother was one of eight children born to Obata Nobuhiro and Obata Kuniko. She was born during World War II, during the height of the war. The constant U.S. air bomb raids over Tokyo and the city emergency evacuation bells ringing non-stop propelled my grandfather to move his family to Osaka to seek shelter. This is the environment in which my mother grew up. She was only 7 years old when the War ended in 1945.

As a result of the War, my grandfather lost much of his wealth and sold most of his properties to feed his eight children. My mother grew up as the eldest daughter and the fourth sibling among her brothers and sisters. Her four elder brothers were born to different mothers. It is important to note that my grandfather was previously married twice losing his first wife to illness and losing his second to the War. My grandmother was wife number three. My grandmother was only twenty years old when she first started working at my grandfather's liquor shop. Despite the 30 year age gap (my grandfather was over 50 years old at the time), the two married. My grandmother gave him 4 new offspring – and his first daughter, my mother, Obata Etsuko.

My mother grew up in an era where women were expected to become housewives. My grandfather's plan was to send her to the best schools and have her marry early. My mother learned calligraphy, abacus, and flower arrangement during her teenage years and was told that a woman should only have a high school education. My grandfather, who only had a fifth grade education, believed like so many men of his generation, that a women's role was to marry and take care of the home. He was convinced that no man would ever marry a woman who was more educated or smarter than him. In response, my ambitious mother began secretly attending university through correspondence school.

My mother would tutor neighborhood children and use the money she earned to pay for her college fees. She was accepted to Keio University, and unknown to my grandfather, had the university send her homework via mail to a postbox. She graduated in five years. To my grandfather's surprise, my mother not only spurred the men that my grandfather chose for her as potential marriage candidates, but also had the audacity to tell my grandfather that she planned to attend graduate school in the U.S. My grandfather did not agree, but I believe later approved of my mother's decision when he learned that she had not only obtained a PhD, but actually found a man willing to marry her! Unfortunately, my grandfather passed away after hearing that I was born, so I never had the honor of meeting him. But his story and legacy remain with me to this day.

My mother would spend the rest of her life teaching in Arizona and would return to Japan each summer, taking me with her. She applied for my Japanese citizenship, passport, and made arrangements for me to attend Japanese public school. I enjoyed those summers in Japan carrying my black backpack, wearing my yellow cap, and attending class with my Japanese classmates, although I also felt a bit sad that I couldn't spend summer vacation playing in the U.S. with my American friends. Instead, I was studying. But I have to admit I enjoyed eating my grandmother's home cooking, reading manga, and hanging out with my Japanese friends. My experience is rather unique in that I never attended international schools in Japan. I was fortunate to get a real taste, a first-hand experience of the Japanese public education system.

As the eldest daughter, my mother was expected to be responsible for taking care of my grandmother. But the fact that she was living in the U.S. meant that primary responsibility would fall on her brothers and sisters to look after grandma. My mother and I would always stay at my grandmother's house during the summers, but technically that required approval from my mother's elder brother who lived at the same home and ran the liquor store. Their relationship was always lukewarm at best. My mother would help pay some of their bills and take care of looking after my grand-mother during the summers. We would share the same kitchen and bath area with my uncle and his family. My mother's absence from Japan meant that she would not have as much say in handling the affairs of my grandmother. Needless to say, jealousy and tension did exist between my mother and her siblings. Part of that was due to the fact that some of my aunts and uncles did not approve of my mother bringing me with her to live in my grandmother's house. I was shocked when I later learned this through my mother.

My aunts and uncles were always very nice to me in person and often gave me allowance money, so it never occurred to me that what they were really thinking was that I couldn't ever completely be part of their family. Their message was subtle, but it shattered my belief that my "Japanese family" really had my best interests at heart. That painful period left a profound impression, making me realize that nationalism and notions of ethnic and racial unity were false ideologies that could not serve as my guiding principle in life.

Before my mother married my American father, there was considerable debate among my mother's family about my mother marrying a foreigner. They were particularly concerned about how an offspring of an interracial marriage would be treated in Japanese society. Because the Japanese society places a premium on race and ethnicity, they knew it would be tough for a foreigner or someone who looked "foreign" to blend in. They also knew discrimination would be a part of my life. Nowadays, there are many more in-terracial and international marriages than during my mother's generation, but at the time, it was uncommon in Japanese society. I was the only interracial kid in the Japanese neighborhood of Taito Ward, Nihontsutsumi, Minowa. Everyone knew me. Passersby would often shout *gaijin* or foreigner when they saw me in the streets.

Stories of My Grandfather

Growing up in my grandmother's home during the summers, I would always hear about my grandfather through her stories. My grandmother had a large picture of my grandfather in the living room, along with an altar and an incense burner. She would often burn incense and pray in front of my grandfather's picture. Every few months she would visit my grandfather's tomb to wash the stone, cut the weeds, place flowers, and recite the Lotus Sutra. She would bring me with her and I would help her pull weeds and fetch buckets of water used to clean the tombstone. Although my grandfather had been dead for so many years, for my grandmother, his spirit was always present. She would often talk about him and warn me that I was never to do anything that would tarnish the Obata family name nor bring disgrace to my grandfather. I took her words to heart. In Japan, I would always think about whether my actions would receive the approval of my grandfather if he were alive. This discipline helped keep me out of trouble. While praying at the temples, I would think about my Japanese grandfather. My grandmother led me to believe that I could always rely on my grandfather's spirit to protect me. I had no reason to doubt her. She was my greatest role model. And later, even after she passed away during my diplomatic assignment in Beijing, China in 2008, she would continue to guide me as my guardian angel.

Your Gratitude Test

Part of appreciating your worth in the eyes of a creator God is to understand your value. You are uniquely created. You are one of a kind. No one else exists exactly like you. When you understand who you are, and where you came from, you increase your own self-awareness, and create opportunities for success. You also honor the God that created you.

1. *Write down your generational proposition. Think of yourself as belonging to a long line of great men and women. Take a moment to trace your lineage back to individuals that you admire, your generational advocates.* What can you learn from those individuals and what did they give you? If you have a photo of them, perhaps you can carry that with a key message you can write on the back that reminds you of the generational gifts you have received.

2. *On a simple card, think about what your generational legacy will be. What are the actions you are taking to ensure the next generation (whether your children or not) will benefit from your gifts?* Perhaps your gifts are financial or your time or a creative activity like art or writing in which you hope to leave your imprint. Whatever it might be, understand that you have enough, God gave you enough gifts, to leave to others. What you do with your gifts can have a generational impact. Never forget that!

3. *Write a thank you letter to your loved one who has passed. This could be your way to grieve, honor them, and carry their legacy with you.* Here's mine below:

Dear Grandma Kuniko,

You left this world with a heart of gold and made me aware of my own self-worth. You saved me from death, multiple times. You taught me to live and to love and to honor Japan and Japanese people because they are part of your family. Thank you for giving me another family. Thank you for loving me enough and showering me with unconditional love like no other person in this world. You know that I feel awful that I did not visit you upon entering the U.S. Foreign Service because I was so afraid that the State Department would indefinitely preclude me from serving in Japan if I visited you. The fear and threat that I had to somehow hide my feelings toward Japan to prove my loyalty to America crippled me. All I ever wanted was to be sent to Japan as a U.S. diplomat to make you proud so that you could brag to your neighbors and be proud that your investment in me was not in vain. Please forgive me for abandoning you when you never left my side. You were always in my heart even when you were battling Alzheimer's and could not remember my name. Whether I was handling plane crashes in Nigeria, persuading the Government of China to liberalize its health and insurance markets for the benefit of U.S. firms, or traveling by boat through the jungles of Guyana to dedicate a pumping well to a local hospital, your spirit was always with me.

Even in death you gave me a blessing that I did not deserve. Your death turned me to Christ. No one can ever say that the only way to Christ is through a Christian. God chose a Buddhist, a humble lady raised on a farm with only a middle school education, to show me his love. God is great. And you were the messenger of his infinite love. I miss you every day. You are always with me along with my grandfather whom I know you loved dearly. I carry both of you in my heart. I am never alone. Thank you for your generational gifts. Thank you for making me the man I am today.

Love,

Ken Obata Reiman

No matter what your family circumstance, whether you came from a broken family, do not know your family, or have a wonderful supportive family, you are never alone. You are the living testament of a greater, generational love that transcends space and time. Own it. Own you. Someone you love lives in, with, and through you to impact others. Adopt an angel, role model, family member, or simply lean on God to remind yourself that you are worth more than this entire world. Live and succeed for them and for the next generation.

Chapter Four

DID YOUR PARENTS MEET AT A MILITARY
BASE OR A GEISHA HOUSE?

I often encounter questions about my parents and often the assumption is that my parents met on some military base. My father did serve in the Army in Okinawa but he certainly did not meet my mother there. They met in graduate school where my mother was pursuing a PhD in Asian languages and linguistics and my father was studying Eastern philosophy and religion including Hinduism and Buddhism. When I mention to people that my father served in the U.S. Army and was stationed in Okinawa in the 1960s and that my mother is Japanese, the assumption is that they met in Japan in some military capacity.

Worse still—is the assumption that some strangers make—that perhaps my mother was a geisha and that is how my father met her. Nothing could be farther from the truth. My mother cannot even sing much less play the *shamisen* (a three-stringed guitar-like Japanese musical instrument). I can't help but think the bestselling

American novel *Memoirs of a Geisha* and subsequent Academy award winning film had some role in perpetuating some stereotypes. Just to set the record straight, *no*, there was neither a military nor geisha connection to my parents union.

Speaking of strange lines of questioning, I distinctly recall similar ridiculous questions that were asked about my mother during an interview for a scholarship to study in Japan during my sophomore year at Georgetown. This time, the interviewers were all U.S. citizens, predominantly white, who represented some association for the advancement of female rights and had no connection to Georgetown University. Funny, there was only one female in the entire room of seven or more interviewers. I applied for the society's scholarship to study in Japan and made the final round for an interview. Rather than asking questions about my interests and desires to study in Japan, one interviewer asked me if my mother was Japanese. I replied "yes." He then asked me how my parents met and if they met on a military base. I was shocked. I did not feel his question was relevant nor had anything to do with my qualifications. I simply replied "the same as your parents . . . on a date." I never did get that particular scholarship. But I did eventually receive a full scholarship from the Japanese Ministry of Education to study one year at one of Japan's leading private universities, Keio University in Tokyo, Japan.

KEIO UNIVERSITY

I spent my junior year as an exchange student at Japan's Keio University. Because my language ability far surpassed most of my exchange student classmates, I attended regular Japanese classes that the third and fourth year Japanese Keio students attended. I spent most of my time with Japanese students speaking Japanese rather than mixing with English speaking foreigners. As far as I was concerned, the reason for going to Japan was to further polish my Japanese and interact with Japanese people, not to spend my time speaking English with foreigners. If that was my purpose, I might as well never have left the United States to study in Japan in the first place. I knew my priorities and goals. My own goals included doing everything possible to master the language and polish my reading and writing skills so I spent time reading and attending seminars in Japanese.

One seminar I attended was a course on Fukuzawa Yukichi, the founder of Keio University, and a leading Meiji period intellectual. My Professor, Mr. Takao Kawai, assigned one book per week for us to read. For me this took some time as the books were written by Yukichi himself and the characters and phrases used were from an older generation requiring me to consult my dictionary frequently. The Japanese language has changed considerably from pre to post World War II Japan. It probably took me twice the amount of time to finish reading the books assigned than my Japanese classmates. We read such classics such as *The Autobiography of Fukuzawa Yukichi* and *Gakumon no Susume* (Advancing Education). The first book we were assigned was an autobiography of Yukichi and we were told to come prepared to discuss the book for the next seminar meeting. I did just that.

The Professor went around the room asking each student his or her opinion of the book and the life of Yukichi. As he went across the room I could tell that many had not read the book or thought deeply about the subject matter. I was the last person he asked. I came prepared and it showed. The Professor was shocked and the first thing he said was "Mr. Reiman, you read the book." Of course, I read the book. That was the homework assignment and I was shocked that the Professor assumed I would not come prepared. He never doubted me again and would often meet me outside of class to talk about various topics including life in Yamagata Prefecture where he was from and his student days at Princeton University.

Generally speaking, I enjoyed my year at Keio University. But, I realized that the academic standards were not as rigorous as those I was used to at Georgetown. For many Japanese students, college was a time for fun, a way to finally escape the rigors of test-taking and rote memorization, and have a life before joining a company. I noticed a very big difference in the quality and caliber of students based on whether they entered Keio University through examination or were selected based on other criteria (i.e., attended Keio primary school to high school and were exempt from taking the examination, were students that grew up abroad, celebrities, or individuals from prominent families).

The students that had to cram and study hard to enter Keio University through examination tended to be the most serious and academically advanced students. Many of the third and fourth year students did not always attend class or study so seriously because their energies were focused on job searches. Of course, a few students pursued the graduate school route, but most chose to enter a Japanese company. When I asked why many students did not study so rigorously and the standards were rather loose compared to some of the leading U.S. universities, the unanimous reply was that Japanese students studied so hard from primary to high school and that once they pass the university examination it was time to relax. The real "education" would begin once they entered a Japanese company. So the prevailing idea was that students should enjoy their college experience while it lasts.

After studying and attending classes at Keio's Mita campus in Tokyo, I would take the train to return to the all-male dormitory in Higashi Ojima. This dorm included Japanese businessmen, students, and a handful of exchange students from countries such as the U.S., Germany, Australia, Brazil, Tanzania, Uganda, and others. Of the over 130 residents, over 120 were Japanese. Many of the residents were students cramming for one year to try to pass university examinations to enter medical school or law school or to pass a government examination to become an accountant and so forth. Many had taken such exams before and failed, but wanted one more chance to pursue their dreams. If they did not pass the examination, there was no way for them to become a doctor or accountant, architect, etc.

Kyoritsu Maintenance, a private company specializing in building and maintaining affordable large housing compounds owned the dorm and Keio University rented a few rooms out for its exchange students. The dorm manager and his wife were from Asahikawa in Hokkaido and the manager was a former soldier in the Japan Self Defense Forces. There was a cafeteria, washing machine and dryer room, and large *ofuro* (bath) used by the residents. I found it a wonderful experience to live with other Japanese and also meet exchange students from a variety of different countries. Many were already successful lawyers, tax specialists, teachers, and civil servants back in their home countries. They were sent by their respective governments to spend a year in Japan. We all enjoyed our experience together, quickly became friends, and learned from each other.

The commute from the Mita campus to the dorm by train was roughly 45 minutes. A beautiful park was located near the dorm and stores and restaurants to grab noodles or buy snacks were plentiful. The dorm was also conveniently located near a train station so we could easily take the train to visit Shibuya, Shinjuku, and other places where college students tended to gather. My year abroad was magical and I could not have asked for a better place to live than the cozy and quiet dormitory.

WORKING IN JAPAN

Before entering Keio University, I was fortunate to land an internship with a Japanese finance/lease company called ORIX the summer of my sophomore year in college. ORIX had a winning Japanese professional baseball team, the ORIX Blue Wave, which had won the Japanese World Series at the time and featured Ichiro Suzuki, their star player, who later moved on to play professional baseball in the U.S. I wanted to gain work experience and pay for my summer in Japan so I applied to the Forval Foundation. The Forval Foundation has an internship program where they select university students from the U.S. and other countries. Once selected, the Forval Foundation, in conjunction with several Japanese companies, determines the company for which an intern should work based on his or her interests and the needs of the company.

Fortunately, I was selected to work at ORIX headquarters located inside Japan's World Trade Center in *Shimbashi*. I was given a monthly allowance and stayed at an all-male ORIX company dormitory located at *Toda Koen Mae* in Saitama Prefecture. In essence, I lived the life of a Japanese salary worker for two months. I took the packed train from the dormitory to work every morning and at night would often accompany my supervisors for Karaoke and drinking. While I enjoyed the experience, I realized I could never be a salary worker in Japan. My interests were elsewhere.

Upon graduating from Georgetown University, I was determined to be in Japan for the summer to spend time with my girlfriend who was working at a Japanese bank at the time. But I did not have money and needed a job. So I decided to live at my grandmother's place in Minowa, Taito Ward in Tokyo for a few months. Having spent nearly every summer at my grandmother's place, I was familiar and comfortable with my surroundings. Although my grandmother was showing signs of Alzheimer's at the time, we enjoyed each other's company. I decided to work at a convenience store called Lawson located less than 10 minutes from my home and near a *sento* or public bath. The store owner was hiring and he hired me for 800 yen (roughly 8 dollars) an hour on a temporary basis. Because I would work the night shift, I could also gain an additional 200 yen (roughly 2 dollars) per hour. I took the job for both the money and the experience, which turned out to be great.

Customers would often come in and say, "you speak great Japanese" or ask, "Japanese is a hard language, isn't it?" I would reply, "Your Japanese isn't bad either" or "We should study Japanese together since it is such a hard language," which would always catch my customers by surprise because they never anticipated a foreigner providing such replies. Little did they know I grew up right across the street from them and probably attended the same neighborhood activities as one of their children. I had fun changing widely held misperceptions about foreigners, Americans in particular. I loved being able to showcase American values of openness and free speech while maintaining Japanese values of humility and group harmony. I learned through these encounters at the convenience store that with hard work and effort, one could master any language and any culture. If you want it bad enough, you will put in the time to perfect your craft. That process never ends. I also learned that no one country owns a monopoly over the true essence of what it means to be "Japanese" or "American." The notion that only a Japanese person born and raised in Japan can be truly Japanese or has a Japanese spirit is false. Similarly, the notion that only a person born and raised in America can be truly American or love America is also false. Let's merge positive values found in both cultures to promote a *Jamericanness*. Dual nationals like myself live it every day.

LAWSON CONVENIENCE STORE

Convenience stores in the U.S. and Japan vary greatly when it comes to use of technology and customer service. By far, Japanese convenience stores outrank U.S. convenience stores in those areas. Unlike in Arizona where Circle K was the most popular chain convenience store around, in Japan the top convenience store chains are Lawson, 7/11, and Family Mart. These convenience stores are often equipped with delivery services like taking dry cleaning, luggage parcels, library books for drop-off, and mail delivery. Other services include printing digital camera photos, concert ticket purchases, and paying utility, gas, cell phone, and insurance bills at the convenience store cash register. In some stores one can electronically process and submit government documents like change of address and registry without having to visit the local ward office.

When I worked part-time in Lawson we would have electronic computer registrars we used that included weather forecasts which allowed us to order more or less of certain items we knew would be popular on rainy versus sunny days. We had chopsticks, plastic forks, spoons, and other items ready to provide to customers, hot water for instant noodles, a microwave to heat items, and Lawson food item brands like *Karaage Kun* (fried-chicken nuggets) always popular, corn dogs, and *oden* (dish containing all kinds of ingredients like hard-boiled egg, Japanese white radish, and other items in a special broth). On forecasted sunny days we would order more ice cream bars, and on rainy days, other items popular among customers.

Affectionately known as *konbini* in Japanese, these stores have revolutionized the way Japanese consumers shop. Open 24 hours a day, seven days a week, a consumer can get most of his or her needs without having to go long distances to the supermarket. One can buy freshly made lunches, choose from a variety of food and drink items, purchase fruits and vegetables, buy cigarettes, video games, batteries, soap, magazines, comic books, stockings, cosmetics, candy, snacks, umbrellas and more. Competition from these *konbini* have made it difficult for supermarkets and liquor shops to survive. Many of the old mom-and-pop stores went out of business or were bought out by these *konbini*, which now number more than 50,000. Located in rural areas and providing ATM machines, copy and fax machines as well, consumers can conveniently take care of their needs in these one-stop shops.

Customer service was also a key part of the *konbini* experience. All of us were trained to use the proper language and learn set phrases in dealing with customers. We would wear our uniforms, place items in the appropriate size bag, place all utensils there, warm up food, respectfully bow, and thank customers for coming. Working at a *konbini* is a great way to learn Japanese business etiquette and language. In addition to weather forecast information, we also collected demographic data such as gender, age, and regional preferences to ensure we knew our customers. I was amazed at how much detail went into pleasing the customer. In the shop where I worked, because it was located next to a public bath, we knew that around 6pm or later customers who frequented the public bath would come for beer, ice cream, and other items and we were prepared for them. Lunchtime was also a peak period for us. Food items such as *onigiri* (rice balls), sandwiches, fruit, and vegetables would be delivered on average two to four times a day.

The Japanese consumer is extremely picky and sensitive to customer service, so any business that wishes to survive, particularly chain stores, must exceed customer expectations. Innovation and creativity is therefore fostered to meet the high expectations of Japanese consumers who demand the highest goods and services. Competition among the major operators is fierce. Each has to find a way to distinguish itself from others. Lawson, for example, started a convenience store called 100 in which all products are sold for 100 yen including fruit juices, vegetables, and other items (excluding sales tax). They also created a store for mothers to take young children to purchase children's items, baby food, and more where mothers can relax, chat, eat, and drink while allowing their kids to play in an indoor playground. These stores collect, study, and analyze demographic data to effectively target customers living in the respective *konbini* areas to meet their needs.

I would not have secured the job at a convenience store nor visited Japan if I had not fallen head over heels in love with a Japanese exchange student I met in Georgetown my freshman year. I was determined to chase after her. And chase after her I did.

LOVE BROUGHT ME TO JAPAN AND
NOT THE MIDDLE EAST

As a young man new to the Washington DC area and for the first time really away from family, I was quite lonely during my freshman year at Georgetown. My roommate at the time smoked marijuana, drank heavily, and did not share the same values I did. He came from a well-to-do family in Albany, New York and didn't seem to put studies first. For my parents and me, a Georgetown education was a very expensive financial proposal and I couldn't afford to let them down by not focusing on studying as hard as I could. Had I chosen to remain in Arizona I could have attended any state university on scholarship, greatly reducing the financial burden of a college education on my parents. But I had chosen to go to Georgetown specifically because it was a Jesuit University and because of the School of Foreign Service. But little did I know I couldn't choose my roommate for my freshman year. Initially, I recall a Japanese exchange student was scheduled to be my roommate, but he decided at the last minute not to attend Georgetown University. Wherever he is now I hope his life is full of love and happiness.

Partly because I felt so "unclean" sharing a dorm room with my roommate and partly because I had a strong sense of wanting to do something "useful" with my life, I had a notion of leaving Georgetown during my freshman year to become a Buddhist monk in Taiwan and join the Tzu Chi Foundation. I couldn't think of a nobler thing to do than to volunteer and serve humanity. But I ended up meeting a young Japanese girl instead who filled an empty void in my life.

Two years older than me, she was an exchange student from Sophia University, a Jesuit University in Tokyo, Japan. She spoke English, Japanese, and French and came to Georgetown on a one-year exchange program. I was attracted to her the moment I was first introduced to her by her roommate. We began dating and she changed my life. She visited my home in Fountain Hills, Arizona, spent Christmas with my parents and me, and we became a couple. I decided my junior year to attend Keio University in Tokyo, Japan so that I could be closer to her, giving up my previous plans of studying Arabic and attending a university in Cairo. We stayed together even as she started working for a bank in Japan and I began graduate studies at Stanford University. It was natural for us to think about marriage. As soon as I joined the State Department, we became engaged and began to plan for our wedding.

The wedding was to occur legally on March 27 and the official ceremony was scheduled for May 23, 2004. Let me explain why we needed to get married legally first. Unless we were married legally first, she could not be added to my travel orders as the spouse of an American diplomat nor enjoy the full privileges of diplomatic immunity that accompany that status. Complicating matters once again was the requirement by Diplomatic Security (hereafter "DS") that any Department of State employee planning to marry a foreign national must notify DS 180 days prior to the wedding and submit a complete background application form so that DS can investigate that person's background.

I also had to complete a background check prior to joining the State Department and had to renew this process every five years in order to update my security clearance and be eligible to continue to serve as a Foreign Service Officer. The background form asks if one has any immediate family members that are foreign nationals or has an intimate or on-going relationship with any foreign nationals. I listed my mother, my grandmother, and my fiancée (all three Japanese nationals) on my form. Listing three Japanese nationals made me nervous because the DS culture uses that information to preclude people from serving in countries where they have "ties" that DS believes would somehow not be in the interests of the organization. I know plenty of Foreign Service Officers married to Japanese women or who have immediate relatives that are non-American that are barred from serving in the country where one has family ties.

But ultimately I did not marry my college sweetheart. One of the factors that made me decide not to marry her was I did not want her Japanese background to hinder my own chance of serving in Japan. I thought that eliminating one more name from the DS background form would give me a better shot at acceptance and would prevent folks from questioning my loyalty. Another factor was I didn't believe the Foreign Service life, which entails a commitment to "worldwide availability," would suit my fiancée. Becoming a Foreign Service Officer means one may have to take assignments in dangerous locations or in the developing world and that was not something I thought my fiancée would be prepared to accept. She made it clear that she preferred Paris, I made it clear that I preferred service in Africa. Finally, at the time I wanted to marry someone with faith, particularly a Christian with whom I could grow together, not just emotionally and physically, but also spiritually. We ended up not marrying and separating after eight years. And, that was the hardest decision I ever made. I made that decision out of "love" but I felt I had died that morning of March 27, 2004 at 11am when we last spoke. I felt we were too young, had divergent career goals, and that I could not be the man she wanted me to be. Needless to say, my heart was broken, and I know her heart was broken too.

While DS and the Foreign Service were not the sole reasons for the break-up, the pressure that DS places on individuals contemplating marrying foreign nationals and the restrictions it places did have a big impact on my decision-making at the time. Looking back it was naive to think that not marrying her would boost my chances to serve in Japan – the only thing I ever asked from the State Department. There is nothing like your first love, which, by definition, only comes once. And the illogical system of barring people with language skills and cultural background from serving in the country in which he/she has ties— *impacts lives*. I don't want any other person to have to face the sense of inequality, devastation, and loss I felt—so I share this with you. The Foreign Service needs to do a better job of utilizing its "cultural treasures" and resources or else many individuals will leave to find an environment in which one's background can be viewed as an "asset" as opposed to a "liability." My service came at a very high price at the cost of two significant relationships (my grandmother and my fiancée).

Regardless of whether I should or should not have married that Japanese woman, I never had a chance to meet her again. We communicated periodically via email after that day, but after a time, that communication also stopped. Not because I wanted it to, but because she no longer desired to maintain a friendship. Up until then, she was the only woman I had ever truly loved and desired to make my wife. However, six years later, God gave me the opportunity to meet a woman who perfectly fit into my life, the woman I would eventually call my wife. We would travel together to Guyana, and in time, have two wonderful sons.

3 Lessons Learned:

- In diplomacy and in life, as I look back, I can say to others, never sacrifice those you love for a career. Your career will end at some point. Invest in the relationships that matter TODAY!

- Learn from your failures and share the mistakes you made so that others can benefit. In doing so, you turn a negative into a positive and turn your loss into a gain for others. Your suffering is not in vain if it can be used to help others and make the world a better place.

- Write, paint, or engage in other creative outlets that can help you process and heal. You can rebound from any setback and succeed. If I can do it, so can you!

Your silence says something. If you do not speak up or express your views then someone else will shape the narrative for you. Own your destiny. Own your story. Own your life. Own your successes and failures. But most importantly, own your duality. Have the courage to confront prejudice and stand up for what is right. Lack of authenticity is detrimental to diplomacy and life. Both the United States and Japanese governments need to allow dual nationals to be authentically themselves and authentically and unapologetically love both.

Chapter Five

Going After My Dreams: Diplomacy Here I Come!

Graduate School

Before graduating from Georgetown, I decided I wanted to continue my passion for East Asian affairs by pursuing further study at graduate school. I applied to many schools including Stanford University and Columbia, but chose Stanford because of its location and vicinity near to Arizona. I wanted to be closer to home. I passed the first hurdle of getting accepted, but I still needed money to pay for graduate school. I applied for the DACOR Bacon House scholarship given to one student at Georgetown's School of Foreign Service. Two students were selected for interview with only one receiving the scholarship. DACOR consists of a group of retired former Foreign Service Ambassadors and Consul Generals. We were invited to attend one of their periodic meetings and I was impressed with the enthusiasm and energy in which these gentlemen discussed foreign affairs. Each had previously served in different countries and it was refreshing to hear the perspective of former Ambassadors regarding their lives and experiences in the Foreign Service. That left a positive impression on me and made me consider pursuing a career in the Foreign Service.

The fact that I won the scholarship also helped. The scholarship was for 10,000 dollars, but I had also applied for another scholarship, the Woodrow Wilson scholarship, that would cover all my graduate school expenses including room and board. I was waiting for the final results of that scholarship. I eventually won a Woodrow Wilson Foundation Scholarship so I had to decline the DACOR scholarship. But I credit the DACOR foundation for increasing my interest in joining the U.S. diplomatic corps by believing in me, and providing me with a positive experience.

Under the agreements of the Woodrow Wilson Foundation, I would have all graduate school expenses paid for with the condition that I would serve in the Foreign Service for at least three years. The only catch was that I would have to pass the written and oral examinations for the Foreign Service. I would also have to do an internship in the State Department in DC for one summer and spend another summer as an intern at an Embassy abroad. If I failed to meet my contract obligations, I would have to pay the Foundation back for all expenses. The fact that we would have to pay back all expenses motivated me to honor my contract and study hard to pass the Foreign Service exam. Luckily, I did. I then entered the Foreign Service in September 2002 after obtaining a Master's degree from Stanford's Center for East Asian studies.

At Stanford, I chose to do research on Japan's colonization of Korea and its impact on North Korea. I had a wonderful mentor and expert on Korean nationalism and sociology as my thesis adviser. Professor Gi-Wook Shin had recently arrived at Stanford's Asia Pacific Research Center (APARC) to establish a first class Korean Studies Program and he had taught previously at UCLA. Under his guidance, I studied the impact of Japanese colonization on Korea. But I wanted to study more about North Korea and the impact of

Japanese colonization in shaping post-World War II North Korean education. I studied moral education textbooks used by Japanese colonizers in Korea during the colonial period and compared that to current moral education textbooks used in North Korea's primary and secondary schools. I concluded that the North Korean regime, despite its Stalinist/Leninist communist rhetoric and denial of utilizing anything Japanese, employed a combination of tactics used by their former Japanese occupiers to instill a sense of ethnic or racial nationalism to unite the populace around a central emperor-type figure through their education system.

The so-called experts could not understand why the North Korean regime did not crumble after the fall of communism in Russia, Romania, and Germany. The reason was simple. North Korea is not truly a Stalinist/Leninist regime as they pretend to be in their official public pronouncements. Rather, it operates more on Confucian principles and a political structure that in many ways resembles that of Japan's pre-World War II military government led by a central emperor figure. State Shinto ideology was merely replaced with North Korean *Juche* ideology and the Japanese emperor was replaced by Kim Il-Sung and later his son Kim Jong-Il. I learned that to truly understand present day North Korea, one must study the impact of Japanese colonialism and Korean history prior to the Japanese occupation.

I studied Korean language at Stanford as well to do my research. Finding textbooks and authoritative sources on North Korea was problematic. Primary sources were scarce. However, the Hoover Institute and Professor John Lewis who frequently visited North Korea came to the rescue. I read the Japanese moral education textbooks that Korean primary and secondary students were forced to study during the colonial period. One of the primary reasons I wanted to study North Korean history was because of its close proximity to Japan and I did not fully understand why the two Asian neighbors were bitter enemies. I remember when I was an exchange student at

Keio University some dorm mates and I were eating in the Higashi Ojima Dorm cafeteria when news arrived that North Korea had launched a Taepedong Missile across Japan. I also later learned that North Korea had kidnapped several Japanese citizens in the past and that was another issue of contention between the Japanese and North Korean governments.

I wanted to learn what made the North Korean regime tick and what mechanisms were used to keep the populace loyal to the ruling Kim family. My research at Stanford allowed me to do just that. I wrote my Master's thesis on the impact of Japanese colonization and use of moral education in shaping North Korea's political and education systems. The thesis is still held at the Hoover Institute Archives at Stanford University. If we want to be effective diplomats and problem solvers, we need to understand history and learn how to apply historical lessons to modern society.

History Matters

With friends from Korea, China, Taiwan, and Japan, it saddens me to see continued friction regarding Japan's role in World War II. The history issue of Japanese textbooks whitewashing atrocities committed by Japanese troops during World War II continues to serve as a point of contention. We hear about Chinese and Korean "comfort woman" used by Japanese troops as sex slaves. We hear about the 731 medical unit's biological and chemical experiments on innocent Chinese. The list goes on and on. What is tragic is that there has never been a national debate among the Japanese people regarding responsibility for the War. While Japan's Foreign Ministry's position is that Japan has officially apologized over 17 times towards the countries it had colonized, the apology does not resonate as "sincere" among Japan's neighbors. Frequent visits by Japanese heads of state to the Yasukuni Shrine to pay official homage to Japan's fallen warriors, including 14 Class-A War Criminals, continue to remain a thorn in Japan's diplomatic relations with its Asian neighbors.

Papua New Guinea is a country where many Japanese young soldiers were sent during World War II prior to the Philippines becoming the strategic base of importance. Many 18 and 19 year olds were sent to this region and died not from fighting in battle but from starvation. The Japanese military government literally left these soldiers to starve. These soldiers and countless other Japanese youth were victims of the war as were the mothers and children left in Japan to support soldiers in the field. I often have to remind friends in China and Korea (some of whom have never met or had a relationship with a Japanese person) that many Japanese people were also victims of WWII. Unfortunately, in China, the government controls the media and many PRC citizens are not taught the suffering endured by many Japanese citizens during WWII, which leads many Chinese to label Japan, and by association all Japanese people, as "aggressors." Chinese media often broadcast programs rife with anti-Japanese sentiment, especially programs dealing with WWII. A Chinese national watching such programs inevitably learns to equate Chinese nationalism with "anti-Japanism." It is only when a Chinese person meets a Japanese person or visits Japan that his/her perception changes. Exposure beyond the media is key.

I frequently hear from Chinese friends upon returning from Japan or making Japanese friends that they are surprised at how different the reality about Japan and Japanese people is versus what they learned growing up in China. Often, after having these experiences, these individuals express admiration and an increased sense of respect toward their Japanese neighbors. In Korea, anti-Japanese sentiment is also quite common and expressed in Korean nationalism. But I have found that both Koreans and Chinese that have never made Japanese friends or visited Japan tend to have a more negative view of Japan than those who have Japanese friends or have visited the country. In the same way, I also know of many Japanese people who get it wrong when it comes to Korea and China. The biases and prejudices go both ways. Many Japanese people are also guilty of not quite understanding their Korean and Chinese neighbors. But I know that people to people exchanges are one way to break this cycle of mistrust and promote coexistence in peace and harmony.

Exposure is crucial. People to people diplomacy is essential. And the more exchanges between Chinese people and Japanese people, Japanese people and Korean people, the better. Ultimately, you want to engage in business with partners you trust. Those relationships lead to greater trade and investment and business opportunities that can benefit both sides.

History matters. Education matters. More should be done to educate citizens in China, Korea, and Japan about the common history and periods of mutual cooperation and trade between these neighboring countries to emphasize the commonality and similarities between them rather than focus only on differences. Chinese characters, Confucianism, Buddhism, architecture, art, and many other cultural treasures while taking different forms in these three countries nonetheless are commonly shared. A common "Asian" heritage should be emphasized in which all members can take pride. There is no need for any country to serve as the sole representative of Asia, just as there is no need for any European country to serve as the sole representative of Europe. There is more that unites us than divides us.

Am I less American because I speak Japanese, like Japanese food, and love my Japanese heritage? Absolutely not. Am I less Japanese because I speak English, respect American values and institutions, and love barbeque and apple pie? Absolutely not.

Chapter Six

No Way, the U.S. Government Does Not Discriminate!

Next to physical survival, the greatest need of a human being is psychological survival—to be understood, to be affirmed, to be validated, to be appreciated.

~Stephen Covey

The Department of State does a poor job providing the psychological support dual nationals need to survive, much less thrive in an environment that fundamentally views dual nationals as liabilities rather than assets. It does little to practice what it preaches when it comes to diversity. That does not bode well for the future of U.S. diplomacy and weakens U.S. national interests at home and abroad if not corrected. Lack of authenticity in promoting diversity eventually will be exposed and asking Congress and the American taxpayer for more money when the Department does not take advantage of the human capital it does have (i.e., denying dual nationals eager and ready to serve in their country of national origin), is not only inexcusable, but also wasteful. Asian American diplomats without dual nationality still face very high bars and hurdles to be sent to their country of national origin even though many have the expertise and language skills to effectively serve. This practice needs to end immediately. It undermines organizational effectiveness, impacts morale, stymies innovation, and is an unnecessary hardship placed on an employee and his or her family. We have enough external enemies to defeat. Let's not cast dual nationals and loyal Asian Americans into the same enemy camp. We need to work with and not against them. After 16 years, we have no progress. If anything, policies toward dual nationals have only tightened.

Commercially and economically, it makes sense to value Asian Americans. According to the Nelson Report, the buying power of Asian Americans is to hit $1 trillion in 2018. Asian American purchasing power grew faster than any other racial demographic. This group presents a dream niche for companies who are eager to find as much data on Asian American consumers as possible. The fastest growing multicultural segment in the United States is not a segment to ignore. When you add to that mix dual nationals who can navigate the United States and their country of origin, you are able to tap into two minds for the price of one. The trade between two of the world's economic titans, the U.S. and Japan, alone makes for a compelling argument to curry favor with dual nationals who can provide instant access and credibility.

It makes sense not just morally but economically to affirm, validate, and appreciate what Asian Americans can offer. We should view dual nationals as the conduit to tap into two huge commercial markets. Connect the diplomatic dots and empower dual nationals, and they then will empower you and your organization to reach new heights. But some may ask how can dual nationals save the U.S. government and American taxpayer money?

A fluent Mandarin or Japanese or Arabic speaker saves the American taxpayer at least two years of language and area studies training, which amounts to considerable ROI for the taxpayer. In fact, even with two years of intense language training, non-native speakers will not have the type of fluency in language and culture nuance as their dual national counterparts. Imagine the millions of dollars the Department of State wastes of American taxpayer money by not sending dual nationals to serve in their country of national origin. Add to that the millions of dollars spent on recruiting diversity candidates, many with strong ties to their country of national origin, including dual nationals, only to bar them from serving in the country where they would most effectively perform. Don't you believe American taxpayers deserve better returns on their investment? I do. Each year that passes represents another wasted opportunity and the American taxpayer deserves to know the truth.

We're thinking about dual nationality in the wrong way and acting out on those prejudices based more on fear than anything else. When we view dual nationals as assets and not liabilities, we affirm, validate, and appreciate the diversity they bring. If you do not believe dual nationals can effectively serve the United States Government, do not hire them. If you are suspicious that they cannot serve U.S. interests abroad because of potential conflicts of loyalty, do not recruit them. However, studies have shown that employing diversity candidates increases an organization's efficiency and can lead to greater innovation. Barring dual nationals from serving in the country of their national origin makes neither financial nor human resource nor psychological sense. It only makes sense if you are against diversity, inclusion, and equity. The key is to leverage the strengths of dual nationals. Organizations can do so by employing dual nationals, embracing their uniqueness, empowering them to succeed through education and training, and promoting them.

A recent 2017 State Department policy on Dual Nationality found in 3 FAM 2424.5 confirms the Department's anti-dual nationality posture, a policy that was not in effect nor made clear to me when I was first recruited in 2000. I held on to my hope since entering the U.S. Foreign Service in 2002 that I would eventually be sent to Japan, dual national or not. I believed the Department would come to its senses and do the right thing. I gave the Department the benefit of the doubt for 16 years. I loyally took my marching orders thinking one day my hard work and perseverance would pay off. One day, the Department would realize its mistake, see the value of dual nationals as assets, and allow my dream and that of my family to come true along with countless other dual nationals stuck in the same boat. That boat is sinking and has been for some time. Only you and I can salvage the wreck. I believe in the power of civil society to influence governments. I believe in the American and Japanese people; I believe that together we can create a dual environment for success.

Clearly, the Department of State could have done a better job communicating to dual nationals at the beginning of the recruitment process what a career in the U.S. Foreign Service requires of them. Candidates should be informed from the start that they must renounce their non-U.S. citizenship to have any expectation of an assignment in their country of origin. This gives the employee a choice to take his or her services elsewhere and find organizations that will affirm, validate, and appreciate them. You save the employee and the organization heartache. Expectations would be clear and dual national resources could be utilized in an environment of duality that actually values diversity.

These dual national assets are willing to work on behalf of America to promote U.S. interests. Why not let them do so? Barring them from serving in the country where they have expertise, know the language, and have a desire to serve denies them their inherent duality, diversity, and trust in the ideals of America. That is why my mother came to this country. She believed in the American dream. She obtained it. It was unimaginably difficult for my mother and I to learn that the same country in which we both served would deny us our dream to serve it better.

For 16 years, I gave the Department of State the benefit of the doubt. If only I work harder, if I deny my Japanese heritage, if I prove my loyalty by not visiting Japan, if I persuade my relatives to become U.S. citizens, if I do not apply for dual nationality for my children, if I avoid contacting Japanese people—I could avoid foreign contact reporting that indicated strong ties to Japan, etc. etc. My mind played out so many scenarios just to prove my loyalty to the United States. Did any of that help? Nope. It did the opposite. You know what all that did to me? It impacted my health, my relationships, and nearly lost me my life. Wanting so badly to be accepted, I sacrificed my personal health, relationships, and welfare.

Based on my 16 years of experience as a State Department Foreign Service Officer based in DC and overseas, having had to file two equal employment opportunity or EEO cases for discrimination against two white Senior Foreign Service Officers on two separate occasions, and having been precluded from serving in the one country I wanted to serve since day 1 in the Foreign Service, I cannot recommend dual nationals to join. At least not until they are afforded the same opportunities to maximize their talents as others. Given my bilingual background, I had always wanted to bridge the gap between the U.S. and Japan. I thought entering Georgetown's School of Foreign Service was the first step toward that goal. I never intended to join the Foreign Service, but what I did know was that I wanted to do something international, hopefully connected to Japan. I took advantage of Georgetown's exchange program with Keio University in Tokyo, Japan and spent my junior year studying in Tokyo. I was fortunate to be included in classes that included Chinese, Korean, Russian, Uzbek, and German exchange students. During a sociology course on Japanese festival traditions, my teacher and two fellow Korean students asked me whether I felt the U.S. government discriminated against Asian Americans. I replied without hesitation "no."

According to them, their friends had confessed that there was a ceiling for Asian Americans trying to rise up in the ranks of government and an inherent bias towards them. They cited the internment of Japanese Americans during World War II and the period in which the Department of State did not allow Japanese-Americans to serve. I was too naive and had no life experiences with government to ever feel that was the case back then. However, the seed was planted in my head that perhaps what these gentlemen and scholars were saying might have some truth. Upon further research, I discovered a few startling facts.

First, there have been less than ten Asian American Ambassadors in the history of the U.S. Department of State, and until 2011, the majority never served in an Asian country of significant strategic importance to the U.S. such as Beijing, Tokyo, or Seoul. It was only in 2011 that Gary Locke, a Chinese American, became U.S. Ambassador to China and Sung Kim, a Korean American, became U.S. Ambassador to Korea. To date, however, there has never been a Japanese American Ambassador to Japan. There was only one person who reached the ranks of Assistant Secretary, and that role was more of a token position with little real power, given to a non-career officer with political connections. Unfortunately, the Department of State has a poor record of hiring and recruiting Asian Americans into their ranks and allowing them to rise within the system. The numbers do not lie. The same can be said about Native American recruitment. When it comes to senior management positions, it is extremely difficult to find a career Ambassador with Native American heritage. I could only find one career Foreign Service Officer, Dennis P. Barret, who rose to become U.S. Ambassador to Madagascar (term of appointment December, 1992 to November 1995) listed as having strong Native American roots. Ironic, isn't it given that the only true "Americans" are Native Americans whose land we stole and continue to occupy to this day.

There are plenty of Asian Americans that speak Japanese, Mandarin, Taiwanese, Vietnamese, Cambodian, and other Asian languages that are as capable of doing a stellar job as any non-Asian American assigned abroad to a U.S. mission. Given the number of Korean Americans, Chinese Americans, Japanese Americans and other Asian Americans, why do we not have more prominent figures representing us abroad in powers of position in the top embassies in Asia (i.e., Beijing, Tokyo, and Seoul)? There has never been any substantive "Asian-American" or "Pacific Islander" history month celebrated with much fervor within government circles. Rather than trusting and conceding more authority and power to Asian Americans, what appears is an inherent bias against us that deems us somehow less "American" among conservative organizations within the Department of State such as the Bureau of Diplomatic Security.

Diplomatic Security has a history of preventing qualified individuals with talent and language ability from serving in positions abroad where they can use their language skills and cultural background. DS frequently prevents such individuals from serving in locations based on the individual's ethnic background and cultural ties. This exclusion applies to officers who marry foreigners, have a foreign mother or father or relative, or who have close and intimate ties with individuals from countries that DS deems inappropriate. This can also include dual passport holders. This is a shame. Some of our best talent comes from this pool. If we stringently adhere to such outdated models, we will never be able to present the "best and the brightest" U.S. representatives abroad.

I was barred from serving in Japan for the first five years upon entering the Foreign Service because my mother was Japanese and because DS thought I had too many ties to Japan. I never felt more humiliated in my life. Raised to believe that my Japanese heritage and background was an asset, I learned that somehow that became a liability, preventing me from serving in the country in which I had always wanted to serve. One of the primary reasons for joining Georgetown's School of Foreign Service, studying North Korean politics and education system at Stanford's Center for East Asian Studies, and entering the Foreign Service was to utilize my language abilities and passion for promoting U.S.-Japan relations. I was greatly disappointed to learn that the U.S. government, for all of its recruitment talk about equal opportunity, would sideline me from playing on a field they claimed was "even." I found out that was false advertising meant to pay lip service to an American public increasingly sensitive to topics of political correctness and equal opportunity.

In reality, my preclusion from serving in Japan meant I could not even apply or have the opportunity to apply for jobs in Japan, effectively eliminating my dreams. That, to me, did not make much sense, especially during a period when the Department claimed it experienced severe shortages of qualified officers fluent in one of the "super hard" languages, including Japanese, and that they were recruiting people specifically with such language skills to serve in those missions. I found out that only included people of "appropriate" ethnic or cultural background with limited or no ties to the country they wanted to serve. If you only want to send mediocre candidates, the best way to do so is to eliminate from the competition the top Asian language speakers, many of whom have family or ties to that country. I do not believe that is the correct policy for any agency to pursue, particularly one with primary responsibility for promoting diplomatic ties abroad.

I remember applying for a position in the Central Intelligence Agency (CIA) and National Security Agency (NSA) during my Georgetown years. My dual citizenship and fact that my mother is Japanese was a "negative" for recruiters in these agencies. They found me to be a "security" liability. If they were smart, they would have hired me to serve as a double agent. I did not realize the bias these individuals had towards people of dual nationality and exclusionary policies they pursued in the hiring and recruitment process. What my fellow exchange student classmates from Keio University had told me about inherent biases found within the U.S. government toward Asian Americans became reality for me. I did not understand why I was not considered "American" enough to serve my country and risk my life for that cause, even though my paper credentials and qualifications far surpassed any of the requirements for entry set out by both the CIA and NSA. The message was loud and clear—"your duality threatens us." I encountered the same results when applying for the Defense Intelligence Agency (DIA) and other intelligence branches. Where does this fear come from? False assumptions, ignorance, and pure prejudice.

Foreign family members including immediate relatives and spouses of government employees are encouraged to change citizenship to U.S. citizenship. That policy is understandable. However, whether an individual's mother or father is a citizen of another country or not, should not have bearing on assigning an individual to a country where he or she has a desire to serve. I cannot change the fact that my mother is a Japanese citizen. But, I do not feel she must change citizenship simply to allow me greater job opportunities to serve in one of many U.S. posts in Japan (Embassy Tokyo, Consulate Sapporo, Consulate Kobe, Consulate Fukuoka, and Consulate Okinawa).

If I passed all the security and background requirements to enter, why would you then not "trust" me enough to serve my country with pride in Tokyo? That was the question that kept running in my head as I had to eliminate a job in Tokyo that I wanted to apply for when I first entered the diplomatic corps. I was sent to my second choice—Taipei, Taiwan and given seven months of Mandarin language training in Washington, DC before serving two years in Taipei as a Consular Officer issuing visas. I do not regret my experiences in Taiwan nor the opportunity I was given to learn Mandarin Chinese, but I did resent the fact that I could not even apply for jobs in Japan.

In government circles, things do not change unless someone causes a stir and gains the attention of the "higher" ups. I was not willing to go to the Assistant Secretary of State for East Asian and Pacific Affairs as a newly minted Foreign Service Officer to complain about the preclusion placed by DS barring me from serving in Japan. After all, when we sign up for the Foreign Service we do agree to be available for "worldwide" service and not just to the countries we want to serve. I understood that and did not want to make a fuss. So, I begrudgingly accepted my fate. However, I decided that enough was enough and that I would contact DS myself to have whoever reviewed my file reassess my case and re-move the preclusion. I had to fight to have this preclusion removed. They finally agreed to remove my preclusion, but only after service in Lagos, Nigeria—one of the toughest places to serve in the Foreign Service, where I thrived.

Through all of these unpleasant experiences, I was reminded of two historic facts. First, the only country the U.S. ever dropped not one, but two atomic bombs on was Japan. Second, the only American citizens the U.S. government placed in military intern-ment camps during World War II were Japanese Americans. From these two historic realities, one can conclude that the present bias towards Japanese Americans is simply a continuation of racist and discriminatory policies since the time of the Franklin D. Roosevelt administration. Prior cases of discrimination towards the "Yellow Peril" or flow of immigrants from Asian countries and the immi-gration ban policies placed on Asians in the early 20th century attest to the government's poor record in including Asian people into the political discourse and seats of power.

I did not have my property or belongings stripped by the U.S. government like Japanese Americans interned during World War II, but my dignity was stripped and my heritage defiled when a ban was placed on me from serving in Japan. Really? A kid born in Iowa and raised in Arizona with zero military ties to Japan, cannot serve in the one country he has the language skills and cultural back-ground to serve immediately on behalf of the American taxpayer. I was dumbfounded. I believe that America, and American values must be about helping people achieve their dreams regardless of race, religion, ethnicity, gender or dual nationality. If we do not let our U.S. diplomats, dual national diplomats, achieve their destinies and utilize their skills, then we're failing them, the American tax-payer, the country, and the bilateral relationship.

I ask myself, "What progress has been made since the days of Japanese-American internment to provide opportunities for Japanese Americans to attain prominent positions of power within government?" Sadly, I do not see much progress. Sure, there may be a token nomination for an individual to serve as Secretary of Transportation, Secretary of Labor or Secretary of Veteran Affairs, but what about other posts? It does not surprise me that many Asian Americans opt not to take jobs in the public sector. With the inherent biases towards them and a government culture that still caters to an older mindset that does not know how to fully incorporate the Asian American experience into the mainstream culture, it is no wonder that few Asian Americans feel they "owe" government anything.

∞∞∞

AN UNJUST EVALUATION

In the Foreign Service, officers are evaluated every year through the EER or employee evaluation report. You have a rating officer and reviewing officer. The rating officer is your direct supervisor and the reviewing officer is typically your supervisor's immediate boss. Each writes an evaluation and provide examples of performance. These examples are supposed to be based on the core precepts which are: leadership, management, substantive knowledge, intellectual skills, communication (oral and written), and more. In my Foreign Service career I have had supervisors that wanted to draft the EER for me, but more often than not I was expected to draft my own EER and my supervisor would decide what to include and omit. Each EER has an "Area for Improvement" section, which only allows space for a few sentences. I always found it odd that we were told to include a "real" area for improvement as opposed to a "throw away" and yet we were never given any space on the form to really provide concrete examples and elaborate on that area. If we are really honest with ourselves, there are probably a lot of "areas for improvement" that we could talk about but you really need more, probably half a page as opposed to room for three sentences if you are really serious about providing a "real" area for improvement.

The final page of the EER includes the Rated Employee's statement otherwise known as the "suicide" box. It is known as the "suicide" box because what one writes in that area can have an impact on how a Review Panel Board evaluates you and can hurt your chances for promotion. I was always told not to completely fill the entire page but to leave some white space. Writing less tended to be safer than writing too much. The unspoken word was also, in some form, to always praise your supervisors, to talk about your future plans in the Foreign Service and to acknowledge any area for improvement.

Once an EER is complete, the EER goes to an EER Review Board within the Embassy or Consulate and a Panel Chair provides feedback and edits. The Rated Employee then incorporates the Board's edits and suggestions, changes areas that need fixing and then resubmits with the Rating Officer, Reviewing Officer, and Rated employee all signing. Once that is complete the Review Panel Chair signs the EER and it is sent to the State Department's Office of Employee Performance.

Review Boards in Washington DC then review the thousands of EERs they receive each year to determine eligibility for promotion. I have had the opportunity to serve on a Promotion Panel twice. Boards usually have members of each cone – political, economic, consular, management, and public diplomacy review an EER and also include someone outside of the Foreign Service such as a professor, academic, or other non-State Department person to review. Each officer is reviewed based on his or her in-cone experience and outside cone experience. For example, a political coned officer who spent the past year on a non-political cone assignment may not receive an in-cone promotion, but may have done exceptionally well to merit an out-of-cone promotion. A promotion is a promotion either way, but typically Boards do look at how much work an officer performs in his or her own respective cone and takes into account experience in Washington, DC.

How well an EER is written is key to promotion in the Foreign Service. No matter how well one performed or how poorly one performed, the key is having a well-written evaluation. What is written in the EER is that which Promotion Boards review.

I have had very good EERs throughout my career and have received numerous State Department awards including: Superior Group Honor Award for political reporting in Taiwan, Meritorious Honor Award in Nigeria for economic work and a Meritorious Honor Award in Nigeria for consular work. I was tenured and promoted as a 03 Foreign Service Officer as quickly as the process allowed. My second EER in Beijing, however, was not stellar. My immediate supervisor seemed to despise me for curtailing my assignment early as I was suffering from severe respiratory problems that kept me bedridden. She chose to enact revenge via my EER. She knew, once I departed Beijing, I would be rendered helpless with no HR support, and intentionally waited until I left Beijing to draft an EER that not only was sloppy but also inaccurate and spiteful.

I had provided her examples of performance and a draft two weeks in advance of my departure from Beijing around November 20 and she chose to sit on it until the very last minute on April 13 when the EER was due on April 15 to draft it. Not only did she write an Area for Improvement that was grossly inaccurate but she had never discussed it with me nor solicited my feedback despite the fact that she knew I was in Japan powerless to fight back. I distinctly remember one of her emails in which she asked me if I planned to stay at Westinghouse Japan permanently (where I was taking leave without pay from the Department to recover my health and pay homage to my grandmother who had passed away during my tour in Japan) or return to the Foreign Service, as if that had anything to do with writing an accurate EER and giving credit where credit was due. Needless to say, I will never serve in another post with some of the individuals I met in Beijing who did not have my best career or health interests in mind. Lesson learned. She was a Caucasian female who became a Senior Foreign Service Officer and served as Deputy Chief of Mission in Asia twice after.

When I had protested via email about the language in the EER and decided to honestly state my side of the story in the Rated Employee Statement of my EER I was threatened by my Reviewing Officer not to expose the truth. He said in not so subtle words in an email to me that there would be "consequences" in doing so. I wrote it anyway. And, yes, that led to retaliation and an EER I was not pleased to receive. And that horrendous experience in Beijing definitely hurt my career in terms of promotions. My Reviewing Officer, a Caucasian male also became a Member of the Senior Foreign Service and Deputy Chief of Mission in Asia twice.

Rather than play the victim, I discussed what had happened to me during my time in Beijing with the American Foreign Service Association legal team in Washington, DC. They told me that I definitely had a case and connected me with one of their lawyers. I submitted my case via email to them after heading to Embassy Georgetown, Guyana in South America in late 2009. The most they could promise is that changes would be made to my EER and that I would have another one to two years extra time to be eligible for promotion.

A GRIEVANCE FILED

The AFSA lawyer helped me file a grievance. We sent the grievance through State Department Bureau of Human Resources

Grievance Staff. The Department of State actually has a Director of Grievance Staff to handle all grievances. That fact goes to show that there are likely a lot of grievances from Foreign Service Officers around the world sent to that office. We submitted the document package to the Director of Grievance Staff who sent me a letter acknowledging receipt of my document package on March 18, 2010. The letter notified me that my case was being handled by a member of the Grievance Staff, received a case number, and that they must resolve my grievance within 90 days of receipt.

On May 14, I received an email from a case officer from the Human Resources Office of Grievances asking me further questions. On May 19, the individual offered a settlement—to expunge my last EER from Beijing from the record as I had requested. I agreed. However, I will always keep that last EER as a reminder and reference. You never know when you may need to use it again.

UNDERAPPRECIATED IN THE U.S.

Japanese and Asian Americans are often labeled as being "whiter" than white, a phrase that portrays the community of members as having higher education levels, higher paying jobs, and overall higher quality of life than the white majority. The myth assumes that because we are more successful, we don't need government aid or special funding or help. There is a lot more Americans need to learn about Asian Americans. Our history is often overlooked and ignored. There are plenty of Japanese Americans and Asian Americans that don't fit the mold of the successful "whiter than white" model that the media in the U.S. seems to love to portray. You just don't read about their stories because Japanese American and Asian Americans don't control the media in the U.S. We don't really have too many Asian American role models in the media if you think about it.

I do believe Asian Americans in the United States are underappreciated. Because we are underappreciated and we do not do a better job of organizing ourselves and lobbying, we are often overlooked and our concerns ignored. The same can be said within the State Department. The number of high-ranking government officials in groups like Asian Americans in Government, while growing, is still remarkably small. You might ask why? The answer is that Asian Americans in this country are often asked to self-negate the "Asian" part of their Americanness. We don't need to do that. That is one of the central messages I hope you gain from reading my story. We should be proud of our Asian or bicultural heritage, study it, accept it, and let people deal with us on our own terms!

Governments and countries too often underappreciate and overlook the importance of accepting people of "dual, triple" and even more nationalities. As a government employee, I wanted to shout at the top of my lungs, "Don't just pay lip service to diversity, accept and embrace it America!" The road ahead for Asian Americans still needs to be paved by us. And we need to pour our own concrete, this time not for others to walk all over us, but for us to allow the next generation to have a smoother, brighter path ahead on which to run.

UNDERAPPRECIATED IN JAPAN TOO

Amazingly, I discovered the path to acceptance being both Japanese and American (i.e., my duality) in Japan was even harder. Japanese often looked at my "foreign" appearance and accepted my American side while dismissing my Japanese side. It was only until speaking with me in Japanese and understanding my cultural roots and experience in Japan that they slowly came to realize I knew and understood Japan, but that didn't automatically translate into me being accepted into their club. I have found that Japanese

Americans that are not fluent in Japanese are often viewed with discrimination or a sense of disdain, as if their lack of speaking the language was their fault. It does pain me to see Japanese not fully embracing and welcoming one of their own simply because he or she does not speak the language or was not raised in Japan. There is this sense among many Japanese people that Japanese that have left the islands of Japan and didn't return to lay roots in Japan are no longer Japanese. It's almost a sense of second class citizenship or worse, unrealistic expectations that you should speak and understand Japanese culture, language, and society because you "look" Japanese and your ancestors are from Japan.

Given Japan's aging population and changing economy, it becomes increasingly important for Japan to embrace Japanese educated abroad and Japanese Americans as important people that can lead society. I am comforted that Japan is now accepting people of former *Buraku* ancestry (people who came from families of undertakers, butchers, leather-makers who are often looked down upon as outcasts) to assume positions of real leadership. The former Chief Cabinet Secretary of Japan's Liberal Democratic Party Hiromu Nonaka is someone from *Buraku* ancestry. There is still prejudice in Japan against *Buraku* as well as Korean Japanese, Chinese Japanese, and foreigners in general. This attitude needs to change.

Japan, in many ways, is a closed society. There is a need for more doctors and nurses in Japan. However, Japan does not hire doctors trained outside Japan. The association of medical professionals in Japan strictly recruits individuals that have gone through the Japanese medical education system. Due to the shortages of nurses, Japan has recruited nurses from the Philippines to work, but has not hired United States nurses.

There are several qualified doctors and nurses around the world, but unless you have gone through the Japanese medical training and education program, your medical degree is worthless in landing you a job in Japan. Law is the same. Obtaining a law degree from the United States may allow you to land a job in a U.S. company in Japan, but your options are limited when it comes to practicing law. Japanese companies and foreign companies will typically hire lawyers that have gone through the Japanese legal system and passed their exams to practice law. For someone like myself wanting to work in Japan, going to law school or medical school was not an option. Diplomacy I found was also a dead end. That left only teaching or business.

DISCRIMINATION KEEPS OCCURRING

During my last overseas assignment in Burkina Faso, I was appalled when my supervisor, the Deputy Chief of Mission (DCM), refused to grant special compensatory time off for work performed for a 12-person ambassadorial road show for the Front Office over a weekend. The same individual would later deny me a three-day training course on Cultural Affairs Resource Management, a training course I needed to perform my job. I had arrived in Burkina Faso one month early to fill a two-person gap and therefore could neither take the three-week Cultural Affairs Officer tradecraft course nor the one-week social media course which my Deputy was allowed to take. I did not think asking for a three-day training course was an unreasonable demand.

Unfortunately, my tour in Burkina Faso was also rife with an Ambassador who wanted to hold 27-person road shows and waste taxpayer money. He called his adventure to go hiking with his family while using U.S. government resources, including from my Public Affairs Section, a "cultural" activity to justify his abuse of resources. I had told my DCM earlier that I did not think these road shows were very strategic nor a good use of resources. There was a reason why no one in our Embassy wanted to do them. But, of course the DCM just wanted to go along with the Ambassador and did not listen.

The same DCM would ask me to process his private voucher

for him even though he had his own secretary to do so and illegally try to ask my Section to use Public Diplomacy funds to host an internal private Christmas party at his residence. His plan was to have me, and the Section I led, invite enough Public Diplomacy Section contacts to his internal party to allow him to avoid paying funds out-of-pocket. If half of the invited guests are official foreign guests, you can claim it as an official representational expense and get reimbursed for any money spent. When I objected, he continued to apply pressure on the local staff to fund his event. For a person of integrity like myself, I could not tolerate witnessing, nor being part of such abuse. Foreign Service Officers do not leave the State Department because of the work or the challenges of the work; they leave because of bad bosses. There are dedicated officers like myself who signed up to serve to protect the Constitution and work on behalf of the American taxpayer. I could not simply look the other way and stay silent. American taxpayers deserve to know the truth.

When I reported waste, fraud, and abuse to the Ambassador and DCM during my exit interview with both of them, I thought they would have appreciated that honest feedback so that they could understand why I had to leave. The toxic work environment which they created forced me to leave after six months as I was unwilling to engage in waste, fraud, or abuse and did not want anything to do with an abusive Front Office eager to mistreat me, waste U.S. taxpayer money, and ruin the lives of families. I stood up to this and said, "No, thank you." The result, however, was that after I left they tried to get back at me via retribution by weakening my evaluation report and not recommending me for promotion. Ironically, these two Caucasian males would recommend for immediate promotion my deputy, also a Caucasian male, who had only served them for three months. The Ambassador had lent him his own private vehicle for use, an offer he did not provide my family. When asked why the double standard, neither could offer a convincing argument. Discrimination just keeps on going in the State Department. They did not like that I left Post early and that I did not believe in their methods of leadership. I left Burkina Faso not because they lost confidence in me, but because I lost utter confidence in their leadership and lack of integrity. What a sham! What a shame!

The outcome for me was my medical clearance was reduced, I had to evacuate the family, move the family thrice while in Virginia, and be placed in an office not of my choosing. Instead of the abusers, the victim is always the person that suffers at State. The Front Office would say "we have a strong team" or that Ouagadougou is a "family-friendly post." The reality was far from it. This is another example of how titles, and the accompanying status and power that come with them, can corrupt able men. I've seen it so many times over my career that I can say it happens to able men and women regardless of Bureau. It is a sickness that needs a cure.

Having come out of a tour in Human Resources, I was profoundly disappointed as well with the lack of support by the Human Resources Officer (HRO) at Post who did nothing to help protect employees, their families, nor oppose waste, fraud, and abuse. She supported the Front Office's position of not compensating people for work performed over the weekend. Again, this was an illegal posture that only helped to ruin the health of employees and demoralize good officers. The decision to leave Burkina Faso for health and family was the right one. The cost of leaving an assignment early to preserve my integrity was better than willfully engaging in dishonest and illegal activity. I can live with myself in the mirror each day knowing I did not what was convenient but what was right. Can they?

No Love for Japanese Americans

During my time in the Africa Bureau I had the chance to get to know the Principal Deputy Assistant Secretary of State for African Affairs, Don Yamamoto. Don served in Japan as a staff aid in the

Embassy in Tokyo early in his career, as well as Principal Officer in the Consulate in Fukuoka. A Japanese American himself, Don did very well for himself, including becoming U.S. Ambassador to Djibouti and Ethiopia. Given his experience in Asia and Japan, he would have made a great candidate to serve in a leadership role on Japan affairs. I was told, however, that the Bureau of East Asian and Pacific (EAP) Affairs passed him up for a Deputy Chief of Mission job in Tokyo. He therefore parted with EAP and became a full-time Africa hand. Again, the State Department has always kept Japanese Americans from serving in important Japan policy affair jobs.

There is not a single Deputy Assistant Secretary of State or Assistant Secretary of State for East Asian and Pacific Affairs within the State Department who is Japanese American. There never has been. This makes one question why the State Department is keeping qualified Japanese Americans from assuming such jobs. Having spoken with leaders in the Japanese American community, this seems to have been an ongoing discriminatory trend that has not been resolved even after nearly 73 years. The key Japan policymakers, past and present, tend to remain white males. This list includes Jim Zumwalt, who retired from his position as U.S. Ambassador to Senegal several months early to become the CEO of the Sasakawa Peace Foundation, and who did little to employ, empower, and promote Japanese Americans much less support the cause of dual nationality. The former Japan Desk Office Director under Jim's tenure, Marc Knapper, who became Deputy Chief of Mission in Seoul, Korea also is a white male, later promoted to Deputy Assistant Secretary of State for Japan and Korea. The person who replaced him as Office Director, Joseph Young, who became Deputy Chief of Mission in Tokyo, Japan also is a white male. While these men are undoubtedly talented, hardworking, and capable, I would argue that Japanese Americans have not received a fair chance to represent the Department at the highest levels of policymaking when it comes to U.S.-Japan relations. The State Department preaches diversity and yet in the case of Japanese Americans doesn't practice it.

DANGERS OF SPEAKING UP

The Department is not perfect, and in fact has many management, resource, and morale problems. People need to speak up. Unfortunately, the culture is such that those that make noise may face retribution, are pushed out, or face serious challenges to promotion, obtaining good onward assignments, and advancing in one's career. I find this extremely unfortunate. Too many are suffering in silence. I chose to speak out. Several officers that have served in Iraq or Afghanistan returned home with Post Traumatic Stress Disorder or PTSD. The Department has been woefully slow in meeting the mental health needs of officers. People keep silent and silence is not healthy. Your silence says something. Speak up!

One officer I know wrote a book about his experiences in Iraq. He told the truth about the State Department's waste, fraud, and abuse recounting his experiences in Iraq from 2009-2010 as a member of a Provincial Reconstruction Team. His story is reminiscent of countless others. He just decided to speak his mind and risk his career. Before publishing his book, he spent a year trying to clear it and gain approval from the Department of State, which did not object to his publication of the book. However, as soon as he included portions of his book readily available to the public on his blog, Diplomatic Security decided to suspend his security clearance.

A security clearance suspension means an officer is not allowed to handle classified material and can severely impact one's onward assignments and hence career. He took that risk because he wanted the truth to be known about the $63 billion Iraq reconstruction campaign. His testimony is a reminder that much of the American taxpayers' monies spent on reconstruction efforts were in vain. Clean water, health care, and other projects aimed to assist Iraq became pointless projects because our government mishandled operations. Spending enormous amounts of money on a lavish Ambassador's residence and creation of an "American" Embassy town while Iraqis starve and suffer is not a humanitarian message we need to be sending.

One of the tragedies in all of this is that we often project our own values on other countries without asking them what it is they really need. If a water well is needed more than a gym or a new truck, we need to be using our resources sparingly and effectively to provide access to clean water rather than on projects with little practical value. USAID is notorious for spending aid on pointless projects and wasting vital taxpayer monies abroad that could be spent to rebuild our schools, further education, and implement important domestic programs.

When an officer speaks up, he risks his career, chances for promotion, and desirable assignments. In many cases, officers have security clearances suspended to prevent them from speaking further. We need to foster a culture of open communication to address weaknesses within the State Department, and cease punishing those that demonstrate integrity and a desire to create real change by speaking up against fraud, misuse, and waste of taxpayer funds.

Publishing this book also creates risks for me. But, I am willing to share my thoughts because I serve the American people who pay my salary. Too often, government officers, particularly Foreign Service Officers, forget whom they are serving. It should not be, although it *is* the Ambassador or Secretary of State who is considered first. It should be the American taxpayer we think about most in implementing policies and programs that provide them with the most returns on their taxpayer investments.

Self-Negation

The most unpleasant experience for me in entering the U.S. Department of State was the constant struggle to prove my loyalty. I had to deny my Japanese heritage and inner self to fit in. I worked tirelessly to prove to others that I was just as "American" as anyone else so that I exhausted myself. I wasn't true to my own identity. And, it wasn't healthy. The Japanese values that my grandmother had instilled in me were very much a part of me. I felt ashamed that it was only after her death did I realize how stupid I was in engaging in a self-destructive path of self-negation. I felt ashamed that I did not visit her once during my Foreign Service career, all because I didn't want DS to doubt my loyalty. My grandmother had battled a form of Alzheimer's for several years, but I had missed my chance to say farewell. I felt a total failure as a grandson.

One of the reasons I am writing my story is because whether or not you are Japanese American, Cuban American, Italian American or have a mixture of ethnic backgrounds blended together, never forget that the only person you need to stay true to is yourself. And I didn't during my years in the State Department. Don't ever take the mistaken path I took. Don't let other people disparage you or make you feel small as though your diversity is a liability not an asset.

I was taught that my diverse background was an asset and something beautiful. And, it is. But, somewhere along the way as I left my parents' loving nest, I found many people whether from jealousy or ignorance take snipes at what I held as more valuable than gold— my heritage. This happened on both sides of the Pacific. We are all human. If someone has not studied another country or culture or is not exposed to various viewpoints, a natural bias exists to support the cultural norms he or she grew up with. But the world is changing. There are increasingly more and more children of mixed backgrounds with dual nationality. Governments may be slow in recognizing and embracing this new breed of citizenry, but we, as a people, need to begin to accept these rainbow of colors and diverse backgrounds as critical members of our society. Let them not choose one side or the other. Rather, allow them to be both. I choose to be both Japanese and American. No one has the right to take either side away from me.

Lack of Dissent, Innovation, and Creativity

Inevitably, when an organization lacks funds, people, and resources, it makes it difficult to effectively carry out a job. In the State Department, I discovered that many people are afraid to voice dissent. No one wants to be perceived as a complainer. But healthy discussion about problems is necessary for any organization to move forward. And the State Department is not an exception. The problem with the State Department, however, is that the culture does not allow for people to voice dissent without being labeled, stigmatized, or ridiculed as troublemakers or even worse, not considered to be "team players." People are afraid they will not receive promotions or get the assignments they desire if they voice dissent. I'm sure this is true of several organizations and not just the State Department, but I do find the lack of channels to voice dissent (without reprimand) as troubling.

I also understand that when you are short of people and funding, there is no time for people to engage in dissenting views. However, this leads to another problem, lack of creativity, and innovation. We need creative and innovative solutions to fix many of our world's problems. We also need to effectively utilize our resources by sending those with language skills and cultural knowledge to countries where they can effectively put their language skills to use instead of precluding them. Sending people with the language skills saves the government money in terms of language training. It also sends a message to those individuals that the government does value the cultural background he or she brings. Precluding them hurts morale, is counterproductive, and goes against American ideals and values.

If an individual has a Syrian mother, speaks fluent Arabic, wants to serve in Damascus, and is a United States citizen that passed the Foreign Service exam and has no criminal background, send him or her to Damascus. If we trusted someone enough to represent our country by hiring that person in the first place, then what are we doing precluding that individual? I realize that September 11 changed our security environment and created stringent security rules. But, we need to be fighting the terrorists, not fighting American citizens or branding our own people as security threats.

INTERNMENT OF JAPANESE AMERICANS

Prior to the full-scale internment of Japanese Americans in the United States there were discriminatory laws against Japanese immigrants. Most notably, the 1924 Japanese Exclusion Act prohibited Japanese from immigrating to the U.S. Prior to that, discriminatory laws aimed at both the Chinese and Japanese immigrants existed, barring them from marrying outside their race, denying Japanese the right to own land and homes, and prohibiting them from becoming U.S. citizens. During WWII, the U.S. government tracked and monitored people of Japanese ancestry. President Franklin Delano Roosevelt signed Executive Order 9066 authorizing the forceful removal and relocation of over 120,000 Japanese Americans on February 19, 1942. Not only was this unconstitutional, but government documents indicated that many Japanese Americans were loyal to the United States. FDR's actions ripped the Japanese American community apart stripping innocent Japanese Americans of their dignity, livelihood, and basic human rights. Most of the internment camps were located on the West Coast in California, Arizona, Colorado, and Utah. Other camps were located in Idaho, Arkansas, and Wyoming. The U.S. Department of Justice also had detention camps in Texas, North

Dakota, Montana, New Mexico, and Idaho. Prior to the war and immediately after, many Japanese were barred from choice jobs and had to send some of their children to segregated schools.

The U.S. State Department had a discriminatory policy against Japanese Americans as well. There was a period of time in which people of Japanese ancestry were not allowed to enter the U.S. Foreign Service. In addition, many Japanese Americans were pressured to work for the U.S. military and government as the only way to regain their rights as Americans and prove their loyalty. The U.S. government acknowledged its actions towards Japanese Americans was wrong, but it took 34 years before the next U.S. President, Gerald Ford, would rescind Executive Order 9066 and another 14 years before surviving internees (many had died by 1990) would receive individual redress payments and a letter of apology.

The U.S. government has a history of hiding the full extent of its actions regarding the imprisonment of Japanese Americans on U.S. soil. Immediately after Pearl Harbor, the FBI conducted raids without search warrants on many Japanese American residents in Hawaii. These loyal citizens were treated as prisoners of war. Most of the Japanese Americans were interned outside of Hawaii. Although Hawaii did have Japanese American internees, the U.S. government could not round them up and relocate them in Hawaii for political and economic reasons. Japanese Americans in Hawaii were a very large ethnic group comprising over 35 percent of the population of Hawaii at the time and they were prime movers of the economy. In addition, earlier raids by the U.S. government to arrest suspected persons of espionage ensured that Hawaii was secure.

We need to discuss the history of U.S. government actions and human rights abuses targeted at Japanese American citizens in our schools and history books. There is a legacy of discrimination against Japanese Americans that needs to stop. Many of those sent to internment prisons have died. Many who worked for the U.S. government had to sign notices or swear allegiance that they would not discuss the crimes committed against Japanese Americans. We all have a responsibility to tell their story. All of us as part of the human race.

Morality of Hiroshima and Nagasaki

In war, there are inevitably civilian casualties. However, the targeting of civilians is never justified in my view. The decision to drop the atomic bombs on Hiroshima and Nagasaki I would argue was more an "ethnic" rather than "ethical" decision. President Truman and his advisers were men that fit the WASP stereotype, colored in their own biases towards ethnic minorities, and supportive of policies that discriminated against Japanese Americans and Asians in general. Internment of Japanese Americans, ban on interracial marriages, immigration policies that limited entry for "Orientals" and other discriminatory federal and state laws were rampant during that era and preceding. No atomic bombs were dropped on Germany or Italy.

The argument that the bombing saved countless lives is sheer propaganda. Targeting military personnel is justifiable, but the wanton use of force on women and children in Hiroshima and Nagasaki is not forgivable. The U.S. should officially apologize to the Japanese people and nation for using its people and soil as a guinea pig experiment to unleash the destructive powers of atomic energy. The decision to do so was based on hate, ignorance of the beauty of Japanese people and culture, and racism. American lives were saved, but Japanese suffered. The U.S. has a moral obligation to admit that the decision to drop the atomic bomb was immoral and unjustified.

It was not until 2012 when a U.S. Ambassador to Japan attended the Peace Memorial ceremonies held respectively in Hiroshima on August 6 and Nagasaki on August 9, 1945 that the U.S. paid respect to the victims of the atomic bombs. Previous U.S. ambassadors never attended these official events sponsored by the mayors of both cities. No sitting U.S. president has ever attended the ceremony except for President Barack Obama who visited the Hiroshima Peace Memorial in 2016, 71 years after the U.S. dropped its first atomic bomb in Hiroshima City. Other U.S. presidents have stayed away from participating in the ceremonies. President Obama's speech fell short of an apology, but his presence was supported. If the U.S. cannot apologize, how can it expect other countries to do so? We need to examine ourselves before we criticize other countries. Human suffering is human suffering. Perhaps if a U.S. president one day can apologize to the Japanese for that atrocity, that would show a sign of leadership and humility that could influence a Japanese prime minister to do the same toward other neighbors in Asia that were victims of Japanese brutality.

Several *hibakusha* or victims exposed to radiation from the atomic bombings are alive in Japan and receive medical allowances. The memorials in both cities contain lists of *hibakusha* who passed away since the bombings. The Japanese citizens living in those cities at the time were not the only victims; there were Koreans and citizens of other countries who were also victims.

The U.S. government intentionally censored photos and articles in Japanese media depicting the cruelty of Hiroshima and Nagasaki until the 1950s. They did so to contain Japanese outrage and prevent anti-American sentiment. Had the Nazis dropped an atomic bomb in Europe and lost the war, they would have been tried for war crimes. The U.S. avoided any war crime trials for dropping two atomic bombs because it was the victor in World War II. Pure and simple. The U.S. government experimented with the two attacks to see the effects of radiation and never took responsibility for the total devastation. The U.S. government never cared for these victims. And, as the colonized country, the Japanese government also largely ignored the needs of these victims and did nothing to fight for them until the victims organized themselves and lobbied the government.

The *hibakusha* deserve the Nobel Peace Prize for raising awareness of the terrible impact of atomic weapons and for advocating for a nuclear free world. They have my vote.

~3 STEPS TO PUT INTO ACTION~

1. *Find champions inside and outside your organization. Take the duality principle and make it your dual advantage.* Seek champions who will support you, motivate you, and look out for you. It can help your life evolve to the next level, find new opportunities for personal growth and launch a whole new career for you.

When you're faced with hostility and an unwelcoming environment, find champions who can help you succeed and navigate choppy waters. Following the principal of duality—that two is better than one—seek to find mentors *within* and *outside* your organization. This has dual advantages. First, you get to know leaders within and outside your organization who can serve as mentors as well as your advocates. Second, you allow yourself an opportunity for further exploration and growth and appreciation for what others do and how you might fit in to assist them. When I could not find role models within the State Department that I wanted to be like, I sought leaders in the military and the private sector.

In addition, I sought membership in the Federal Asian Pacific American Council (FAPAC), an affinity group that brings Asian Pacific Americans in Federal Government together to thrive. In fact, in 2018 I was selected to their career development program which exposed me to other agencies, thought leaders, and mentors. I was the only State Department representative at FAPAC among various Asian American leaders who represented departments of Defense, Transportation, Commerce, Labor, Interior, Agriculture, Justice as well as NASA, Office of Personnel Management and numerous other federal agencies.

State's lack of participation and involvement once again indicated a lack of support for Asian Pacific American communities. During the 2018 annual FAPAC leadership conference in May in DC, not a single State Department senior leader attended. May is Asian heritage month. It is sad that the State Department does not find value in joining other interagency colleagues to support the development and growth of Asian Pacific Americans.

2. *Be an inclusive diversity hero.* Even if your own organization does not practice what it preaches or has a poor record of leadership on the diversity front, that does not mean you have to do the same. We need champions who are willing to mentor others. I learn as much from my mentees as they do from me so that there is a dual benefit.

People that you champion within your organization and empower to succeed will remember your gift to them. The best gift of leadership is helping someone else succeed. They will remember that for life. Mentoring can also make you feel "useful" and that is empowering. It makes you feel good about yourself and what you're doing, and creates more diplomatic dots for future success. As a mentor to both Foreign Service and Civil Service employees throughout my 16 year career, I found this to be true service.

It is not easy to fight discrimination. Stand up to any form of harassment; your integrity is worth more than your career. Let me repeat that. *Your integrity is worth more than your career.* You can always switch careers. But you do not want to compromise your core values. It simply is not worth it.

3. *Cultivate impeccable integrity.* No one will follow a leader that lacks ethics and integrity, at least not for the long run.

Report waste, fraud, and abuse immediately but also leave any supervisor or toxic environment that does not abide by the highest ethical standards as soon as you can. You do not want to learn bad habits and you do not want to associate with those who demonstrate a lack of integrity.

One way to cultivate integrity is to stay true to who you are, practice self-regulation, and abstain from trying to be someone else. Be you. Be all of you. When you aren't being who you are, you risk more than your health and relationships; you risk your integrity. Do not make the same mistakes I did in trying to compromise my duality so that others would accept me. I experimented in negative negation. Experiment in positive affirmation! I'm not striving to just be the best American. I'm striving also to be the best Japanese. Doing so requires me to cultivate impeccable integrity as a person who values duality to the core and wants others to understand and appreciate the United States and Japan at a deeper, more human level.

Loving each side does not mean sugarcoating our weaknesses or being exclusive. Loving both means honestly assessing the good, the bad, and the ugly in either side. When we do so, we both succeed and lift others to also reach for the skies.

If any organization prevents her most valued assets—people—from achieving their destinies, something is wrong with that organization and it is time to leave and move on. Plenty of other organizations exist that would gladly utilize your talents.

Chapter Seven

First Diplomatic Tour Taiwan: Test of Perseverance

My first assignment in the Foreign Service was at the American Institute in Taiwan, better known as AIT, where I served from 2003-2005 after completing six months of language training in Mandarin and three months of consular training at the Foreign Service Institute in Arlington, Virginia. I enjoyed my assignment to Taipei, Taiwan and made some lasting friendships. But two incidents stand out during that experience. The first involves a group of aspiring Taiwanese diplomats who came to AIT to hear the then Director, Doug Paal, speak about diplomacy. The graduate students were then given an opportunity to interact with the Entry Level (i.e., first-tour) U.S. Foreign Service Officers to ask them questions individually. I distinctly recall students gravitated toward the Caucasian officers. When students gathered near me, the first question they asked me was "where are you from?" I said the U.S. They then asked me where my parents were from. I told them to guess.

I received various answers from Uzbekistan, Mexico, Mongolia and so forth. When I said my mother was from Japan and my father from New York, there was silence. They did not know what questions to ask next. I remember similar questions were never asked of my Caucasian colleagues. I felt greatly disappointed that of all the questions these aspiring Taiwanese diplomats could ask an American diplomat, they could not go beyond race or ethnicity. That was my first experience in Taiwan where I directly felt that my "mixed" background caused others not to know how to begin or continue a normal conversation. And it also confirmed for me the notion that many foreigners continue to assume a "real" American is white with blue eyes and blond hair. I guess I must have disappointed them with my brown eyes, dark brown hair, and almond shaped Asian eyes—not the picture of the Hollywood star they may have imagined from the movies.

The second experience I remember involved another Foreign Service Officer. We were eating at a restaurant during a diplomatic function where we were entertaining some Japanese government officials. I was naturally speaking to them in Japanese. The Japanese officials complimented me on my Japanese. My Foreign Service colleague who had studied Japanese interjected in Japanese and replied "his mother is Japanese." I was furious that my American colleague would make such a comment, but I knew it came from jealousy (i.e., my Japanese language ability far exceeded hers) and it would have been inappropriate for me to say something in front of the guests. I let it go. But such comments reveal the typical ignorant assumptions that people make. They think because someone's parent is Japanese that the child automatically speaks the language, which is preposterous.

I know several Japanese, Chinese, and Korean Americans whose parents are from those countries but they themselves do not necessarily speak the language proficiently, or at all. Yes, there is an advantage if a parent is from a foreign country and teaches the language to the child. However, there is only so much a parent can teach. The rest depends on the amount of time and effort the child spends perfecting the language. I have to say that my Japanese language ability came from countless hours of practice and study that I initiated on my own. Every summer and in my spare time I practiced writing characters, reading books, and listening to Japanese to improve my level of fluency. I did not appreciate such comments that appeared to "whitewash" my efforts. Furthermore, I found it ironic that the American officer that made the comment was married to a Taiwanese American who did not speak a word of Taiwanese or Mandarin despite the fact that both of his parents were born and bred in Taiwan. I didn't bother to remind her of this fact. There are some battles that are not worth fighting. I chose not to engage in argument. I believe one day the same person will realize that raising bilingual children is not an easy task, and like most things in life, requires tremendous commitment and study on the part of the child.

Speaking of language training, I do distinctly recall a teacher at the Foreign Service Institute Language Training department making an inappropriate comment about Japanese people. The teacher was Taiwanese and her role was to try to have her students (sent to Mandarin language speaking posts abroad) pronounce Mandarin as accurately as possible. I was having difficulty pronouncing the "q" sound when the teacher told me, "that's because Japanese people don't know how to pronounce the 'q' sound." I was shocked and did not know how to reply. Even more disturbing was a fellow classmate, the spouse of a Foreign Service Officer sent to Shenyang, China, who said "your facial structure" is the problem. I was so stunned that it took me two days to process what she said and realize these folks had made racist comments towards me. I did not know what to do. I thought about speaking to the director of the Mandarin Language program, the teacher, and the spouse from Georgia who had made the comment, but in the end did not do so. I was so naive I did not even know how to go about responding and did not want to cause a stir as I only had a few more months of language training left before I was due in Taiwan.

Taiwanese Attitudes Toward Japan

My experience in Taiwan was that a majority of Taiwanese have favorable attitudes towards Japan. Although a former Japanese colony, many Taiwanese do not have the same type of animosity towards Japan as compared with their Mainland Chinese and South Korean neighbors. In fact, many of the older generation of Taiwanese in their 80s and 90s speak Japanese. There are also several TV channels in Taiwan that broadcast reruns of old Japanese shows, comedy, and singing programs targeting the older generation. For Japanese businessmen based in Taiwan, the island provides a favorable social and cultural environment for Japanese to feel comfortable.

Strong trade ties between Japan and Taiwan, their dependent reliance on the U.S. for security against Mainland China, and post-WWII education systems rooted in American ideals of democracy and capitalism make for shared bonds. The Japanese also helped develop Taiwan's modern education system and infrastructure backbone during its occupation of Taiwan that many Taiwanese acknowledge as a time of turning points in their history. That's not to say that the older generation of Taiwanese believe that the Japanese occupation of Taiwan was morally acceptable or not at times harsh, but they have a much more benign attitude towards the occupation in general.

One theory behind this is that Japanese occupation strategy differed based on whether the Japanese Imperial Army or Japanese Imperial Navy served as chief military occupier. In Korea and Mainland China, the Japanese Imperial Army ruled with an iron hand. In

Taiwan, Indonesia, and the Philippines, the Japanese Imperial Navy was in control. Several scholars have stated that in places like Taiwan, Indonesia, and Philippines, Japanese conquerors took a more benign approach to occupation by allowing local people to have more of a say in self-rule and governance. In other words, the occupation strategy employed by the Japanese Navy was less strict than that of the Japanese Imperial Army.

Whether one accepts that theory or not, Taiwanese both young and old tend to have a much more favorable opinion of their island neighbor than the Koreans or Mainland Chinese. During Japan's economic golden years and development starting in the 1970s and lasting until the late 1980s, Taiwan looked toward Japan as the economic model in Asia to emulate.

DUAL TAIWANESE AND AMERICAN NEIGHBORS

During my first tour in Taipei, I lived alone in a modern apartment known as "Dunhua." The apartment was within walking distance to Taiwan University, Meihua Movie Theater, and the Far Eastern Plaza Hotel. I was fortunate that my neighbor on the same floor was Dr. Kun-Yen Huang. Dr. Huang loved the Japanese game of *Go* and was born in Taiwan during the Japanese occupation. He had received a Japanese education through middle school and spoke Japanese, Mandarin, English, German, and Taiwanese. As a leading epidemiologist and former dean of Taiwan's Cheng Kung Medical School, he was a very famous person in the field of medicine. He and I would chat together, read Japanese books, and play on occasion the game of *Go*. His wife, Amy, also was a doctor and successful in her own right.

Dr. Huang and Amy lived a rich life full of political and geographic transitions. Educated in Japanese schools in Taipei during the Japanese occupation, he then learned Mandarin and Taiwanese after the Japanese left, and subsequently studied English to pursue a medical education in the U.S. His children were born in the U.S. where he practiced medicine and obtained citizenship. He returned to Taiwan to lead Taiwan's Cheng Kung University Medical School in 1984. Dr. Huang had published a memoir in Mandarin and was working on his autobiography during my time in Taipei. When it was finally published in Mandarin, he sent me a copy which includes a portion of one of the conversations he and I had during my tour there.

Although his passion was medicine, Dr. Huang also enjoyed hearing my views on politics, the U.S.-Japan and U.S.-Taiwan relationship, and speaking Japanese. He passed away in Bethesda, Maryland in 2012 and Amy passed away four years later in Bethesda, Maryland in 2016. They will always be part of my life and Foreign Service journey. I miss them both.

Loss of Fiancée

During my diplomatic assignment in Taiwan I was all set to marry my girlfriend of eight years whom I had started dating my freshman year at Georgetown. Upon entering the U.S. Foreign Service in 2002, we felt it was time we should seal the deal. We had determined the wedding location, menu for the wedding reception, guest lists, and even wedding dress and attire. I had visited Japan during my tour in Taiwan to meet and stay with her family in Yokohama and work out wedding details. She had also completed the background security questionnaire required by the State Department as I had notified the Department in advance of our impending wedding plans. What happened next completely threw me.

We got into an argument the very morning when we were supposed to go to the local ward to legally register our marriage. And the argument could not have been more petty and inconsequential. Talk about the worst timing! She had said she just needed a few seconds to get ready . . . those few seconds turned to an hour . . . as the frustration built, I expressed my displeasure, and she lashed out back at me. Well, things escalated from there and before you knew it, I was on a bus heading over to stay the night with a friend at the U.S. Embassy compound in Tokyo.

The experience was so negative for me that I called off the wedding and flew back to Taiwan shortly thereafter. A number of reasons influenced my decision. First, in my eight years of knowing her, it dawned on me that I had always been the person who apologized in the relationship. Even when she hurt me, I never received an apology. I realized that marrying someone unwilling to ever apologize would not be an ideal situation. Had she simply said sorry on the phone call before my return to Taiwan the healing process could begin and maybe we could have reconciled. The other factor was ever since I met her mother when I was an exchange student at Keio University, I sensed she didn't approve of my dating her daughter. While she never said this vocally, I could see her concern and it bothered me. Professionally, my fiancée constantly complained to me that she would have to give up her career in banking to join me in the Foreign Service. I didn't want to have that guilt trip over my shoulders, especially if the locations she desired for me to serve didn't fit with my career aspirations. If I could have been assigned to Tokyo, maybe this would not have mattered so much. The final factor was knowing I wanted to develop my faith and grow in my relationship with God. I didn't see my fiancée as ready to join me on that spiritual journey.

The bottom line is we were too young, had divergent career goals, and didn't share the same values. Better to wait ten years to marry the right woman than be in a miserable relationship for ten years. I was heart-broken and so was she when I called the wedding off. And it took me a long time to overcome the loss, pain, sense of failure, and guilt. All my Foreign Service colleagues, bosses, and friends in Taipei expected me to come back with the news that I was officially married. Our actual wedding was scheduled to take place later in the summer. Imagine my pain when I had to tell everyone without going into details that I called the wedding off. I was walking the streets of Taipei at night alone, crying, and trying to figure out what had just happened. I would walk until I got exhausted so the pain in my legs could help erase the pain felt in my heart. Many a night I cried myself to sleep over her. And I asked God how this could happen. In fact, I questioned the very existence of God. I came to the conclusion in my darkest hours that God must exist because he alone could grant me hope that life was worth living and that my life had meaning. With her gone from my life, I couldn't see the daylight.

But time heals wounds. It takes patience to overcome any loss. I learned that when you are in your early twenties, sometimes you just need the time to discover yourself before you can make someone else happy. Two people who only know each other might need to separate when the stakes go beyond just dating to getting married and starting a family. I knew that I wanted children but not as soon as she wanted children. I think I wasn't ready for the commitment to her just yet. I was still contemplating what God wanted for my life. I was later relieved to learn that she married and started a family in Japan. To this day, I hope she and her family are prosperous and doing well. And I thank her for the eight years of love she gave me. My experience with her taught me how to deal with loss, how to mourn, and how to move on.

Although it took five years from our breakup until I met and married the woman of my dreams and mother of my two children, ultimately I came to realize it was all part of God's plan. I had to trust in Him and wait in faith. The manner in which I met and married my current wife was equally dramatic. The lesson learned is if you follow God with all your heart, he will find a way to fill any void in your life *in His time*. He certainly did intervene in my life and He can perform similar miracles in your life. Faith is so crucial in crises—whether personal or diplomatic. Similar to my freshman year when I considered possibly joining a Taiwanese Buddhist organization as a monk, as a first tour Foreign Service Officer who ended an eight year relationship, I started thinking about whether I should join a religious community. But this time, I thought about Catholic religious orders and actually began sending emails to various orders to research what it would mean to join as a seminarian. I seriously considered the priesthood as an option and consulted with Jesuits I had befriended at Georgetown and in Taiwan to learn more about their way of life.

Ricci Center in Taipei

As a product of a Jesuit education, I was very eager to explore the Jesuit influence in Taiwan and see whether I should consider a career in the priesthood. My adviser at Georgetown University, Professor John Witek, S.J., was the leading scholar on Matteo Ricci, a Jesuit who had learned Mandarin and spread Christianity to China. Father Witek became the Chair of Georgetown's history department and was a scholar like no other. His knowledge of Asia was vast and he studied the classics. I would always seek his council and visit him prior to every overseas assignment to pick his brain and learn from him. I sought his counsel until he passed away in 2010 during my fourth diplomatic assignment in Guyana.

Upon acceptance into the Foreign Service in 2002, one of the first people I met to share the news was Fr. Witek. He had been more than an advisor to me but a trusted confidant and friend who I knew cared about me. We talked about my preclusion to Japan. He offered his thoughts and agreed that the preclusion made no sense. To encourage me, he shared stories of another Japanese American officer who had initially faced difficulties in being assigned to Japan, but eventually made it to Japan as a Foreign Service Officer. I worked under her as an intern in 2002 on the Japan Desk. She did not possess dual nationality. But the very fact that she was Japanese

American, a Georgetown alum, and a mentor made me feel like I too could one day go to Japan to represent the United States.

Little did Fr. Witek nor I know that the Foreign Service would impose such a restrictive and discriminatory policy toward dual nationals that would shatter my dreams of serving as a U.S. diplomat in Japan. As a condition of service after 16 years in the State Department loyally serving America and protecting U.S. citizen lives, I was asked to renounce my Japanese citizenship. Why didn't the State Department just ask me to renounce my dual citizenship before entering? No, that would have been too easy. I was transparent and clear with the State Department about my dual nationality from the start, and yet I was strung along for 16 years on false promises and hopes that Japan was a possibility. Those lies led to nowhere but disappointment, heartache, and thoughts of suicide. If the Department was asking me to disown half of who I am, what kind of life would that be? Certainly not an authentic one. Denying half of who I am, and a very important part of my heritage, led me to contemplate ending my life. But God had other plans for me.

While I was in Taipei, Fr. Witek suggested I visit the Ricci Center in Taipei which I did. I was disappointed that it wasn't as grand as I thought, the building was under construction and the Ricci library needed some work to contain all the books. Nonetheless, the Ricci Center was next to a church and I was able to make some friends there. One person was a novice from Argentina studying to become a deacon and eventually a Jesuit priest, Carlos Aspiroz. His brother was the head of the Dominican Order at the time, but Carlos had chosen to join the Jesuit order instead in order to learn Mandarin and spread Christianity in China through working with leper colonies. He eventually was ordained a Jesuit and was sent to northern China to work among leper colonies where he served the poor as well as the lepers in the region. Carlos was there to comfort me when I asked him what the purpose of life was after he found me in a church in Taipei distraught after my breakup with my Japanese fiancée. He treated me to some dumplings, listened to the sob story of my breakup with my fiancée, and even offered his younger sister in Argentina to be my wife, until he remembered she had already gotten married. It seems God has a sense of humor.

Even to this day, I appreciate Fr. Aspiroz's kindness, and I have to laugh when I recall he temporarily forgot the sister he had in mind was already married. To offer your sister to some guy you just met in church after his breakup is pretty funny. Fr. Aspiroz taught me more than how good homemade empanadas can taste, he taught me that faith and friendship go hand in hand. Faith is about a relationship. When you have a friendship, you have a relationship. And relationships matter even more when you need someone to listen, to empathize, and support you during your darkest moments. Those moments, if you live long enough, will come for all of us. We just do not know the time and hour. What I learned during my time in Taiwan is that even during your most painful periods, food, friendship, and faith can offer the comfort you need to heal. I never had Argentinian empanadas in my life prior to Taiwan, but boy did they taste good.

Chapter Eight

Nigeria and China: Two More Diplomatic Assignments Gone Wrong

When I had the option of choosing which countries to serve after Taiwan, Japan was on the list. However, once again, my preclusion from serving in Japan prevented me from choosing that option. With the breakup with my Japanese fiancée and my own desires to see someplace new, I may not have selected to serve in Japan anyway. But I did not appreciate the fact that I did not have an opportunity to even apply and put my name in the "list" of eligible candidates for jobs in Japan. Reviewing the list of available jobs, I chose a tour in Lagos, Nigeria over Guangzhou, China. We were advised as Entry Level Officers that the Foreign Service we entered demanded officers to have geographic diversity, and at least two different regional bureaus. I thought I would like to have both Asia and Africa as my two regional bureaus. I signed up for Lagos, Nigeria. Lagos had a reputation for being a challenging place to serve even within the Africa Bureau. I wanted the hardest challenge. Nothing I figured would be harder than what I had already faced–losing my fiancée of eight years and being precluded from serving in Japan.

Nigeria was a growing experience for me. I had never visited, much less served in Africa. I took it as a challenge and opportunity. One of my motivations for serving in Nigeria was because one of my best friends was Nigerian American and because I wanted to see some place new besides Asia. I wanted a new challenge and Taiwan became boring for me after my first year. Taiwan is in many respects a first world "country" although we were taught that we cannot say "country" because we do not have official diplomatic relations with Taiwan like we do with Mainland China. Politics aside, Taiwan has a first rate economy, a democratic political system, good health care and education, and a history of friendly relations with the United States. Everything worked. But that also made my work there seem less interesting. I was bored and needed a new challenge. I thought Africa would be a good change of scene. My breakup with my Japanese fiancée and long-time partner for eight years also made me want to spend time far away from Asia. I mistakenly thought that the farther I moved away from her, the more I could erase the pain. I was wrong. I carried the scars with me and I missed having a companion. My desire to serve in Japan only intensified during my time in Nigeria.

Nigeria did not disappoint. There were plenty of challenges from plane crashes, the spread of Avian flu, kidnappings of American and foreign oil workers in the oil-rich Niger Delta, HIV/Aids, and an unstable political government. As an Economic Officer responsible for reporting on aviation, telecommunication, transportation, maritime security, agriculture, and the growing Chinese influence in West Africa, I had more than enough interesting work to cover. My second year I rotated to the Consular Section where I was responsible for doing Immigrant Visa work, fraught with plenty of fraud and challenges itself. But before I could get to my second year, I had to get through my first month.

My first month in Nigeria shook me. As Aviation Officer at Consulate Lagos, I handled my first plane crash my first month on the job which I had to handle with no person nor manual to help prepare me for what was to come. There was no time to sit back and relax. I thought I would be handling aviation agreements, not planes falling out of the sky. Tragedy struck on October 22, 2005 when Bellview Airlines Flight 210 crashed, killing all 117 passengers on board, including a U.S. Embassy official. Deputy Defense Attaché Lieutenant Colonel Joseph Hayden was one of the passengers on that evening flight out of Lagos Murtala Muhammed International Airport heading home to Abuja, the capital city of Nigeria where our Embassy was located. He wouldn't make it back home, and neither would any other passenger on that tragic flight.

The fact that the aircraft was a U.S. Boeing 737-200 meant that an investigative team comprised of U.S. Boeing representatives would soon be in-country to investigate the causes of the plane crash, including whether the crash was caused by pilot error, mechanical failures, or both. I had to prepare for their arrival, the investigation, the chaos of the press, and work on an aviation policy to ensure we had updated protocols in place for U.S. citizens planning on flying on domestic Nigerian carriers. Within two months of the Bellview plane crash, I would have to handle my second plane crash, Sosoliso Airlines Flight 1145, another Nigerian domestic carrier that utilized a U.S. McDonnell Douglas DC-9-32 aircraft to transport passengers.

On December 10, 2005, the plane crashed at Port Harcourt Airport, killing 108 out of 110 passengers. Like the Bellview flight, there were U.S. citizens on board, including several dual national Nigerian Americans. We had to get to work immediately to save any lives we could. My Consular colleagues had to notify the families of U.S. citizens who were on that flight and pass on the horrifying news that their loved ones had died. What made the second plane crash difficult was that 61 high school students from Loyola Jesuit College in Abuja were on that flight, with only one student surviving. What was supposed to be a month of celebration in preparation for the Christmas holidays became a period of mourning and wailing for many Nigerians, Americans, and other nationals who had to make sense of what happened. Two plane crashes within two months created a sense of fear among residents of Nigeria, including among the U.S. and Japanese citizen communities regarding the safety of domestic air travel on domestic airlines. My first four months in Nigeria gave me a first-hand look into crisis management.

Lessons Learned from 2 Plane Crashes in Nigeria

There are a number of challenges one faces in handling a crisis such as a plane crash. The first challenge is gaining access to accurate information and sifting through conflicting reports that bombard you. When the October 22, 2005 Bellview plane crash occurred, we received conflicting reports regarding the site of the location in the initial hours. Some reports claimed the plane fell near the coast of Nigeria or into the ocean, while others identified different locations.

In a developing country plagued with electricity shortages and poor infrastructure, communication served challenging and much of the initial reports we received were inaccurate. The plane had crashed in the jungles in Lisa in Ogun State. The first people on the scene were members of the Red Cross.

As the Aviation Officer at Post, I was tasked with calling all contacts in the government, private sector, and NGO communities with reliable links to the aviation industry to get the latest reports, draft the situational response (SITREP) cables based on the information we knew, and clear through the Front Office before sending to Washington, DC. During this time, I would also receive calls from the Operations Center asking for periodic updates to include in the

Secretary's morning briefings. Since the crash occurred in the jurisdiction of Consulate Lagos, our team and the Consul General took lead in reporting, designating roles, informing the Aviation Minister, defense forces, and Governor of Ogun State to help us secure the crash site.

Confusion over reports around number of survivors is quite common in the beginning stages of a crisis as is speculation surrounding the cause of the crisis. In the case of the Bellview plane crash, there were local media reports claiming 50 survivors. These reports were false as all 117 passengers and crew we learned died immediately on impact. We knew a U.S. Embassy official, Lt. Col. Joseph Hayden, was on that flight so the initial reaction among members of the combined Political/Economic Section where I worked was hope that perhaps he would still be alive. I had arrived at Post barely one month before having to handle my first plane crash and did not personally know Joe Hayden.

As our Section and the Front Office in Lagos was scrambling to gain information, secure an official request from the Government of Nigeria to assist in the investigation, speak with the Aviation Minister, communicate with the Front Office in Abuja, secure a flight manifest, and draft SITREPs, chaos, confusion, and crying occurred. One officer in the Section who had known Joe Hayden had to be calmed down by the Consul General as she could not control a sudden burst of emotions. Witnessing all of that, there was no time to think about our situation or process emotions. We acted and reacted in a race against time. Maybe we can save him, perhaps there are other survivors, all of these emotions raced through our heads, but we had to keep working around the clock. We took shifts. Making sure to eat during a crisis is one sound piece of advice I received from the Assistant Secretary for Consular Affairs during the time. We had Military Meals Ready to Eat (MREs) stored in the Controlled Access Area.

The Assistant Secretary of State for African Affairs had just happened to arrive in Lagos immediately after the plane crash so I briefed her on the latest information I had, along with the Consul General and other members of the Consulate Country Team. Prior to briefing her, I was on the phone with the Aviation Minister and National Security Advisor. One of the challenges our mission faced was we could not officially investigate and have the National Safety and Transportation Board (NTSB) arrive in-country to assist in the investigation until the Nigerian government submitted an official request for assistance. It took a few hours to receive it even with the Consul General pushing for it. In the meantime, I worked on securing a flight manifest so that our Consular Section could use it to check their databases and identify the U.S. citizens aboard the plane. Other foreign missions in Nigeria were also trying to obtain a manifest to identify if some of their citizens were also aboard that plane. This is where cultivating relationships with foreign diplomatic missions proved effective. I called a contact in the Japanese Consulate in Lagos to learn that the Japanese had secured the flight manifest before us. The Japanese diplomat was willing to fax the manifest immediately over to us. Cultivating relationships is important because those contacts save you during a crisis.

Each day the Emergency Action Response Team led by the Consul General was convened, information was shared, and cables were sent back to Washington. Since a U.S. Embassy official was involved we had a missing person's report. The Defense Attaché Office worked to get a Mortuary Affairs officer from European Command (EUCOM) to arrive in Lagos as soon as possible to try to find the remains of Lt. Col. Hayden. Our Legal Attaché (LEGATT) from the FBI had a team inspect whether explosives were on the plane while Boeing representatives arrived with the Head of the NTSB Africa Division to investigate the cause of the crash in cooperation with Nigeria's Civil Aviation Authority.

There were so many things to do, so many moving parts, everyone's adrenaline was running high, reports of wailing in the electronic and paper news media in Nigeria over lost lives; accusations against the Bellview CEO; rumors that this was a terrorist attack; a plot by the opposition to weaken then-President Obasanjo as some of his close aides were aboard; a flash of thunder cited as potentially causing the pilot to panic or that thunder struck the plane out of the sky; and too much for one person to process. In a crisis, coordination is key, and luckily for us every member of the Consulate from the Consul General on down worked to manage the crisis and define points of contact. I became the central point for information and the Consul General's main point of contact.

Pacing is important during a crisis, as is a willingness to ask for help. I do not think I did a good job of doing either. I felt like I had to do more. I even went with the Mortuary Affairs Team to the physical location of the crash site to assist them pick up 15 bags of body parts hoping that maybe some of them would be the remains of Lt. Col. Hayden. Ultimately we only found a piece of cloth from his pants. I will never forget the smell of fumes, the stench of body parts, the huge crater, the tail end of the plane, scattered remains, and objects like shoe laces, toys, and other indications of human beings hanging from the tree branches and spread on the ground. It wasn't in my Work Requirement Statement (an annual performance document for Foreign Service Officers that outlines their continuing work responsibilities and specific duties for the rating period) to assist and look for the remains of an officer I never knew. I went because I felt it was the right thing to do at the time. What I saw at the scene, I was not prepared to witness. Not only did I never receive any briefing or training beforehand, but I also had no group or person with whom to discuss the tragedy afterwards. There was no debriefing for me.

It is easy to get burned out and that is why supervisors need to ensure their subordinates take breaks when they can, receive adequate training, and by all means are part of a group debriefing to handle the aftershocks. I wish I knew beforehand the importance of speaking with specialists and not brush aside all emotions thinking I was "just fine." I had never read a book on dealing with traumatic events prior. I wish I had. I never received training on whom to contact. I wish I did. I was given a fantasized orientation of all the positives of a Foreign Service career would entail without the harsh realities. I did not quite know what I was getting myself into. The question wasn't what someone in my position would face in a crisis in a Foreign Service career; the question was *when*. Preparing diplomats for the challenges that lie ahead is a daunting task, but a necessary one. The Department now spends more resources on crisis management training than when I entered given the number of officers who have had to serve in war zones or terrorist prone areas in Iraq, Afghanistan, and Pakistan.

Two of the greatest challenges I faced were first, this was all new to me, so I did not know what to expect, and did not realize that there would be an emotional component that needed to be addressed. I said I was fine and carried on long after the incident had occurred. By the time I had to deal with my second plane crash, I knew exactly whom to call and said to myself "here we go again." But there was no time for me to rest as I had to deal with the stress of the second plane crash, which occurred less than two months after the first one. The Nigerians were wailing as students were involved and this occurred at the worst time possible, right after the Bellview crash, and right before Christmas. There were only two survivors of that Sosoliso crash, one of them, a high school student from Loyola College Preparatory, Kechi Okwuchi. Imagine for a second being Kechi on the plane and surviving as 60 of your classmates died that day. Kechi wrote a poem titled "Tribute to the 60 Angels" which is available online. I have never met him, but I would like to meet him one day.

What Kechi experienced was survivor's guilt. I felt the same way. I just didn't realize I had had it—until much later when I would ask myself "why Joe Hayden and not me?" Again, there was no time, and I held firm to the belief that no debrief was necessary. It caught up to me later. When a Regional Psychiatrist came to Lagos to give a brief and counsel anyone who wanted to speak with that individual, I did not see the need to do so. As far as I knew, I was fine. I did not want to talk about it, but just to forget about it. The lesson is that the brain stores trauma and reacts to scenes that are reminders of that incident, whether it be an odor, watching a documentary on planes, or another trigger. We never know when our bodies react. But there is a way to process it and it's essential to address it. People do not need to serve in Iraq or Afghanistan to face a traumatic event. The loss of a loved one can be a traumatic event. It's perfectly natural to seek help. Do so.

I wish I knew about the Bureau of Medical Services or MED earlier and their role in assisting officers prior to my tour in Nigeria. I also wish someone would have told me that there would be emotional stresses, how to handle them, and would also have told me that what I was experiencing was normal, and that seeking help is important for long-term health and well-being. I wish someone would have told me the five stages of emotions one experiences having been a first responder to a traumatic experience. Anger, guilt, sadness, helplessness, and other emotions flooded my psyche. I was so busy handling the crises, one after another, that upon return from the Bellview crash site, I experienced chest pains and could not swallow. I thought the Indian food I ate might have caused some heartburn, but quickly realized that it was becoming increasingly more painful to swallow with each bite. Even swallowing my own saliva hurt. It turned out the anti-malaria pill I was required to take during my tour in Nigeria was caught in my esophagus, creating an ulcer. I was medically evacuated to London where I was patched up and sent back to Lagos shortly thereafter, just in time to handle my second plane crash. When facing high stress, it is wise to drink a full glass of water with any necessary pills.

In addition to plenty of water with medicine, here are some other tips to prepare for crises: know the medical resources available, read about Post Traumatic Stress Disorder, learn breathing techniques, understand that avoiding emotions only delays recovery, eat and rest, and find ways to talk with other individuals who have had similar experiences. Join a group. Also, grieving and mourning is part of the closure process. Allow for that time. Find joy in simple things. Practice gratitude and remember the blessings in life. Foster resilience by using pain and lessons learned to help others in need. Finally, the only other advice I have for Foreign Service Officers or others interested in a career in diplomacy is to read the embassy's Emergency Action Plan ahead of time and become familiar with it. We never had time to do so when the crisis was occurring.

For managers, I recommend finding ways to give your subordinates breaks, prepare for events and what to expect as a team beforehand, and conduct debriefs afterwards. Invite all members involved to funerals and other events to allow the grieving process. Also, be aware that people may need some time alone. Grant a few days of leave if it would help the employee. Offer positive encouragement and remind subordinates to eat, rest, and understand that survivor's guilt is natural, but that he/she is safe now and is not at fault. Support each other. Encourage subordinates to speak with a Regional Psychiatrist reassuring them that this will not hurt their career or look "bad" on their record. Let them know that you find no shame in anyone seeking counseling and will grant them flexibility in their work schedule to address appropriately and meet appointments.

Nigeria Was the Hardest but Most Rewarding Tour

One of the reasons I chose to serve in Nigeria was the amount of responsibility I could shoulder early on in my career and gain valuable experience working with government elites from the Aviation Minister to CEOs of large American and Nigerian companies, something impossible for a second tour or even senior officer to experience in a place like London or Paris. I was the lead person interacting with a Cabinet Member official on aviation matters. I was the person that received the call at 2am in the morning from Nigeria's National Security Advisor when a plane crash occurred in the jungles of Nigeria involving American citizens. I also wanted to prove to the State Department that I was willing to serve in the hardest, most dangerous operating environments to pay my dues and receive the call to finally serve in Japan. After two years of service in Nigeria, Diplomatic Security finally lifted my preclusion from serving in Japan in 2007; I felt now was my time to finally get the chance to utilize my Japan background and skills.

I distinctly recall that drinking after work or talking about different categories of visas never appealed to me as a way to decompress. I may have alienated a number of colleagues who enjoyed drinking, watching and discussing the latest TV shows – activities I avoided. A teetotaler since childhood, I never enjoyed drinking and often settled for a soft drink or water. I preferred making friends with Nigerians and expats and exploring the art scenes. I was too consumed with trying to study and maintain Mandarin as well as exercising so I did not want to spend time engaging in activities that were not for me. In addition, my work consumed me. As an officer overseas, especially during a crisis in which you are the lead, you are essentially on call 24/7, at least that was my experience and how I felt at that time.

Respecting each other at work is a given. But people—even Foreign Service Officers—can be ignorant and make erroneous assumptions about an individual's cultural or ethnic background. I remember one day when I did not respond the way a colleague thought I would regarding some trivial matter, she remarked "that's the Japanese side of you." I was rather shocked that this fellow colleague had the nerve to tell me what side of me is Japanese and what is not. She never thought that it could have been my personality or other factors that dictated my reaction. Although the individual had no ill-intention, I was offended by that comment. It made me think once again—why do I have to keep defending myself against such ignorance. She and I are friends, but it made me defensive around her for the remainder of my tour. I certainly could not bring up certain topics with her—but that is natural too. We can choose to whom and to what extent we are willing to share our lives with others. Setting boundaries is a healthy part of the process.

Although generally positive, I do remember a few encounters that made me conscious of how others perceived me. First, as an Economic Officer I often visited my contacts to gain updates about various aspects of the economy. I recall one Nigerian gentleman asking me where I am from. I replied the U.S. He then said, "you do not sound like an American." I asked him what he meant. He explained that he has two children studying in the U.S., that he has visited the U.S. on numerous occasions, and that I do not sound like the Americans he is used to conversing with. He may have meant I do not "look" and "speak" like the Americans he interacts with. I simply took that as a compliment.

I also recall a few Nigerian store employees working at a Lebanese owned grocery store named "Goodies" calling me, "Chinese, come here." I had to politely tell them I am not Chinese and that I would appreciate it if they would not address me as such. I never had a problem since, but it reminded me that many people cannot differentiate between Chinese, Japanese, Vietnamese, and so forth. It is also quite understandable in Nigeria because the largest Asian population in Lagos is the Chinese population, mostly from Southern China. Due to the People's Republic of China's interest in Nigeria's oil as well as telecommunications, railroads, and manufacturing, the presence of Mainland Chinese technical advisers and workers has been growing each year. In contrast, the Japanese community in Lagos during that time I served from 2005-2007 was roughly around 50 individuals. I can't imagine that number to be significantly higher today. To many, we are all "Chinese" because the vast majority of Nigerians have more contact with Chinese than any other Asian ethnic group. Hence, many people equate Asian with Chinese.

The same could be said within the U.S. Consulate in Lagos where I worked among the Foreign Service National (FSN) staff. There was one other Asian American besides me who worked at the Consulate. He and I look nothing alike. He is Chinese American and we have completely different names. However, at times local staff members would call me by his name. That became annoying at times, but I knew it was not done out of malice. And, I came to appreciate how hard the local staff members worked despite the daily hardships they and their families endured—inadequate health care, constant electricity blackouts, poor water and sanitation, and horrendous traffic. Lagos is the largest city in Africa with a population of between 17 to 20 million people at any given time. The poverty, crime, and malnutrition rampant in the country made me grateful for the many items we take for granted in the United States—access to drinkable tap water, electricity, good roads, and a vibrant and viable legal, political, and economic base structure.

SAVING LIVES IN NIGERIA – A PROUD MOMENT

During my second year in Nigeria I worked in the Consular Section issuing and refusing visas. The visa refusal rate in Nigeria was one of the highest in the world, rife with fraud and thousands of applicants wishing to visit the U.S. Consular work in Nigeria is challenging. You get used to people lying to you. But, there are also several individuals that do qualify for either a non-immigrant or immigrant visa. I remember one case in which a mother had a baby that was going to die unless her baby received medical treatment. The Jesuit community was willing to pay for the baby's operation at Harvard Medical School since the mother was the sister of a

Jesuit priest in the U.S. This woman had been refused three times prior, was a single mother, and did not have a stable job. She didn't qualify for a non-immigrant visa. However, I received an email from a very high level State Department senior official asking if we could review the case. I asked the Consular Section Chief and Deputy Chief of Mission what to do. Ordinarily, we would have asked this person to gain a waiver from the Department of Homeland Security (DHS) on humanitarian grounds, but we knew if we did that this woman's baby would die before she could receive a reply from DHS.

We made the decision to grant her a limited tourist visa annotating the visa to indicate the hospital where she and her baby would go and the dates for her trip. That was one of my proudest moments knowing that the bureaucracy didn't win. Had we not shown compassion towards this request, we very well could have received a backlash from the Nigerian media for negligence not to mention heat from the senior State Department official. I was glad to be a part of saving someone's life.

At the same time, there are millions of other people in similar situations that will never receive a visa. She was one of the lucky ones. She knew the right people and the right people were advocating on her behalf. Most people don't get that chance.

The Japanese in Lagos

The Japanese community in Lagos was very small. The Japanese Embassy (now in Abuja) used to be located in Lagos. The former Japanese Embassy was located very close to the U.S. Consulate Lagos (which also previously served as an Embassy before moving to Abuja). The office in Lagos served as a Liaison office that included a Liaison head, one Consular officer, a Security officer, and a temporary contract security worker. The Japanese government officers in Lagos resided in the compound located inside the Liaison office equipped with two large tennis courts and 24-hour Nigerian security. The Japan External Trade and Relations Office (better known as JETRO) was also only a few minutes away from the Liaison office. The Japanese association of Lagos routinely held receptions at the JETRO location or Liaison office for Japanese citizens and their families representing companies such as Honda, Toyota, Mitsubishi, Ajinomoto, JGC Gas, and others.

When I initially arrived in Lagos, I was invited to a dinner reception at the home of the Liaison office Head. I was the only American invited. The Liaison Head was married to a Swedish lady and had two sons that were "mixed" like me. The only difference was that his children spoke little or no Japanese. I remember the Liaison Head treating me with utmost respect, often talking about his two sons and their education. I was invited to play tennis with members of the Japanese community at the Liaison compound and gracefully accepted their invitation to play on Saturday mornings. I also introduced members of the Japanese community to American and other English speakers to allow them to practice English. Many officers and their spouses would often ask me for help in English or ask if I knew people who would be willing to teach them English. I gladly assisted. Everything seemed to be going smoothly as I organized a U.S.-Japan softball game in Lagos between the U.S. Consulate community and Japanese Liaison office and business community. It was a smashing success. However, there were a few developments that made me gradually pull away from mingling with many of the Japanese community members.

First, I remember when attending the dinner reception at the Liaison Head's house that one of the Security officers mentioned it was "disgusting" that I spoke Japanese. He did not or could not believe a foreigner could speak Japanese at a native level. He must have thought I was a spy. I ignored what he said as sheer ignorance, and told him I did not think describing my language ability as "disgusting," was appropriate. He nodded his head in acceptance. However, I later learned from a Japanese spouse married to an American Consulate official that the same Officer had asked her why she had married the enemy. The Japanese spouse confided in me how shocked she was to hear this from a Japanese government representative. Even if it was said in jest, it was nonetheless inappropriate and the spouse was offended. I had also learned from Japanese citizens married to Nigerians that the Japanese Consulate community, far from welcoming them, had an exclusive spouses' club that only included Japanese married to other Japanese. I found that policy disgusting, not only because they were discriminating against Japanese married to non-Japanese, but also because it went against the intended purpose of having a Liaison office or Embassy which is to protect and support your country's citizens. It was unfortunate that that was the "unspoken" code they followed. Who one marries should have no bearing on how a diplomatic mission treats its citizens. A Japanese citizen is a Japanese citizen no matter who he or she marries. Japanese government officials can ill afford to be narrow-minded, nor can it alienate the very citizens it is obligated by law to protect. Prejudice has no place in diplomacy.

I gradually stopped playing tennis at the Japanese Liaison office and stopped entirely after one incident in March 2006 that turned me away from wanting to communicate with the officers there. The Security officer had provided me a pass to give to Japanese citizens to enter the Liaison office at will to play tennis. After the U.S.-Japan softball match I helped organize, he mentioned to me in private that I could keep the pass and that I would be given honorary privileges to use the court as a result of my efforts to assist the Japanese community. I was flattered. Little did I know that the next day he would call to tell me that the Japanese government officers of the Liaison office had held a meeting and a decision was made that only "Japanese" could use the court. I was rather shocked since I had been playing on the court every Saturday and the security guards and Liaison office members all knew me. This had occurred when a new Liaison office head had replaced my former friend and made the decision to ban me from using the court on weekdays. Later I learned that the incoming Office head despised the former Office head and that the feeling was mutual. Although I was later told I could use the court on Saturdays with other Japanese, I no longer had the desire to do so. If the Japanese representatives in Lagos wanted the court to be used only by Japanese, so be it. I would play on courts used by other Americans and invite one or two Japanese friends to play tennis there. I never returned to play tennis at the Liaison office again.

While I avoided the Japanese Liaison office afterwards, I did try to maintain friendship with some members of the Japanese community. At the end of my tour, I was able to count a few Japanese expatriates sent to Nigeria including a couple from Ajinomoto, the Director of JETRO Nigeria Office, a couple working for a trading company, and the Managing Director of Honda Nigeria as friends. Through these individuals, I was able to eat Japanese food, learn about current affairs in Japan, maintain my Japanese language, and preserve the Japanese link that is part of who I am.

I never told the Japanese in government or business circles that my mother was Japanese. I knew it would change their attitudes and behavior towards me. I wanted to observe their reactions to me and have a meaningful dialogue that was not based on race or ethnicity. As much as possible, I have always strived to break down the barriers of communication and make my Japanese friends realize that foreigners can speak Japanese and that the idea that only a Japanese can truly understand Japanese culture was a myth. As soon as a Japanese friend learned that my mother was Japanese, the conversations changed from talking about the economy and life in general to racial or ethnic questions about my mother. Where is she from, what is her background, and so forth. I politely informed my friend that I do not feel like talking about my mother and that whether my mother was Japanese or not should not have any bearing on the topics of discussion.

BEIJING, CHINA FOR MY THIRD
OVERSEAS ASSIGNMENT

During my tour in Nigeria, I began bidding for jobs for my third tour. With my preclusion from serving in Japan I knew that Japan was out of the question. I knew I wanted to return to East Asia and hone my Mandarin. But, was there a job that would interest me? I came across a newly created "Virtual Presence Post" job opening for Beijing, China. Virtual Presence Posts (VPP) and American Presence Posts (APP) were jobs created with the intention of having officers do more public outreach in second and third tier cities outside the host nation's capital. These positions were newly created under Secretary Condoleezza Rice's "Transformational Diplomacy" initiative which, unfortunately, as I discovered later, was neither well defined, funded nor implemented. It was a failure from the beginning. But officers like me had no idea that was the case when initially applying for the job, naively thinking this was an opportunity for us to do public speaking, utilize Mandarin in day-to-day work, travel outside Beijing, and engage in people-to-people diplomacy. The prospect of moving from Nigeria, the most populous country in Africa, to the most populous country in the world, China, right before the 2008 Olympics excited me. It would also mean I would at least be geographically closer to Japan.

I expressed interest in the job and the person making assignment decisions on the China Desk in Washington, DC gave me a "hand shake," or an informal commitment to give me the job. I was naturally excited. The job, however, required having a 3/3 level in Mandarin. This meant I had to have proficiency in speaking and reading Mandarin at a level that would allow me to engage Chinese officials. Having spent my first tour in Taiwan and having continued to study Mandarin on my own in Nigeria, my Mandarin level was at a 3/2+—just shy of the necessary score. The China Desk agreed to allow me to take intensive language courses in Beijing to obtain the necessary 3/3 score for the job. Most officers received one to two years of full Mandarin language training to obtain that score; my case was an exception. I would only receive less than four months training, yet did better than what everyone expected. Hard work and knowledge of Japanese paid off in allowing me to obtain the required language score without two years of intensive Mandarin Chinese.

Mandarin Language Training in Beijing

The language school where I would take short-term intensive Mandarin courses was located near a music conservatory college in Beijing. Classes were held at the Foreign Affairs Office Monday through Friday from 8am-4pm with Thursday as an administration day. Our teachers were native Chinese and only U.S. diplomats were taught at the school. Our classes were taught one-on-one. Naturally, some teachers had more experience teaching U.S. Foreign Service Officers than others. The motivation for the teachers was essentially to raise our proficiency level to such a degree that we could pass the language exam. Passing a language exam does not necessarily mean one is fluent in the language, but the Foreign Service has its methods of language testing and I was happy to receive language training and get paid doing so.

One teacher in particular had a knack for teaching diplomats and everyone wanted to take her course. This created some jealousy among the other teachers, but we all knew certain teachers were better at preparing us for our exams than others. One of my favorite teachers was affiliated with Tsinghua University (one of China's top universities along with Beijing University) where her mother was a Professor and her husband, the Director of the Physics Department. She was an expert at teaching us Chinese proverbs and

I thoroughly enjoyed her classes. Thanks to her help and others, I scored a 3+/3+ on my Mandarin exam.

During my period of intensive study, I never talked about my Japanese background or Japanese language skills with my Chinese teachers. I didn't want that to "distract" us from our ultimate aim—passing the exam. And, I knew that some teachers wanted to state the reason for my fast advancement was due to my "Japanese" background. I wasn't going to even let that come into the equation. No need to let them use "race" or ethnic background to make assumptions about my language progress. Having Japanese language did help in terms of character recognition, but my countless hours of study both inside and outside the classroom was what led to rapid advancement. Besides, I didn't feel there was any relevance to discuss my Japanese background in class. In addition, we were all taught that we could not rule out the possibility that the Chinese affiliated with the Embassy, even our teachers, likely reported to the Chinese Security Bureau. The classrooms where we were being taught (inside the Foreign Affairs Department) might also have had listening devices. So, that gave me even more reason not to want to reveal much about my background.

Empty Promises

Having been promised the VPP job I was naturally disappointed to learn that the China Desk hadn't kept its promises. Six months before arriving in Beijing, I had sent an email to my supervisors asking for a job description and work requirement statement for the VPP job. No one replied. Strange. I sent it again and the result was the same. This made me rather worried, but I figured that I would have four months of language training prior to beginning work so that we could negotiate and work something out.

Arriving in June, 2007 to Beijing International Airport I was greeted upon arrival by the then Deputy Economic Section Chief.

I was so happy to see someone there. He helped me with my bags and guided me to the vehicle that awaited us to take me to the apartment where I would live during my entire tour in Beijing. He handed me the keys to my apartment and my mobile phone as well as a list of critical contact numbers. During this time he told me that I would not be doing the VPP job as people had promised. Instead, I would be doing economic work covering high-tech and telecommunications. This, of course, was a disappointment to me, but I figured high-tech and telecommunications sounded cool too. Besides, for the first four months I would be in language training so I didn't let it bother me.

Every Thursday was administration day which meant we could go to the Embassy to get cash from the Embassy cashier, pick up mail, check our State Department emails and take care of any pending administrative matters. Some Thursdays I stayed at the language school reviewing my language materials. On other Thursdays I went to the Embassy to check email and get acquaint- ed with members of the Embassy community. It was during these periods that I went to meet with my supervisor to inquire more about my job responsibilities. He also promised me that I would work in the Economic Section's External Unit covering high-tech and telecommunications. Three weeks before my language exam, the supervisor that I had spoken to had to depart Post because his wife had developed breast cancer. We never had the chance to work together as he had to immediately leave Post with his family. Nonetheless, I had assumed that what he had promised and what the Deputy Section Chief had earlier promised would hold true in terms of my portfolio.

Naturally, I was again disappointed when I learned one week prior to my language exam that my portfolio would entail covering construction, engineering, architecture services, insurance, legal services, government procurement, retail, and distribution. I was hearing this for the first time and had never agreed to cover these topics. My portfolio had changed three times in the course of four months before even beginning my new assignment and my input didn't matter. I was furious. But I had to focus on preparing for my language exam and afterwards take time to compose myself and prepare to assume duties as an Economic Officer in mid-October. I made the most of my portfolio including organizing the U.S.-China Construction Dialogue, U.S.-China Insurance Dialogue, and later becoming the point-of-contact for our VPP Qingdao, China Team.

Management is a key problem in the Foreign Service. An easy way to have avoided such problems was simply to give people the portfolio promised them. Later I found out that the high-tech and telecommunications portfolio had been given to another officer in my Unit that had initially applied to do that job but had been assigned to handle Intellectual Property Right (IPR) issues instead. Give people the jobs you promised them. If not, tell them in advance and be honest if the job description is not going to be the same. You cannot expect happy workers if you are not honest with them or randomly make management decisions without gaining employee input. Had I known that I would not be doing a VPP job in Beijing, I would not have applied for the job. Nevertheless, I worked hard to contribute to the Economic Section and Mission's success.

VPP Scam

I accepted my fate that I would be doing economic work first and in my spare time (virtually non-existent) do VPP work. I was selected to be part of the Qingdao VPP Team. Qingdao is a port city in Shandong Province. Home to the famous Qingdao Beer, Qingdao was a former German colony with nice beaches and the sight for the 2008 Olympic Sailing events. I loved being part of the VPP team, speaking with Qingdao city officials as well as the American business community. I felt the work mattered and most importantly, this is what I had signed up to do in the first place. Each time I visited, I felt even more depressed that I could not engage in such activities full-time. Besides Qingdao, the Embassy had designated VPP Teams for Urumqi, Xi'an, Wuhan, Tianjin, Xiamen, and more. We would go in teams of three (one consular officer, one political officer, and one economic officer) to represent the Embassy. The VPP jobs were created because Secretary of State Rice wanted to create these jobs under her "Transformational Diplomacy" initiative. The stated objective was to create additional jobs in places like China where officers would be sent to important cities outside Beijing to do outreach. We would create, in essence "virtual" consulates where we would have websites for VPP cities and try to offer traditional diplomatic services in those locations. Obviously, this initiative was not very well defined, resourced, nor funded, as people who were designated to fill those jobs more often than not, discovered they were in for an unpleasant surprise.

COVERING UP THE TRUTH – MEDICAL DISASTER

Four months after arriving in Beijing and completing my language studies, I reported to work as an Economic Officer working in the External Unit (previously known as the WTO Unit) at our old Embassy located on Number 3 Xiu Shui Road. I worked at office number 200 in a compound known in Chinese as "San Ban" or Third Compound, an area only accessible to cleared U.S. citizens. My office was on the second floor which I shared with three other colleagues. Most of the Economic Section was located on the second floor and the Ambassador and Front Office was also located on the same floor. Since beginning my job at the office in October 2007, I began to encounter symptoms of asthma, a persistent cough, wheezing and breathlessness that eventually led to development of full blown asthma. Despite repeated visits to

Embassy Beijing's Medical Unit and repeated requests for medical evacuation to examine my condition, each request was denied, prolonging and worsening my respiratory problems.

Visits to an outside pulmonologist referred by the Medical Unit proved fruitless. I will never forget that the Regional Medical Officer (RMO) at the time categorically denied that the toxic air had anything to do with my coughing. I was shocked. The same RMO wrote a glowing medical report about conditions in Beijing that caused our hardship pay to be lowered, another slap in the face to community members that could not take their children outside to play and suffered from some of the worst air pollution in the world. Certainly, the lowering of the hardship pay hurt Embassy morale.

Oh, and the Embassy didn't bother to install a state-of-the-art air filtration system in the building where we worked. The air filtration system in the old Embassy, at least the office where we worked, was inadequate. We were breathing toxic air and people were covering it up. Management knew this. They were more interested in avoiding lawsuits than taking care of the people that worked inside those buildings. When we moved to the new Embassy compound in November 2008, we were told management had installed a state-of-the-art air filtration system. Yes, but what about the years of lung damage and respiratory illness people faced by not having state-of-the-art air filtration systems placed in the old office buildings? Again, this was an example of negligence and an indicator to me that the Department was not taking care of the health of its employees who were sacrificing their health and that of their families to be there.

Although I have had no prior history of smoking, no history of respiratory illness, and never experienced persistent coughing until starting work in Beijing, no one wanted to admit acute toxic exposure to atmospheric pollutants in the air was causing my coughing. If they sent one of us home, they would have to send all of us home. At the time, I did not fully understand the political game that was going on, but after departing, I realized I was denied proper and immediate medical evacuation from Embassy Beijing due to political as opposed to health reasons. I had been coughing persistently for 11-months. Clearly my body and lungs had suffered and instead of paying for a medical evacuation, the Medical Unit again denied my request. Why? Because medical evacuations cost money. And the bar for meeting a medical evacuation is set so high that they are rarely granted. I was unlucky to have a RMO who cared more about maintaining the perception that all was fine with the air in Beijing, rather than my health. How can we expect our diplomats to perform when we deny them the proper medical care? Had I been coughing for only three months that would be, perhaps, another story. But 11 months is serious. It made me question the integrity of the Department's Bureau of Medical Services.

Since beginning the job in October, I noticed my coughing becoming worse. Despite remaining indoors inside my apartment as much as possible where I had two air filter systems blasting on high 24-hours and limiting my activities outside (including outdoor sports I loved such as basketball and tennis), my condition had not improved. My coughing became so severe in March/April 2008 that I requested to be medically evacuated to have my condition examined. My request was denied. By this time I felt scared to even meet the RMO because I felt he did not have my best health interests in mind. Instead, he seemed more preoccupied with saving costs than saving lungs. Beijing has some of the worst air pollution if not the worst air pollution in the world, but I didn't quite realize what that would mean for my health and body until experiencing it first-hand for 18 months. I had never visited the Medical Unit as frequently as I had than when working in Beijing, China.

Despite reading daily Embassy reports that stated hazardous air pollution levels, every request for evacuation was denied. Not only was it denied in April but the pulmonologist to whom the Medical Unit at the Embassy referred me misdiagnosed my cough as related to gastro esophageal reflux disease (GERD) and not exposure to toxic air despite daily atmospheric reports from Beijing registering unhealthy air. Before he even examined me, the pulmonologist from Beijing United Hospital insisted that no air pollution existed in Beijing. He had to do so, for admitting the air was the root cause would mean losing his contract with the Chinese government and potentially, his job. His findings were then reported to Embassy Beijing's Medical Unit. The Embassy then added that psychological reasons could be behind my coughing. Rather than examining my claim that exposure to toxic air was at the root cause of my coughing and dwindling health, the Medical Unit cited GERD and psychological reasons to avoid examining my claim.

No job is worth ruining your lungs. And, clearly I had to leave Beijing or risk greater health risks. Health is non-negotiable. And I was disappointed that the Medical Unit was not flexible and more reasonable in handling my case. I can only imagine that several other individuals had to suffer in silence like I did, and it is not right that we treat people this way. Had the Medical Unit evacuated me outside Beijing when I requested this in April 2008, I believe doctors would have discovered that I was unfit to serve in Beijing, reassigned me, and I would not have had to request leave without pay. I also believe I would not have developed asthma.

I had to spend so much time fighting for my cause that it literally exhausted me. My health was in jeopardy, my lungs were damaged, and my spirits plummeted. Besides one senior human resource officer, no one at the Embassy seemed to be doing much to support my case. I had only two options left—resignation from the Foreign Service or requesting leave without pay. Despite having a terrible time and feeling miserable both physically and emotionally, I opted to request leave without pay. Thank God for the Deputy Chief of Mission who supported my decision to curtail my assignment and depart from Beijing. He, however, resigned in the summer of 2009.

MY GRANDMOTHER'S DEATH

My Japanese grandmother died on September 22, 2007 during my Beijing assignment. I was unaware of her passing until late October when my mother came to visit me in Beijing. Only during her visit did my mother tell me that my grandmother had died. Naturally, I was very upset with my mother for not telling me about my grandmother's death but she didn't want to tell me the bad news until after I passed my Mandarin exam in early October. I had missed my grandmother's funeral. My grandmother was the person who played the role of "mother" in raising me during my summers in Japan. She had cooked meals, taught me Japanese, and cared for me while my mother was busy doing research. In many ways my grandmother was the driving force behind my decision to enter the Foreign Service. Now she had died and I had no way to see her again. I loved her so much and it hurt to lose such a special person in my life.

In front of my grandmother's tomb, I reflected upon the greatest gift one human being can give another—unconditional love. She only had a middle school education, but she understood the meaning of life. And, she lived her life in fulfillment of others. She sacrificed herself to allow her eight children a bright future. She is the most impressive and warm-hearted woman I have ever encountered in my life. Much of my success I owe to her. As I said my final prayers I made a vow. I vowed to her that I would never negate myself nor deny my Japanese heritage and background ever again for any reason. In the face of adversity and trials, I will remain as much Japanese as I am American. The internment of 120,000 loyal Japanese Americans during World War II reminds us of the brutal actions governments can resort to when racially motivated policies are enacted based out of fear and prejudice. My grandmother showed me another route to take—love. When we enact policies based out of love and not fear, viewing loyal dual-national Americans as valuable assets and bridges to unite people and businesses, we all prosper.

For the past six years during my time as a Foreign Service Officer I never visited my Japanese grandmother in Japan out of fear that Diplomatic Security would cite that as another reason to preclude me from serving in Japan. All I had ever wanted to do was to return to Japan to make her proud. My grandmother had raised eight children, my mother being the eldest daughter. While I knew my uncles and aunts and cousins growing up as a child in Japan, I really didn't have much of a strong connection with any person besides my grandmother. My aunts and uncles occasionally visited and gave me *otoshidama* or allowance money, but I didn't live with them. I thought my grandmother would be so proud of me if I returned to Japan as a diplomat working on U.S.-Japan relations that this was motivation enough for me to continue working at the State Department until my chance came.

Little did I know that so many obstacles would stand in the way for me to attain that goal. Most disappointing was that the obstacles came from the very organization that hired me, claiming they needed people with hard language skills like Japanese when recruiting me. I felt deceived. I felt angry. I felt foolish that I had given so much to an organization and now my grandmother had died and I had nothing left, not even my health.

First I had the sad experience with my Japanese fiancée, then I witnessed the struggles my mother had to face in giving up Japanese citizenship to obtain U.S. citizenship, just to give me a better chance to serve, fighting Diplomatic Service to remove my preclusion. And now that I had lost my Japanese grandmother, I felt I had lost everything. My grandmother's death made me reevaluate my priorities. I wanted to return to Japan, the birthplace of my grandmother.

LEAVE WITHOUT PAY

When my coughing condition became severe in April 2008 I had gone to my then supervisor and told her I was thinking about resigning from the Foreign Service. That shocked her. I had performed well, had a very good evaluation, and she was concerned. She recommended that rather than resigning, I should have the Medical Unit evacuate me or consider leave without pay. I tried the medical evacuation option, but that failed. The doctors made me think the origins of physical illness began mentally. So, I tried to convince myself that mental toughness would allow me to persevere. Obviously, the only solution to a problem with the air would be to limit exposure to toxicity. Try as I may, I could not do so. Taking leave without pay made sense because it would give me time to think before acting and recover my health. It would also give me time to reassess my career and reevaluate the Foreign Service. In the end, having stayed in Beijing for an additional eight months, it was time to accept the facts. I was not going to get better in Beijing. I had to request leave without pay for one year as the only means for me to leave the work environment in Beijing and recover my health.

I also submitted a claim to the Department of Labor providing medical proof that my asthma was work-related. In February 2009, the Labor Department concurred with the 80-page document I submitted full of doctor reports from my doctor in Arizona and in Washington DC siding in my favor. Rather than collect a worker's compensation check, however, I decided to accept a job working as a Business Development Manager for Westinghouse Corporation in Tokyo, Japan.

I believe in the idea that one should not make life changing decisions in haste or under stress. The one year leave without pay period was necessary for me to reconnect with my parents with whom I very rarely had the opportunity to spend time during my career abroad in the Foreign Service, and I would also have time to ask the question "what went wrong?"

CREATING THE RIGHT ENVIRONMENT

Several things went wrong, but the most important factors were that I was in the wrong place at the wrong time, performing the wrong job. And I had sacrificed time with family and my health to be there. During my assignment in Beijing I had again lobbied for a job in Embassy Japan. I had plenty of reasons for wanting to serve in Tokyo. My Japanese grandmother had recently passed away, my mother was planning on retiring in Japan, I wanted to meet and marry a Japanese lady and I wanted to utilize my language skills. In other words, I felt at home and comfortable in Japan. And, even though I would be with officers that may not have the same amount of appreciation for Japan, its language and its people as I had, I knew I could have a life outside the Embassy community, and if nothing else eat food that I grew up eating as a child—the Japanese food I loved. Besides, having served in hardship posts, paying my dues taking anti-malaria pills in Nigeria, and breathing the bad Beijing air, I felt I deserved to serve in Japan. Not only that, myself and my family, particularly my mother, had to endure a lot of suffering as a result of Diplomatic Security, placing an unreasonable security preclusion on me from serving in Japan. My mother felt guilty that because of her I could not serve in Japan. She took the step of becoming a U.S. citizen, an act considered by the Japanese government as renouncing her Japanese citizenship, just to give me a chance to follow my dreams and serve in Japan.

When I was told I would not receive an assignment anywhere in Japan including our consulates in Osaka, Okinawa, Nagoya, and Sapporo, I was devastated. After finally having my security preclusion removed, I was still told "No." I took this personally and decided if the State Department could not find a way to utilize someone with my background and skills then I needed to seriously think about finding a place that would. Several U.S. companies and friends I knew had suggested I seek opportunities outside of the State Department. I decided what they said made sense. With Japanese and Mandarin under my belt and having international work experience, I felt good about finding a job in Japan even if it did not offer the same lucrative benefits and salary as the State Department. I found out that a number of people were interested. That made me feel valued and appreciated again. I was going to see if I could take advantage of my one year leave without pay to send myself to Japan and gain some valuable private sector work experience in the process. I am so glad I made that choice.

Seven years into my career, I had lost my fiancée, dealt with the trauma of two plane crashes, an ulcer caused by anti-malaria medication, lost my Japanese grandmother, had my dream of serving in Japan shattered, caused my mother unimaginable pain in renouncing her citizenship, and now I suffered from adult asthma. No one could ever say that I did not sacrifice for the State Department, the American taxpayer, or the United States of America. I served loyally and with distinction. The costs, however, had begun taking an unbearably high toll on my health.

Lessons Learned

After leaving Beijing I had physical exams conducted in DC and Arizona. The x-rays and chest exams revealed asthma. My medical clearance was lowered from Class 1 (the highest medical classification) to Class 2 (which meant I would have to receive Post clearance to serve in certain Posts abroad). What I learned from my experience in Beijing was that I had to protect and defend myself.

The system would not do so. Second, the State Department culture breeds a fear among Foreign Service Officers against openly fighting the system and demanding more from our bureaucracy. We often decide fighting the bureaucracy is not worth the stigma placed on those that do and not worth the effort. People are afraid that voicing dissent would affect their jobs and translate into lack of promotions. What we need is not only the courage to serve, but also courage to admit our faults and demand more from the State Department. Too often the problem lies not in Foreign Service Officers meeting the State Department's expectations, but in the State Department failing to meet the expectations of its employees.

We spend so much time asking other countries to be more transparent. Yet we don't set an example of transparency within our own government system. True transparency means being more open about health risks in a country, being forthcoming in the assignment process, about dual nationality, and valuing honesty in everything we do. We owe that much to the men and women serving in hardship places, in Sudan, Iraq, Afghanistan, and elsewhere around the world. That is the only way we can build trust. Paying lip service is not enough.

2008 BEIJING OLYMPICS

My tour in Beijing was not completely filled with sad memories. I had the chance to be a part of Olympic history and watch some of the 2008 Beijing Summer Olympic games live. Several months prior to the Olympic events, the Beijing city government announced policies to reduce the number of CO_2 emissions by having Beijing residents take buses, subways and limiting the number of vehicles on the roads. They did this by enforcing a rule that vehicles with odd number license plates could not drive on the road on even number days and vehicles with even number license plates likewise could not drive on the road on odd number days. The only exception of course were diplomats who could drive on any day with their diplomatic license plates. While this rule did not fix Beijing's air pollution, it did temporarily halt increasing CO_2 emissions and made traffic lighter on the streets of Beijing immediately before and during the Olympics. Beijing city also created a special Olympic lane for vehicles affiliated with the Olympic events to allow such vehicles to cruise past the traffic.

Initially, I had not purchased Olympic tickets either through friends or online, thinking we would be so busy at the Embassy with visitors and work that I would not be able to attend such events even if I obtained tickets. I assumed that the only individuals lucky enough to see the games would be high level VIPs. I'm glad this thought turned out to be wrong. The Embassy Community Liaison Office received a number of extra tickets and allowed Embassy community members the chance to secure free tickets. Our supervisors were also kind enough to allow us to go to games on our spare time (most of them were doing the same). Also, friends that decided last minute that they could not attend certain games offered a few tickets to me. I saw three Olympic baseball games (Japan vs. Netherlands, Japan vs. Korea, and U.S. vs Japan). The final Olympic baseball game I attended was an Olympic bronze medal match between the U.S. and Japan. The U.S. won that match. Prior to the game some Japanese TV crew interviewed me thinking I only understood English and I predicted in Japanese that the U.S. would beat Japan. I had some artist on the street paint USA red, white, and blue flags on both cheeks to indicate I was rooting for the U.S. In my heart I wanted both to do well.

What was amazing was that the Chinese crowds would invariably root for any team matched against the Japanese. In the case of the U.S. vs. Japan match, the Chinese were rooting for the U.S. team. Same with the Japan vs. Korea match. I felt sorry for some of the Japanese fans that flew all the way from Japan and paid probably three or four times the price of the ticket to attend the games only to have the crowds rooting against team Japan. It had to be unpleasant. During the Japan vs. Nigeria soccer match I attended in Tianjin, the Chinese crowds were rooting for Nigeria. Nigeria did win that soccer game and won enough games to make it to the gold medal match. I was happy to see the Nigerian soccer team win the gold medal. They deserved to win.

Other games I attended included a field hockey match between Pakistan and Canada and a track and field gold medal event where I witnessed the U.S. 400 meter men's and women's relay teams respectively take the gold medal. That was a wonderful experience. Sitting next to me were three Embassy friends that shared that magical moment with me.

The Olympics were magical. The U.S. Olympic basketball games were always sold out and tickets were in high demand. Michael Phelps also made Olympic swimming history. The Chinese media played out his victory scenes with enthusiasm. The Chinese had more gold medals than any other country and took pride in letting all of us know that even if the U.S. obtained more overall medals, China was number one when it came to Olympic gold for 2008.

In the apartment complex lobby where I lived, there was an Olympic medals score sheet that constantly reminded us how each country fared in the medal standings. The Olympics were a time of pride for the Chinese. The Chinese officials must have felt relieved when the Olympics concluded without any terrorist incidents, civilian riots, or major accidents. With the entire world watching Beijing, the Chinese government certainly did not want their event on the world scene to be marred with tragedy.

Prior to the Olympics, China had to contend with violence in Tibet, a major earthquake in Sichuan in May 2008, a railroad accident, and snowstorms that ravaged the country early in 2008. The Chinese leadership did not want to see any hiccups in the Olympics. Their number one priority was security not economics. The Chinese government implemented a strict visa policy limiting the number of foreigners allowed to enter or remain in the country during the Olympics (less foreigners meant less security concerns). Many hotels and local businesses that spent millions of *renminbi* to prepare for foreign tourists were disappointed when they learned strict visa policies meant less people occupying hotel rooms and spending money to boost the local economy. Nonetheless, the overall sentiment in China was that the Olympics were a resounding success, especially since Chinese athletes won so many gold medals.

The one disappointment for Chinese viewers was that their star Olympic hurdler, Liu Xiang, who had won Olympic gold in Sydney and was expected to win another in Beijing, failed to win a medal due to injuries. Yao Ming and the Chinese national basketball team continued to gain support from Chinese fans and it was fitting that Yao held the Chinese flag leading the way in introducing the Chinese Olympic players during the opening ceremony where each country's Olympic athletes wore their nation's colors and introduced themselves to the world. Roger Federer, Kobe Bryant, Manu Ginobili, Usain Bolt, and Michael Phelps were just some of the stars in attendance that opening night.

As each country's Olympic members waved their nation's flags, leading VIPs from those countries (President Bush for the U.S., President Hu for China, etc.) stood proudly to salute or acknowledge their countrymen. The Chinese media would spotlight heads of state and leading dignitaries in the Olympic stands during the opening ceremony waving and cheering when it was time for their country to be announced and their countrymen dutifully marched on the field.

It was surprising that when the Japanese team was announced the Japanese Prime Minister Fukuda Yasuo not only did not wave or salute the Japanese Olympic athletes but did not even stand up from his seat. His wife was standing and clapping her hands in place of the Prime Minister. Millions of people witnessed this as it was broadcast throughout media channels around the world. The Japanese media also picked up on this, and it caused embarrassment to the Japanese government. Later, I was told by a Japanese diplomat working at the Japanese Embassy in Beijing that the Japanese Ambassador to China held a private "internal" meeting afterwards with his staff criticizing the fact that no one informed the Prime Minister to stand or at least cheer and to draw lessons from that media disaster to ensure such an incident does not occur again. It wasn't long after that embarrassing incident that Prime Minister Fukuda resigned from his post as Prime Minister.

TEA WITH FORMER PREMIER ZHU RONGJI'S DAUGHTER

One of the perks of being a diplomat is you gain access to the business and political elite. And, in the process, you build trust. I remember having lunch with the wife of former Chinese Minister of Foreign Affairs Li Zhaoxing at a European restaurant called Wine and Dine across from the Canadian Embassy. Mrs. Qin Xiaomei and her husband Foreign Minister Li had served in New York and had a solid understanding of the U.S. I enjoyed hearing stories about conversations Minister Li had with former Secretary of State Madeleine Albright regarding U.S.-China relations.

One other contact with whom I enjoyed discussing U.S.-China relations and other topics was one of Zhu Rongji's daughters (I'm protecting her anonymity). She was well-educated, well-traveled, had worked in England and enjoyed talking about a topic that most Chinese avoided – religion. Not only that, she admitted to being a follower of the Dalai Lama's teaching. As you know, the PRC government views the Dalai Lama as a threat and keeps close watch over followers of Tibetan Buddhism. The Dalai Lama is viewed as a troublemaker trying to incite a rebellion for Tibetan independence, something the Chinese government wants to avoid at all costs.

My contact not only was admitting to me that she believed in what the Dalai Lama teaches, but also that she did not agree with the current Chinese government leadership's treatment of the Dalai Lama nor government policies guiding treatment of religious organizations. Coming from one of the Communist Party's elite family members this took me by surprise. But, it also reminded me that contrary to Chinese media broadcasts, there are Chinese citizens among the political elite that don't always buy into what the Chinese government is preaching or teaching on matters of faith. I found that reassuring.

PRESIDENT BUSH AND FAMILY
OPEN THE NEW EMBASSY IN BEIJING

During the Olympics, President Bush, First Lady Laura Bush, one of their daughters, and George H.W. Bush visited the new Embassy for a ribbon-cutting ceremony commemorating the opening of a new Embassy compound. During the President's visit, he gave a speech to the Embassy community, shook hands with Embassy community members, and took a photo shoot with Embassy children. U.S. Ambassador to China, Clark T. Randt, gave introductory remarks and President Bush followed-up to say a few words of appreciation. We were assembled at the new Embassy's indoor basketball gymnasium and each of us had a chance to take photos and shake the President and First Lady's hands.

It would be another several months before we would actually move from the old Embassy compound to the new Embassy located on *Nuren Jie* or "women's road." Outside the new Embassy were lines of flower shops facing the consular section, a few hotels or inns behind the Embassy parking lot and embassies of the Republic of Korea, Malaysia, and Israel nearby. The advantage of the new Embassy was that it had a state-of-the-art air filtration system and every agency and section could conveniently be located in one location. One did not have to travel via vehicle to another building complex, for example, to meet members of the Foreign Commercial Service, Public Affairs Section or Department of Energy. Everyone was located in the same building which made it easier to meet and coordinate. The disadvantage, however, was that it lacked the charm and history of the old Embassy neighborhood. The old Embassy on Xiu Shui Road had more trees and greenery. The old Embassy was hidden among the trees and adjacent embassies that scattered the neighborhood. A pleasant park called *Ritan* Park was located nearby.

Next to the old Embassy compounds referred to as *Er Ban* (second compound) and *San Ban* (third compound) one could find the Bulgarian Embassy, Egyptian Embassy, and the Embassy of the Republic of Ireland. The Singaporean, British, Mongolian, Japanese, Ethiopian, Cuban, Vietnamese, and Indian chanceries were also nearby. The U.S. Ambassador to China's residence was also located next to the Greek Embassy with the Kuwaiti and Brazilian chanceries nearby. While I would definitely trade air filtration systems, I enjoyed the greenery and neighborhood of the old Embassy more than the new Embassy. Besides, there was an excellent but overpriced tea house called *Heping Yiyuan* overlooking *Ritan* Park that had the best bowl of *Zha Jiang Mian* noodles for *renminbi* 38 (roughly USD 5-6) in town. After eating the noodles, the servers would always give you a piece of Wrigley's Peppermint gum. A nice touch to end a bowl of noodles flavored with strong sauces and garlic. Granted you could find cheaper *Zha Jiang Mian* noodle places renminbi 7 (USD 1) in town, but in terms of cleanliness, taste, ambiance, service and of course, the Wrigley's gum, no other place offered the same deal.

HERCULEAN TASK

Anyone that worked in Embassy Beijing from 2007-2009 knows that the VIP visitor workload was endless. Every high level U.S.

official and business person wanted to visit China. During the Olympics, virtually every single person in the Embassy directly or indirectly worked to support a visit. Visits by the Secretary of State, Deputy Secretary of State, Secretary of Defense, Secretary of Commerce, Treasury Secretary, and the President were preceded by preparatory "advance" teams. What this meant is that one was either working on a visit, cleaning up from a visit, or preparing for the next visit. China was the "hot" country and everyone in Washington, DC wanted to be a part of the action. Any and all information related to China gained attention.

In contrast, we had very few visitors to Nigeria. During my time there, we had former President Carter visit and the Assistant Secretary of State for African Affairs visit, but for the most part we did not have many high-level VIPs come to town. No one visited Nigeria just for fun. Everyone had a legitimate purpose for coming.

Beijing, however, was different. So much of the Embassy's resources were devoted to logistical support for visits that it took time away from writing analytical think pieces. Most reports we sent back to Washington, therefore, tended to be short spot reports on discussions held between U.S. officials and Chinese officials. While we individually drafted a lot more cables in the combined Political/Economic Section (each person drafted roughly three cables a week) in Nigeria versus Beijing (maybe one cable a month) the visitor workload was clearly more intense. But, more people back in Washington were reading the cables out of Beijing than out of Nigeria. For someone writing a cable, you always want more readers to read your reports than less.

We also were not issued BlackBerrys in Nigeria. What that meant was once we left the office for home, we could forget about work. Not the case in Beijing. In Beijing, members of the Economic and Political sections were issued BlackBerrys so that we could constantly keep abreast of latest visitor developments and email. That meant that after leaving the office, most of us still continued to work on our BlackBerrys. Even with the 12 hour time difference between Washington and Beijing, with our BlackBerrys we could still interact with our colleagues in DC responding to their inquiries late at night outside of the office. Most people got hooked. The BlackBerry gave you more mobility to interact with colleagues, but it also often made it more difficult for you to escape work during off hours.

Anyone who has worked at the Embassy or been a part of the diplomatic community knows first-hand how hard and how long diplomats in Beijing work. The pace and workload is incredible. So is the stress. The Embassy can be a cold and lonely place to work with more than 1,000 employees (counting locally hired Chinese staff) that it can intimidate you and make you feel like a small fish in a large pond if you let it. You definitely do not get the same sense of tight community as in a place like Lagos, Nigeria.

But Embassy Beijing certainly had so many talented individuals and a Deputy Chief of Mission (DCM) that was a stress absorber and a people person. The DCM's job is often considered the toughest job in the Foreign Service. One has to manage both the Ambassador and Mission staff. Certainly, serving as DCM in the largest Embassy in Asia (largest in the world second only to Iraq) during a change in administration and an Olympic period is a herculean task for any Foreign Service Officer. Most fail. Thank God we had a DCM that was not only a "China hand," but also a good manager.

Not Always Fun Visitors

When the stakes are high everyone wants to visit. Some visitors came to Beijing not because they really needed to, but because they wanted to partake in the excitement. When you are a control officer for a visitor (i.e., person in charge of setting the schedule, logistics, etc.) you spend an enormous amount of time preparing for a visitor. The higher the rank, the more whistles and bells and demands. Some visitors are conscientious enough to realize how much of a drain on resources a visit can be for the people working at the Embassy and they try to come only when needed; others make it a habit of coming for no other reason than to shop, job hunt, or feel "important." I never had to worry about such visitors in Nigeria. Beijing was an entirely different experience.

Let me begin by saying that there are visitors that came to Beijing to engage the Chinese on legitimate areas of work and then there were visitors that did not. Whenever I had to serve as a control officer for the former, I cringed. I could not believe taxpayer money was being used to assist a high level visitor whose sole purpose for coming to Beijing was to shop and job hunt. When you do this once, it angers you but you get over it. When you have to handle the same individual three times, it becomes annoying. As a mid-level officer, you are the person doing most of the work. Supervisors will often say "yes" to a visitor's coming even if you say "No." I don't mind if a visitor has a legitimate purpose. But, it really bothered me when we had to play chauffeur and set up meetings for individuals that came to town simply to network in the guise that he or she was coming to engage the Chinese on X, Y, or Z when the reality was far from it. It leaves a bitter taste in your mouth when you're spending countless hours arranging meetings for a political appointee on his last "Asia tour," asking you to arrange meetings with CEOs and venture capital tycoons, not because it promotes U.S.-China relations but instead is a way to promote his own business interests. I hated that.

Worse still—are individuals that call you from Washington, DC or Europe asking you to make phone calls on their behalf to ask a Chinese store owner in Chinese whether he can give them good deals on Chinese antiques. That request, in my mind, is an abuse of power. As a mid-level officer, I decided not to argue but listen to these demands and just make the phone call on the individual's behalf. Little did I know that that would result in several emails and phone calls at strange hours of the day or on weekends to satisfy the shopping needs of high-level officials.

Most people do not know how much time is spent preparing briefing books and schedules for VIPs. We treat our dignitaries and officials as our customers and smile and do the job without complaining. The complaining occurs after an individual leaves, and we were very glad when certain individuals left the scene. The trouble is when we do a good job, those same individuals decide to come back and recommend us to their friends. That means we get more demands for the Pearl Market (a popular store in Beijing for foreigners to buy pearls and other gifts) and calls on the weekend for delivering messages in Chinese to store clerks to keep obscure items like Cultural Revolution teapots on hold for VIPs in preparation for their next visit.

Panjiayuan thrift store in Beijing, the Pearl Market, Tiananmen Square, and the Great Wall were favorite attractions for many of our visitors. These VIPs would enjoy Peking duck in the evenings and stay in 5-star hotels with a Foreign Service Officer nearby to handle any crisis or stand prepared to help them in times of need. I remember one colleague had to have his wife search for dresses for a female VIP who lost her luggage in Beijing. That was going beyond the call of duty. But, most of us went the extra mile to ensure a visitor felt satisfied.

Speaking Chinese and constantly trying to use the language to reach out to Chinese government officials served me well in scheduling meetings. If I could join a government official for dinner or attend a social event I would try to do so. These contacts would play their part in assisting us when we needed to schedule that last minute appointment with a Director General or obtain the latest information on new regulations or ministerial directives. Sending text messages in Chinese also helped pave the way for smooth relations.

We even personally delivered moon cakes during the Chinese Mid-Autumn Festival held in mid-September to our Chinese contacts to let them know we valued our relationships. Delivering moon cakes was probably the easiest official meeting I ever had at the Ministry of Housing Urban and Rural Development (formerly known as Ministry of Construction), Chinese Insurance Regulatory Commission (CIRC) and Ministry of Finance (MOF).

MEANINGLESS POSITION: SPECIAL REPRESENTATIVE FOR COMMERCIAL & BUSINESS AFFAIRS

Despite having the U.S. Department of Commerce to advocate on behalf of U.S. commercial interests abroad, the State Department has a position called the Special Representative for Commercial and Business Affairs with the equivalent rank of roughly an assistant secretary. This person is a political appointee who has access to the higher ups at State including the Secretary of State. Unfortunately, this position really has not done a great deal to advocate U.S. business interests abroad. The economic and commercial officers in U.S. embassies and consulates abroad are the ones doing the real work. The Special Representative isn't adding anything more to what the stars on the ground are doing. In fact, the role of U.S. ambassadors, commercial counselors, economic ministers and that of the assistant secretary of state for economic affairs is sufficient to promote U.S. business interests. The only thing the Special Representative for Commercial and Business Affairs adds is more work for everyone else.

These political positions are often abused by individuals who are simply out to make a quick name, travel abroad, collect per diem money and search for private sector jobs while in office, knowing that the time will come when they will have to leave.

Having served as control officer for a Special Representative for Commercial and Business Affairs visit to Beijing three times, I was struck by how each time this individual demanded meetings with venture capitalist firms and other companies for his own job hunting purposes. He was being paid by the U.S. government and through tax payer money to visit several countries abroad only to go shopping and make necessary contacts to land a private sector job later. He would call me on the weekends asking me to speak to an antique dealer in Beijing to reserve a few Cultural Revolution era antiques for him for when he would come for another "official" visit to Beijing. I was disgusted each time by this type of behavior. My supervisors didn't have the courage to refuse a man who outranked him and had access to the Assistant Secretary of State for Economic, Energy and Business Affairs. This was just another position and example of tax dollars wasted. Special envoy and representative positions that are not fulfilling their intended purpose ought to be eliminated.

THE JAPANESE IN BEIJING

Most of the Japanese I knew in Beijing were managing directors, CEOs or presidents of their respective Japanese companies in China and lived in the Chaoyang District of Beijing. Like many Korean businessmen in Beijing, many of the Japanese businessmen left wives and children behind. Most of the businessmen spent time within the Japanese community playing golf on the weekends and drinking with colleagues and associates. Many were forced to work in Beijing against their will. Several had died from overwork, stress or lung difficulty. I always felt very sympathetic that so many Japanese businessmen were sent to Beijing without having the option of having their wife and children join them. Some men decided that their children were at such an age that they needed to remain in Japan for schooling. Other men told me that their wives had careers back in Japan and did not want to live in Beijing.

For the men who were lucky enough to bring their wife and children to Beijing with them, they often found themselves stressed having to find some way for their wives to enjoy their time in Beijing, especially if their wives had no children. Most of the Japanese companies prohibited employees and their spouses to drive in Beijing. Spouses were also prohibited from finding outside employment while accompanying their husbands to Beijing. For women who wanted to work, accompanying their husbands to Beijing was a large and often painful experience. Their saving grace was that a flight from Beijing to Tokyo was only four and a half hours allowing them to return to Japan on relatively short notice.

For Japanese women with children, there was a Japanese mother's club. Members of that club would always gather at a specific hour in the morning to send their young children to school. They would also gather in the afternoon with their children. Most of the Japanese children attended the Beijing Japanese School. Japanese wives without children joined a separate wives club, often joining other wives whose husbands worked for the same company, Toyota for example.

There was a Japanese Citizens Association active in Beijing but participation required being a Japanese citizen. Most of those meetings were meant for businessmen and students to network and talk about how great Japan is versus China. I never enjoyed participating in these very right-wing meetings. Most of my Japanese friends in the business community tended to avoid joining the association as well. For them, joining such a group meant more hassles and headaches, and they also felt this association was too right-wing for their liking.

Beijing had movie theaters, malls, up-scale restaurants, night life, museums, the Great Wall, the Forbidden Palace, hiking clubs and more. The cost of living was cheaper than Tokyo or Washington, DC. One dollar equaled roughly seven *renminbi* and one could enjoy a nice three course meal in a reputable restaurant for under USD 15. Because of the plethora of activities, the Japanese community was not as welcoming as say the Japanese community in Nigeria. Japanese people in China tended to do their own thing and there didn't seem to be the same type of pride or unity in being Japanese in China as in Nigeria. Most grocery stores and department stores had Japanese food items as well, so it was not as if one member of the community needed to interact with others to gain basic necessities. Unlike Lagos, Nigeria, there were multitudes of Japanese restaurants and even Japanese neighborhoods in Beijing. This meant that for family members that wanted to isolate their Japanese children from the rest of China and create an "all-Japanese" environment inside Beijing, it could be done.

Some apartment complexes in Beijing which housed all Japanese citizens were equipped with a recreation area, Japanese restaurant, indoor grocery store stocked with Japanese items, library with Japanese books and *manga* or comics and small soccer field. Only the security guards, restaurant workers, and store clerks were non-Japanese. During the summer, I was always amazed to see some closed Japanese communities hold a *matsuri* or Japanese festival with food, dance, music, games and kimonos, just like in Japan in the heart of Beijing unbeknownst to the rest of the world outside their own gated community.

I always felt that it was great to see Japanese parents teach Japanese to their children and provide as normal a childhood as possible for them in Beijing, but it also made me uneasy that so many parents chose not to have their children learn Chinese or make friends with Chinese kids their own age. Most of the children in Japanese schools were taught to learn English as opposed to Chinese, the idea being that when the children returned to Japan, they would have to have a sufficient level of English ability to pass either the middle school or high school entrance examinations in order to enroll in an academically reputable school back in Japan. These children did not have to face as rigorous an academic program attending Japanese school in China as opposed to Japan, and they even had more freedom for extracurricular activities. However, at the same time, many of these children also received tremendous pressure from parents to prepare for passing examinations upon return to Japan.

I can understand why Japanese parents would want to prepare their children to reacclimate back into Japanese society during their stay in China, but at the same time I always felt a sense of sorrow that many of these children would leave China without having a deep understanding or appreciation of Chinese culture, society, people, and language. The Japanese educational system, unfortunately, breeds a culture of test-taking and rote memorization that creates a deficit in areas like the liberal arts, philosophy, theology, and creative writing. These children have the perfect opportunity to become bridges between Japanese and Chinese society, and yet such opportunities are lost when children are only taught to recognize and study Japanese language, culture, and customs. There is a huge gap in understanding between Japan and China. The responsibility for filling that gap will fall largely on the shoulders of the next generation of Japanese youth. However, at present, I don't see a huge commitment or emphasis to train the next generation of Japanese youth to learn enough about China or Chinese language to make them effective diplomats to China. This I believe is a problem.

Japanese are not accustomed to inviting people into their homes to socialize. Social activities are often conducted outside the home in restaurants or bars. However, I was able to make friends with a number of Japanese families. They would invite me for home cooked Japanese meals and those were some of my best experiences in Beijing. Whenever you are asked by a Japanese family if you would like to join them for a Japanese meal at their home, always say yes! You won't be disappointed. Remember, however, to bring some wine or treats to bring to the dinner table to share with your hosts.

The Japanese diplomats and government officials tended to have their own exclusive cliques in Beijing. I enjoyed working with several diplomats in Beijing, but my friends were always business-men. With diplomats there was always this sense that we had to be careful as if we could not be open because you never knew if the other person wanted to try to gain information from you. The same thing was true for media or journalists. It seemed too much like work to hang out with diplomats and journalists outside of work. So my policy was to keep my distance from both during non-work hours.

JAPANESE AMBASSADOR TO CHINA

The Japanese Ambassador to China, Yuji Miyamoto, had a very good working relationship with our U.S. Ambassador to China Clark T. Randt, as well as a good reputation among both the Japanese embassy and Japanese business communities. A number of us from the U.S. Embassy had an opportunity to attend a *sakurami* or cherry blossom watching event at Ambassador Miyamoto's residence. He and his wife were very gracious hosts. His residence had the most beautiful flower garden equipped with Japanese ponds, a tea house, and cherry blossom trees. Their Management Minister Counselor told me that it was the most expensive flower garden of any Japanese Ambassador's residence in the world. I believe him.

While I never knew the Japanese Ambassador save for a few brief meetings at social gatherings, I did hear a lot about him from the Japanese diplomats that worked for him. I was told by several contacts that the Japanese Ambassador (not just in China but Japanese Ambassadors around the world) received an allowance to import Japanese rice and food items into the host country without incurring custom tax. He also had his own personal chef from Japan cook and prepare meals. It is no wonder that whether in Nigeria or China, the best Japanese cuisine in town is always at the Japanese Ambassador's residence. Never say no to a dinner invitation.

Baptized in China

Despite my Jesuit education throughout high school and college I never received baptism. My parents were not Christian and I was never baptized as a child nor asked to believe in one religious tradition or another. My parents allowed me to study on my own but always encouraged me to respect and take from each religious tradition something positive. I had Muslim, Baptist, Catholic, Buddhist, Shinto, and Jewish friends growing up. My father's experience as a Fulbright student in India and his admiration for India meant I would also get exposure to some of the Hindu traditions and religious stories. My Japanese grandmother's belief in Buddhism meant chanting the Lotus Sutra in Japanese was a given. I read portions of the Mahabharata and Bhagavad Gita, the Koran, the Bible and Japanese Buddhist sutras. But I never chose any one particular religion. An atheist until high school, I figured I would choose all of them, take the best parts of each but never allow myself to be confined to any one religious tradition. That approach no longer worked for me as I faced life changing events and wanted to find a community right for me.

The People's Republic of China officially only recognizes five religions. They are: Buddhism, Taoism, Islam, Catholicism, and Protestantism. That is not to say that worshipers of other religions do not exist. China does have a Jewish and Hindu population. Since the Chinese Communist Party governs the PRC and does not promote any religion, the Chinese authorities keep a watchful eye over religious communities. The Jesuits and other religious orders are prohibited from proselytizing and preaching to Chinese citizens. Mass or temple service or other forms of religious service for foreigners prohibit Chinese to join. As such one always has to show a foreign passport or some form of ID indicating one is not a Chinese citizen in order to participate in a religious gathering meant for the foreign expatriate community. The Jesuit priests would hold mass privately in their apartments or in a school classroom designated for worship among the priests and their students.

On September 22, 2008 I finally took the plunge and received baptism. Funny enough, a priest did the honors and baptized me in his apartment with a friend from the Embassy joining us as a witness. That was an awesome experience for me. Ever since, I've religiously attended mass or Protestant service whenever possible. Curiously enough, the closest place of worship for me in Beijing was at the 21st Century Hotel which was a non-denominational service in Mandarin and English. I initially went by invitation from an Embassy friend. Afterwards, I discovered they had small groups that worshiped on Sundays in various languages. There was a Korean worship group, Japanese worship group, French, Russian, and even African worship group. I would often attend morning service at the Japanese worship group and Catholic mass in the evening on Sundays.

Although very small, I really enjoyed hearing the Word preached in Japanese. I felt very much at home. The Japanese Christian worshipers, however, must have found it very strange to find me worshiping there with them. I never told them I worked at the U.S. Embassy or revealed much about myself. I was there to simply hear a sermon in Japanese, reconnect with my roots, and seek greater knowledge of God. I don't know how successful I have been in increasing my knowledge of God, but I do believe with their help and many others I now have a better relationship with God. And, China will always remain my baptismal birthplace.

Chapter Nine

Love and the Private Sector: Made it to Japan

During my time in Beijing I sent resumés to several private companies in Japan. One company, Westinghouse, was willing to interview me. I visited Japan twice for interviews and also met with their team in Washington, DC. I must have left a favorable enough impression on them for Westinghouse Japan to offer me a job as a business development manager. I jumped at the chance to try something new, use my Japanese, and work for a reputable U.S. company. Although I had never studied in the nuclear energy business, I was very much interested in learning more. The U.S. is the largest consumer of nuclear energy followed by France and Japan before the March 11, 2011 earthquake and nuclear disaster which led Japan to shutdown its nuclear reactors. For resource-strapped countries like France and Japan, building nuclear power plants to meet energy demands made lots of sense, particularly since these countries wanted less dependence on Middle East oil.

In 2006 Toshiba Corporation purchased Westinghouse and it was clear that ensuring a happy marriage between a U.S. company and a Japanese company was crucial for both sides to succeed. Here was an opportunity for me to serve as a "bridge" and I very much found that appealing. I would work for Westinghouse bosses and interact with Toshiba employees to get things done. The only detail that needed to be worked out was the salary. I knew that I would be taking a pay cut of about USD 10,000 and would be unable to contribute to the State Department retirement plan (known as the Thrift Savings Plan) during my leave without pay status, but I was willing to take the chance to begin a new journey and fulfill my desire to be in Japan.

As we had entered a recession and one dollar equaled roughly 90 yen, I was satisfied with the 550000 yen per month salary plus housing in Tokyo (housing allowance of roughly 200000 yen). Westinghouse Japan wanted me to enter Japan on a Japanese passport to begin work immediately. Entering on a Japanese passport would also save the company money in terms of not having to apply for a work permit. But I insisted that Westinghouse apply for a work permit for me to enter on a U.S. passport. I had several reasons for asking. First, technically I was still a State Department official and believed Diplomatic Security would have problems if I entered Japan on a non-U.S. passport. Doing so might affect my security clearance and make folks question my loyalty. Second, if I decided I wanted to return to the State Department after my one-year leave period I wanted to keep that option available. Third, I wanted to protect myself if anyone questioned my loyalty. I could cite my lifelong residence in the U.S., my service in the U.S. Foreign Service, and the fact that I was working for a U.S. company in Japan as evidence that I never took any actions against the U.S. government. Also, I had the additional leverage to say that even though I had a Japanese passport and at times it would have made more financial sense for me to use it, I never once used my Japanese passport while serving as a U.S.

government official. I didn't want to give Diplomatic Security or any other organization a reason to make my life more difficult.

Although the dual nationality and passport issue made me think "here we go again," I understood my situation was rather unique. Had I not been working for the U.S. government, I probably would not have had qualms using one passport or the other to enter and leave the country. I am American and Japanese, and a legitimate citizen of both.

I arrived in Japan on February 13, 2009 and began to visit the Westinghouse Tokyo office first thing on Monday, February 16. I had to wait until March 1 when my work permit was finally approved and could not officially receive a salary until that date. In the meantime, I received an advance to allow me to pay the rent, move into a small, but fully furnished dorm room at Kasai in Edogawa Ward. The commute from my apartment to office in Kamiyacho was about a 35 minute train ride, very reasonable compared to some of my Japanese colleagues who spent an hour or longer commuting. From Kasai I took the Tozai Line to Kayabacho, transferred to the Hibiya Line and went straight to Kamiyacho Station. The Westinghouse Tokyo Office was located right above the Kamiyacho Station located on the 7th Floor of the Toranomon 45 Building. Later when I moved from a monthly dorm room in Edogawa Ward to a real apartment in Higashi-Kanda, I would frequently make the 40-minute bicycle ride to work. I cannot emphasize enough the importance of using a bicycle to explore the city of Tokyo and discover all of the fascinating stores, temples, shrines, restaurants, and history.

My first month at Westinghouse I participated as an observer at conferences with utility customers, such as Kansai Electric Power Company and Kyushu Electric Power Company. I had a chance to visit Tsuruga, Fukui Prefecture as well as Fukuoka City in Kyushu and Kobe during that period. In Tsuruga I visited the Kehi Shrine (over 1,300 years of history) where the great Japanese Haiku Poet Matsuo Basho had passed. Basho would visit Fukui (formerly known at that time as Echizen) to see the moon. He wrote at least six haikus during his visit to Fukui. A monument of Basho is found inside the Kehi Shrine compound. Fukui is also known for its fresh fish, agriculture, Wakasa Bay, and its beautiful surrounding nature. Obama City (famous for sharing the same name as President Obama) is also near Tsuruga. I made friends in Fukui and I have to say that the rural countryside has a greater sense of community and warmth that is not easily found in large cities like Tokyo. The people were extremely warm and kind-hearted. I felt very much at home in Tsuruga and had plenty of time to think and participate in *matsuri* or local festivals, as well as learn more about the lives of Japanese farmers.

My experience at Westinghouse was rewarding. I was part of history and had the opportunity to learn more about the nuclear power plant industry and Japanese politics. I represented Westinghouse in Tokyo at the Carnegie Code of Ethics conference to discuss a nuclear code of ethics among various nuclear power companies. Representatives from all the major nuclear power companies around the world attended in secret. I was excited to participate as an "observer."

During my short eight months at Westinghouse I also met my future Japanese wife. So, I have much to thank Westinghouse for that opportunity. While I was about to receive a permanent offer and competitive salary to remain with Westinghouse as a local hire, ultimately I decided to fulfill my obligations to the State Department and return to duty. Leave without pay status was granted with the assumption that after a certain period I would return to the State Department. Despite all of the heartaches and difficulties faced at State, I decided to return for one simple reason—my wife! We would be heading together to my fourth overseas assignment, Georgetown, Guyana by October, 2010, after less than one year in the private sector in Japan. But before doing so, I would need to take a month of Public Affairs Officer training and we would need to get officially married to allow my spouse to be on my orders and obtain diplomatic immunity.

One of the difficulties that Foreign Service Officers face is the paperwork involved in marrying, especially regarding a marriage to a non-U.S. citizen. Hassles include notifying Diplomatic Security at least 90 days prior to marriage to a foreigner. When I first entered in 2002, the rule was at least 180 days. Not having a spouse on travel orders makes it very difficult for the officer. For example, the spouse will not have the same diplomatic immunity nor have access to the same Embassy resources and perks. If on travel orders, however, the Department will pay for the cost of travel for the spouse, authorize per diem to include the spouse, and assist with visas and travel documents. In addition, the spouse is entitled to a full medical checkup as well and the Department will pay for the cost of a medical evacuation. Many Foreign Service Officers end up getting married in "Foreign Service" fashion, which means marriage at Arlington Courthouse or a nearby county court. We were no exception. My wife's family wanted an elaborate wedding ceremony in Japan, but given timing issues and our desire to be together, we went for the court wedding. My wife and I don't regret the court wedding, but I know her parents, particularly her mother, was really expecting an official wedding with reception to follow in Japan. In Japan, marriage is a family matter. But timing and the Foreign Service career made that impossible for us. Maybe one day we can have that dream wedding to give back to her parents.

Spousal Employment

The Foreign Service is a challenge for spouses seeking employment. More often than not, spouses find difficulty finding employment in the country his or her partner is assigned. Doctors, engineers, lawyers, and other professionals often cannot find employment opportunities in the same field abroad. Many spouses give up lucrative or satisfying careers when their partner enters the Foreign

Service. Many end up seeking a job in the Embassy simply because of lack of alternative choices and receive salaries well below what they were earning before. The Foreign Service is not an easy life for a spouse eager to have a career of his or her own. There are tandem couples in the Foreign Service where each spouse is a Foreign Service Officer, which also creates its own set of unique challenges. For my wife, her lack of U.S. citizenship put her at a disadvantage, as she was ineligible to apply for Embassy jobs.

She gave up a job that she enjoyed in Tokyo as an accountant to join me in Guyana. While she was promised a job initially, it never materialized. My first task while in Guyana was to file a petition for her for a U.S. immigrant visa. Contrary to popular belief, U.S. Foreign Service Officers do not receive a "waiver" for such immigrant visa fees. I paid all the necessary fees to file an immigrant visa for her. She had to collect necessary documents such as a birth certificate, police record from Japan, and complete the process just like everyone else. She and I both knew in advance that it might take close to a year before she would receive her immigrant visa. The next step was applying for her to become a U.S. citizen. We believed that having U.S. citizenship would increase her opportunities for finding a job in embassies or in the U.S. if I was assigned to Washington, DC or chose to find other employment in the U.S.

After nearly five years since marriage my wife obtained her U.S. citizenship on July 22, 2014. The naturalization ceremony took place at the Department of Justice's Great Hall with Attorney General Eric Holder presiding over the ceremony. Eric Holder began by mentioning how his father came from Barbados and became a U.S. citizen and spoke eloquently about the positive impact immigrants have had in making the U.S. the world's number one economy. Eriko was the only Japanese citizen among 72 other immigrants representing 52 countries. It was a fantastic ceremony with lots of happy faces and at the end the new U.S. citizens, including my wife lined up to take individual photos with Eric Holder. I asked one of the professional photographers taking photos at the ceremony if he would be kind enough to take photos of my wife and email them to me. He obliged and sent us those photos of Eriko, which will serve as a constant reminder to our son and others of that special day.

Eriko had taken the U.S. citizenship exam and passed the week before. She was asked ten questions and required to correctly answer six out of the ten questions to pass. Eriko answered the first six correctly and so the examiner did not ask her the next questions since she had met the requisite number to pass. She commented that the exam was very easy. I was very proud of her accomplishment. She was the second Japanese citizen in my family that I had helped obtain U.S. citizenship, the first being my mother. We felt this would also make Diplomatic Security's job easier in granting me my desire to serve in Japan as a U.S. diplomat.

With her newfound citizenship we hoped Eriko would have opportunities to apply for federal and state jobs that she was previously ineligible to apply to or at least be able to work at embassies and consulates abroad as my spouse. One of the ironies in life is that she ended up taking a job in the private sector, which would have allowed her to keep Japanese citizenship without applying for U.S. citizenship. Later, when Secretary of State Rex Tillerson imposed a hiring freeze on Eligible Family Member employment, we lucked out in that Eriko's private sector employer allowed her to telework from overseas. Had we known the U.S. government would not send us to Japan even after my wife and my mother obtained U.S. citizenship, thereby losing their Japanese citizenship, neither would have given theirs up.

Toshiba and Westinghouse

Little did I know that after departing Japan, getting married, and completing a tour in Guyana, I would be called back to serve in

Washington, DC where I would have the opportunity to be invited to a Toshiba gathering and meet the President of Toshiba, a man who spent his career in the nuclear industry. The March 11, 2011 tsunami and earthquake that ravaged Japan, killing nearly 16,000 people and destroying hundreds of thousands of buildings, the costliest natural disaster in history, led to the shutdown of virtually all nuclear power plants and an anti-nuclear sentiment among the Japanese populace. Toshiba as well as other companies in the nuclear sector were facing tough economic times. The cultural divide between the two companies I experienced in Japan was also present in the U.S. during this gathering. Unfortunately, there are not enough bicultural Japanese language speakers who can create the communication links to build trust. The Japanese business culture is different from the U.S. and unless someone is able to explain the unspoken rules of the game, it is difficult for a foreigner to understand. I never quite got the sense that the Japanese senior executives were able to explain the rules of the game, i.e. what part of the American business culture was deemed acceptable and what part of the Japanese system of doing business they wanted seen.

Westinghouse had always had a long-standing relationship with Mitsubishi Heavy Industries (MHI). When Westinghouse was facing financial difficulties and was looking for a buyer, most people thought MHI would be the natural business partner until Toshiba offered a much higher bid than MHI. In hindsight, from a human resource perspective and long-term business outlook, Westinghouse would have benefited more from accepting the lower monetary bid offered by MHI than Toshiba. Instead, a long-term relationship was severed in favor of short-term capital gain. Toshiba was in the Boiling Water Reactor business and for decades had been telling its Japanese customers not to buy Westinghouse products. Once Toshiba acquired Westinghouse, Toshiba was in the awkward position of reversing course, asking its Japanese customers to reconsider Westinghouse.

A marriage without trust is unlikely to last long. Several Westinghouse executives and loyal workers have retired or moved on after seeing that the company, under parent company Toshiba, was moving in a direction that didn't quite blend the two systems—Japanese and American—in an effective manner. This is precisely why bilingual and bicultural managers are increasingly important and needed to solve problems, reduce misunderstandings, and build links based on trust and mutually beneficial partnerships; this serves as another reason why dual nationals fluent in both language and cultures and mindsets can serve as an invaluable asset to navigate both environments.

Business Lessons
What Each Side Can Learn From Each Other

Exposure to different corporate cultures and styles of management allows for the incorporation of models that can benefit each other. There is much that American and Japanese business leaders can learn from each other in the realm of business. We both seek results. We both value loyalty and customer service. We both know that innovation, productivity, and stellar results are going to come from our employees. Here are some key takeaways from my time at Westinghouse/Toshiba:

- The Japanese business culture values loyalty and group think. It may take several meetings for consensus to form, but once a decision is made, the Japanese are quick at implementation.

- The U.S. business culture values risk taking and individualism. Time after work and with families and work-life balance is viewed favorably and promoted to encourage workers to recharge their batteries.

- A combination of loyalty to the group, risk taking, and work-life balance creates a dual business environment for success—meeting both group and individual goals. Why not? It is possible for organizations and individuals to both succeed.

But . . . the challenges include:

- Language and cultural barriers need to be explained and understood. Employment of dual nationals with linguistic and cultural fluency to serve as mediators and communication bridges to tear down these barriers for the benefit of both sides.

- Mutual respect and trust factors. There was an assumption made by Toshiba that because it had acquired Westinghouse, Westinghouse would follow and obey everything Toshiba was suggesting. Senior Westinghouse managers were not going to simply take the view from their Japanese counterparts to follow the Toshiba way or no way. Dual nationals can explain *how* to give and receive feedback in a culturally appropriate way to executives on both sides, assisting them to achieve their common objective: profits while maintaining and strengthening human relationships.

- Relationships over profits. Westinghouse leadership opted to take the Toshiba offer because Toshiba offered a higher bid to acquire it over its long-time partner Mitsubishi Heavy Industries. This may have assisted Westinghouse in the short-term, but in the long-term American greed may have led to weaker results on account of a weaker partnership and relationship, which ultimately did not work out well for either partner.

Conclusion: Employment of dual nationals as consultants to review the business cultures of both, assess the leadership styles of management, and determine which companies may provide a better relational fit for each side can save millions of dollars of heartache for companies in the long-run and mitigate job losses and loss of productivity.

Chapter Ten

From Japan to the Jungles of Guyana: Multicultural Journey

During the period when Westinghouse was considering offering me a permanent package to remain with them, I received a volunteer cable advertising a position at U.S. Embassy Georgetown. The job entailed serving as the Chief of the Political, Economic, and Public Diplomacy sections with supervisory responsibilities over four local Foreign Service Nationals and one entry level Foreign Service Officer. Georgetown is not one of the sought after postings in the Foreign Service. It is a hardship post and obviously the volunteer cable came out because Embassy Georgetown was having difficulty staffing that position. It is worth noting that during my entire time there, we had no U.S. Ambassador. Instead, the Deputy Chief of Mission served as Acting Ambassador or Charge d'Affaires, ad interim (a.i.). The Management Officer was from USAID as the Department could not find any State Department officers willing to take that job.

Initially, I had no interest in the position. But one evening I casually asked my wife-to-be if she was interested in Georgetown, Guyana. Expecting her answer to be "no," I was surprised when she said "yes." When I asked her why, she stated that she wanted to "see the world." I decided I would grant her that wish. So, I applied for the position to see what would occur and I received the job offer. During that entire period, I had told my wife that I would be happy to stay at Westinghouse instead of returning to the Foreign Service if she so wished. She also would be able to continue her work as an accountant surrounded by colleagues she enjoyed working with, could easily see her parents in Osaka, and we could enjoy the comforts of Tokyo and added financial advantages of a dual income. However, we decided to take the plunge and go to Georgetown. We figured that given our language ability and experience we could always return to Japan to find a job, but we decided Guyana offered a once-in-a-lifetime opportunity. It would be a good way to test my health, our marriage, allow her to see if the Foreign Service life appealed to her, and make a positive impact in the second poorest country in the Caribbean after Haiti. She certainly would have a chance to see a world most people only read about in magazines.

The State Department agreed to allow me to take a one-month public diplomacy tradecraft course at the Foreign Service Institute in Virginia in preparation for my new assignment. Since I was coming out of leave without pay status, however, I would not be entitled to any per diem nor locality pay while in DC. Rather than spend a fortune living out of a hotel in DC during that period, I was fortunate to have friends in the neighborhood to stay with. I am very grateful to Greg and Susan Frost for their hospitality and am indebted to them.

Prior to departing for Georgetown, I had a chance to introduce my wife-to-be to senior State Department officials in DC including a former Assistant Secretary and a few former Ambassadors to give her a taste of State Department life. We were warned that the

Japanese community in Guyana was very small, numbering only seven or so people. In addition, we knew that no Japanese embassy or consulate existed in Guyana. The Japanese Ambassador to Trinidad and Tobago concurrently serves as Ambassador to Guyana and we were told that Japanese citizens would need to contact the Japanese Embassy in Trinidad for any visa or other needs. With a population of only 760,000 people, no major Japanese businesses and no Japanese government investment in Guyana, and only a handful of Japanese citizens, the Japanese government could not justify establishing a presence in-country. The Japanese we did meet worked for the UN or CARICOM headquartered in Georgetown. In addition, there were a few individuals on temporary duty representing the Japan International Cooperation Agency (JICA) as volunteer coordinators.

Guyana is a country of less than 800,000 people with the capital of Georgetown holding roughly 250,000 people, the largest city in Guyana. What was interesting is that such a small Caribbean country is actually host to the Caribbean Community (CARICOM) Secretariat comprised of 15 member states including Guyana, Suriname, Haiti, Barbados, Belize, Jamaica, Trinidad and Tobago, Dominica and other states. CARICOM also has five associate members and seven observer states, one of which is Mexico. Based in Georgetown, Guyana, the chair of CARICOM goes to a head of government or head of state on a rotational basis. President Bharrat Jagdeo was chairman from July 1—December 31, 2009, for example, replaced by Prime Minister Roosevelt Skerritt of Dominica. After six months, the chairmanship was scheduled to go to Haiti.

Unfortunately, I found CARICOM hampered by bureaucratic inefficiencies and a lack of strong leadership. The Republic of Korea and People's Republic of China do not have a permanent liaison officer seconded to CARICOM. The Japanese government has had a member of the Japan International Cooperation Agency (JICA) based in Georgetown serve as liaison officer since at least 2000, but there was little to show for implementation of projects. CARICOM asks different countries for funding to support regional initiatives, but does not have a funding mechanism that ensures those funds go towards anything more than sponsorship of conferences and seminars. There are many that believe it a waste of funds to have a permanent position in CARICOM. The Japanese Ministry of Foreign Affairs (MFA) created the position for political reasons. Japan's current Ambassador to Guyana is also accredited to CARICOM, Suriname, and Trinidad and Tobago.

The fact that Japan's MFA has never sent a career diplomat to be based out of Georgetown as liaison officer to CARICOM, indicates that MFA realizes it would neither be worth its time nor resources to send one of its top notch diplomats to fill a largely administrative position. Several contacts from various diplomatic missions and those that interact with CARICOM often voiced their frustrations to me at the lack of responsiveness, capacity, and coordination out of CARICOM. Simple diplomatic correspondence and note verbales can take months for a response.

Several ambassadors based out of Guyana or neighboring countries are also accredited to CARICOM. Until the U.S., Canada, Mexico, EU, and UK see a greater return for supporting CARICOM, the bulk of their correspondence with member states will likely remain focused on a more bilateral basis. In fact, CARICOM's ineffectiveness ensures that these countries will work more with member states on a bilateral basis rather than through CARICOM. For all its rhetoric that CARICOM speaks with one voice, the reality is much different. More often than not, Jamaica and Trinidad and Tobago as well as other member states will go it alone on matters of national interest.

JICA VOLUNTEERS IN GUYANA

I've always been impressed with Japan's International Cooperation Agency (JICA) and its many Japanese volunteers that serve in developing countries. With a budget of over US$8 billion and projects in over 150 countries, JICA serves as the Japanese government's official development assistance (ODA) arm promoting technical assistance, training and programs to improve health, quality of life, and promote poverty reduction. Since the organization was led by former UN High Commissioner for Refugees, Sadako Ogata, it has grown and enjoyed success. In Guyana, JICA did not have an official representative office. However, there was a JICA coordinator that assisted JICA Senior Overseas Volunteers (aged 40-69) that came to Guyana for short three-to-six month assignments. These senior volunteers were true assets. Most had advanced degrees including PhDs and all brought decades of professional experience in various fields ranging from pediatrics, agriculture, and food processing to shrimp cultivation. These volunteers were assigned to hospitals, schools, and NGOs rather than to the central or local government. I had the opportunity and honor to meet several of them during my time in Guyana and each volunteer demonstrated an impressive set of useful skills. Most have either retired or are near retirement and appreciated the opportunity to utilize their skills to make a positive difference in Guyana.

No National Counterterrorism Strategy

During my time in Guyana, there was no national counterterrorism strategy for Latin America and the Caribbean. While strategies existed for the Middle East, Asia, and other regions of the world, the U.S. did not have a national counterterrorism strategy for the above two mentioned regions. Security programs countering narcotics trade and money laundering did exist, but were woefully underfunded to make any real significant impact. For the first time in eight years, the State Department funded a counterterrorism regional conference in Panama in September 2010 for Embassy officials in the region and members in DC to join in information sharing. While that conference served useful in bringing different offices and officers together, there is no substitute for having Latin America and the Caribbean included in a national counterterrorism strategy. Without one, we cannot expect host governments in the region to take us seriously. And Washington, DC needs to formulate a strategy that can be implemented through various Embassy officers assigned abroad. One immediate challenge that needs to be addressed is coordination among the different agencies—State, Treasury, DOD, DEA, FBI and other groups to mount an effective counterterrorism campaign.

The experts focused on Brazil, Venezuela, Panama, and Columbia as areas linking drug trade, trade in arms, and human trafficking as connected to terrorism. Drawing that conclusion seemed extreme as not all criminal activity can be traced to terrorism. Defining the term terrorism is also important. Terrorists and criminal organizations are always trying to be one-step ahead of law enforcement. It is important to remember that places that are under the radar (i.e. Guyana) should not be overlooked as Guyana borders Venezuela and Brazil and is an area that criminals and terrorists could use as an operation base in the future. With its porous borders, lack of border patrol, rampant drug trade, money laundering operations, and increasing links to the Middle East, policymakers should pay attention to Guyana and neighboring Suriname. The recent discovery of oil in Guyana has increased the amount of attention Guyana is receiving among U.S. policymakers, but not to the same degree as Venezuela or Brazil.

USAID Ineffectiveness

The United States Agency for International Development (US-AID) had a very large presence in Guyana during my assignment.

Unfortunately, there seemed to be no real justification for having a USAID presence in Guyana when the organization had not produced results. And, members within the Embassy and outside were aware of this fact. It became embarrassing for State officers to field questions on USAID from our various contacts within the Government of Guyana and CARICOM Secretariat pertaining to its lack of effectiveness and utility in Guyana. The USAID Mission Director present at the time had a terrible working relationship with members of the Embassy, particularly State Department officers. Instead of focusing on enhancing USAID performance, the individual spent time meddling in the affairs of other sections and offices to the detriment of Embassy morale and effective functioning of Embassy operations.

It was unfortunate that USAID would quickly interfere with State reporting and activities without contributing to Embassy reporting or adding value to its programs. USAID would claim to be part of State when convenient to do so (i.e., wanting to comment on State reporting and gain information without doing research on their own), and claim to be different from State when it did not want to pull its weight to contribute to the overall Mission (i.e., not participating in the planning of 4th of July activities). The USAID Mission Director also hired retired contractors that seemed to be out of touch with the realities on the ground and never seemed able to do anything else but harass State Department officers trying to do their jobs. Unfortunately, I have heard too often from several colleagues in other Embassies that too often the relationship between USAID and State is one-dimensional with USAID coming to State for assistance. In Embassy Georgetown, the Department of Defense provided more assistance to Guyana and the development of Guyanese society than USAID ever did.

One example is its Democracy and Governance Program, run by a contractor. Local government elections had not occurred in Guyana since 1994. Yet this contractor's job was extended for another three years when no tangible results came out of the program. Guyana had not improved its governance, local elections, nor instituted judicial reforms. U.S. taxpayer monies were being spent to fuel a corrupt government that did not believe in democracy, but rather communism and socialism. Disillusionment continued when USAID spent $2 million to develop a butter squash farm to export squash produced in Guyana. Was that the best we can do? Again, I would argue otherwise, and be concerned as a taxpayer that our monies were not being put to effective use.

To have an effective USAID program where funding is going toward key Mission priorities and not targets on which it is easiest for USAID to spend funding (typically programs that require minimal effort), requires strong leadership from the Ambassador and Deputy Chief of Mission (i.e., what is known in an Embassy as the Front Office). Unfortunately, very few Front Offices are willing to exert such leadership. Later, I learned that Congress decided to close down USAID's Guyana Mission in 2012. There is no excuse to waste valuable taxpayer money. Only when Congress acts and when officers speak up about waste and inefficiencies can we save collectively taxpayer monies. Closing down programs that are ineffective and have little return on investment for the American taxpayer is the right thing to do.

ETHICAL DILEMMAS FACED IN GUYANA AND THROUGHOUT

What I will always remember during my 16 years in the Foreign Service is the mixed bag of leadership and support. Not every supervisor exhibited poor leadership. I've had some good ones too, and some bad ones. So I'm not sure how fair it would be to characterize broadly, but when one sees day-to-day abuses of power, position, and waste of taxpayer money, it dampens morale. It cheapens the Service and sets a bad example for others. Integrity is non-negotiable. In Guyana, I had an Acting Chief of Mission who had the nerve to ask my section to provide "business contacts" in the mining sector to his wife's relatives, and do so as if we were pro-viding such services to "any other American businessman seeking business opportunities." I never did so. I can't vouch for whether he was able to pressure an entry level officer under my supervision to provide him with that information. Technically, what he was doing may not have been illegal, but it certainly seemed unethical to us. To me it indicated poor judgment, but also a self-serving attitude. There were other instances which made me question this person's leadership. The first was having his unemployed daughter, without a college degree, obtain a job in the Embassy in an office that worked very closely and on the same floor as the Front Office. My bilingual Japanese wife who had been in Guyana for a year, who had quit a $45,000 accounting job in Tokyo to join me, and had a Bachelor's degree in finance from an American University, was unable to obtain an Embassy job. I guess anything goes when you are the Acting Chief of Mission.

The Embassy kept using lack of U.S. citizenship as an excuse not to hire my wife, but there were plenty of local Guyanese working at the Embassy without U.S. citizenship and there were advertised openings. When this new Acting Chief of Mission arrived toward the end of my first year at Post, he had the audacity to ask those he directly supervised to send leave schedules to others for review. He didn't want to be the one to make a decision, and instead of telling people directly whether he approved leave or not, he would want others to do the work for him. My confidence in this person's leadership dropped further. But, that action in itself was not unethical. What made me lose respect for this individual was his asking us to participate in an action (i.e., providing business contacts) that we viewed as unethical.

Despite having a lack of resources to carry out our jobs, the Acting Chief of Mission did nothing to assist us. He chose to stay in the Ambassador's residence for several months even though he was not the Ambassador. He held zero representational events for the Embassy community. The Acting Chief of Mission before him, stayed at the Deputy Chief of Mission residence and held Christmas parties and other events at the Ambassador's residence to boost morale at Embassy Georgetown. We were appalled that the new person de-cided to enjoy the benefits of the Ambassador's residence without utilizing it for the benefit of the community. He should have been removed from his position and sent back to Washington, DC for poor judgment, character, and lack of ability. Rather than fixing problems, his excuse was always "when the Ambassador arrives these problems will be fixed." Passing the buck to a person who had not even arrived at Post showed lack of commitment and care for the employees under his supervision. It came as no surprise to me that at least two Foreign Service Officers left the State Department as a result of this man's lack of leadership and disregard for the welfare of those he was supposedly entrusted to lead. Instead of being removed, this man was promoted.

I know that this man was not exhibiting strong leadership, because my boss in Guyana my first year there exemplified strong leadership, integrity, and solid judgment. She set an example that unfortunately her successor was unable to follow. Integrity matters. As soon as she left, the house unraveled. I was pleased to learn that my first boss was eventually promoted into the Senior Foreign Ser-vice ranks after hardship tours in Afghanistan and would later be rewarded with an ambassadorship in neighboring Suriname.

Chapter Eleven

THE FIGHT FOR RECOVERY AND

REDEMPTION

My tour in Guyana did not lead to a Japan assignment nor allow my wife the opportunity to work. She gave up a good job in Japan to follow me. I had promised her that if the State Department did not work out, we would both go back to find jobs in Japan. In the meantime, the goal was to return to the U.S. to allow her to find a meaningful job and pursue U.S. citizenship. We both thought that I would stay as a diplomat for the rest of my career and hence it would make sense for my wife to obtain her U.S. citizenship so that she would have opportunities to work at embassies or consulates abroad as an Eligible Family Member. I applied for and received a one-year detailed assignment to the U.S. Congress as a State Department Pearson Fellow. But before starting, I would do a "bridge" assignment in the Bureau of Legislative Affairs while looking for a Congressional office to do my Pearson Fellowship.

During my assignment in Guyana I was selected as one of 12 State Department officers to serve as a legislative fellow on Capitol Hill and I left my assignment in Guyana early to pursue that new assignment. There was a gap between the period my Pearson Fellowship would begin and when I left Guyana so I decided to fill that gap by working on congressional affairs. I had the opportunity to cover the March 11, 2011 earthquake in Japan and serve as the State Department representative in daily conference calls with congressional staff to answer questions, gain updates, field questions, and report feedback to my supervisors.

Knowing that my language skills and knowledge of Japan could be used to help the earthquake victims, I immediately sent an email to the Principal Deputy Assistant Secretary of State for East Asian and Pacific Affairs, second in rank only to Assistant Secretary of State for East Asian Affairs Kurt Campbell, offering my services. He thanked me for volunteering and forwarded my email to the person coordinating sending officers to Japan. But I never heard back from her and was never sent to assist and "serve" in Japan even in a temporary capacity.

STATE DEPARTMENT
RESPONSE TO MARCH 11, 2011 EARTHQUAKE

The U.S. Embassy in Japan was charged with assisting U.S. citizens in Japan and evacuating them from affected areas. A Japan earthquake task force was created within the halls of Main State in Foggy Bottom to cover the events. The former Japan Desk Director, who was asked to resign after news that he had called Okinawans "lazy" and "manipulative" in an off the record conversation with American University students earlier that year, was silently working as head of that task force. I say "silently" because the Department and its Assistant Secretary of State for East Asian and Pacific Affairs, Kurt Campbell, didn't want the public to know that this man was still "employed" after he was supposedly "fired" for his remarks.

Kevin Maher, the former Japan Desk Director, left the State Department in 2011 and published a book in Japanese alleging he was framed. Given his past reputation for making controversial remarks in Japan, including during his time as Consul General in Okinawa, however, it is hard to believe that he didn't say those words. Whatever the truth may be, his comments created an uproar in Japan, and in Okinawa and it could not have come at a worse time. Kurt Campbell had to visit Japan to personally apologize to the Japanese Foreign Minister for Director Maher's insensitive remarks. It would have created an even greater controversy if the Japanese public learned that Kurt Campbell had not only allowed Director Maher to remain working in the State Department, but also allowed him to lead an earthquake response task force.

The U.S. response to the earthquake, known as Operation Tomodachi (which means friend in Japanese), helped to restore a positive image of the U.S. and U.S. troops. Public opinion of U.S. actions was generally favorable among the Japanese populace. At the same time, public opinion towards the Japanese government turned sour. The Japanese media and people blamed Prime Minister Naoto Kan for concealing the extent of the nuclear crisis and responding too slowly and ineptly throughout the initial and proceeding stages of the crisis. His approval ratings plummeted and Prime Minister Yoshihiko Noda would be replaced within six months after the March 11, 2011 earthquake.

Noda became the sixth prime minister in six years, marking one of the weakest political leadership periods in Japanese history. While Prime Minister Kan lasted a little over a year, the last Japanese prime minister to survive more than a year on the job and complete a full term in office was Prime Minister Junichiro Koizumi (2001-2006). Before Koizumi, one has to go all the way back to 1982 during

Prime Minister Yasuhiro Nakasone's reign from 1982-1987 to find a prime minister that survived a complete full term in office. The frequent change of prime ministers certainly does not bode well for political certainty. While current Prime Minister Shinzo Abe has survived a full term (2012-2018) that is more the exception than the norm. The institution of the Office of the Prime Minister has historically wielded little influence and power in modern day Japan, while the Liberal Democratic Party (LDP) has remained the dominant political force in the country since World War II.

While the media in Japan and the U.S. broadcasted images of victims and rescue heroes, the State Department was once again left with a perennial challenge. The lack of fluent Japanese language speakers hindered response effectiveness; in fact the lack of fluent Japanese language speaking officers required the State Department to look for Japanese proficient officers in other U.S. embassies and consulates in neighboring countries to volunteer. Officers like myself, fluent in Japanese and available to assist in DC, were not called. It is a shame that during such crisis periods the State Department would once again fail to utilize all of its Japanese American resources.

Given the State Department's poor track record of utilizing dual national resources, particularly of Asian American background, I looked at other avenues to put my background to use on behalf of the American taxpayer. After a short bridge assignment in the Bureau of Legislative Affairs, I was ready to utilize my strengths and not let previous setbacks deter me from finding a way to pursue U.S.-Japan affairs.

I began my year as a Pearson Fellow in the U.S. House of Representatives Foreign Affairs Subcommittee on Asia and the Pacific working for the Chairman of the Subcommittee, Mr. Donald Manzullo in May 2011. The Congressman interviewed me for the position and asked if I could cover the topic of rare earths in China during my fellowship period with him. I agreed to do so. I was thrilled to finally get the opportunity to work on Asia policy and put my Mandarin, Japanese, and foreign affairs background to use. Working in the House of Representatives I immediately noticed how young most of the Members' staff were; in many cases they were straight out of college. Yet, these young professionals were involved in telling a Member how to vote, drafting legislation and letters for Member signature, corresponding with constituents, coming up with hearings, and controlling Member schedules and movements. I quickly learned that to get anything done in Congress, you must form key relationships with staff because these are the people that are doing the behind-the-scenes work that helps Members look good publicly, control the schedule, and help individuals get reelected.

I was fortunate to work under a Member concerned about unemployment, reducing government waste, and protecting American businesses. He treated me well and gave me exciting and important substantive work to pursue. No one was working on rare earth metals and China. Rare earth elements or metals are found in electronics, automobiles, wind turbines, missiles, and medical applications, just to name a few. The Chairman was a champion of U.S. manufacturers and heard constituent complaints, particularly in the automobile industry, over China's use of its monopoly over the rare earths metals industry to exponentially raise prices, increasing costs for U.S. automobile suppliers and manufacturers to produce modern vehicles, including hybrid and electric cars.

Noting constituent concerns, we held the first ever hearing on China's monopoly over rare earth metals in the Subcommittee on Asia and the Pacific on September 21, 2011. I played a direct role in drafting the memo, writing questions for the Chairman and other Members, arranging witnesses, and creating a briefing book for him. To my pleasant surprise, he mentioned my name during the televised hearing on rare earths and credited me for working on this topic. The hearing brought a private panel of experts to discuss the impact of rare earth metals on U.S. manufacturing, defense, national security, and foreign affairs.

Besides private hearings, the Subcommittee held oversight hearings involving USAID and State Department senior officials. One hearing involved climate change funding for China. The unanimous opinion of the Chairman and majority was that U.S. taxpayer money should not go to China to help China steal our manufacturing technology (wind turbines, solar panels, etc.) and jobs. With a $1.5 trillion debt, most of which is held in U.S. Treasury bonds by the Chinese government, the rationale was why borrow money from China to pay them to clean up their own environmental mess when China has plenty of revenue to do so on its own? Moreover, China was dumping wind turbine, solar panel, and other clean energy technology products on the market to price out U.S. manufacturers of clean energy. The Committee decided to place a hold on the roughly $4 million for USAID on climate change programs in China as a result. With no USAID mission in China, the Regional Development Mission to Asia is based out of Bangkok, it became clear that USAID had little monitoring capacity to ensure these climate change programs were being effectively implemented. My time in Congress was invaluable in giving me another perspective on State Department programs and the importance of being able to justify to Congress every American taxpayer dollar spent on diplomacy.

During my one-year fellowship, the Subcommittee held a number of hearings. The first hearing was on Japan's future post-March 11 Tohoku earthquake and tsunami that devastated Japan and triggered a nuclear crisis. The 9.0 magnitude earthquake created tsunami waves that led to nuclear accidents in the Fukushima Daiichi nuclear power plant destroying hundreds of thousands of buildings and homes, leaving over 21,000 people dead. The psychological impact of the triple effects of the earthquake, tsunami, and nuclear disasters took its toll on the Japanese people. I was heartbroken to see so many Japanese lose everything as a result of the Tohoku earthquake. It was fitting that the Chairman held a hearing on Japan's future to reiterate the importance of U.S.-Japan relations and cooperation. The Japanese Ambassador to the U.S., Fujisaki Ichiro, came to address the Subcommittee at the hearing to share his views and updates on the tragedy. It was the first time a Japanese Ambassador briefed the Subcommittee during a hearing in the entire history of the U.S. House of Representatives. I was proud to be part of that moment and witness a new chapter in U.S.-Japan relations.

Ambassador Fujisaki emphasized his gratitude to the U.S. for providing assistance to help the victims of the natural disasters. The Japanese people showed tremendous courage and strength in the aftermath of these disasters and the world took notice. I was honored that the first hearing I would be directly involved in as a Pearson Fellow was on Japan, a country I knew and love. Japan experts like Michael Green came to testify. It was a successful hearing, but not many Members of the Subcommittee, unfortunately, came to participate which was disappointing. Most Members of Congress have European heritage or background. There are not many Asian American Members of Congress. When you are the minority, you have less impact and say. Your voice is weaker when your numbers are weaker. We need more Asian Americans to enter politics in order to represent and solidify the ties between the U.S. and Asian countries.

Despite the lack of Member participation, Japanese media certainly came to cover the hearing and Ambassador Fujisaki's comments were aired in the major Japanese media outlets. We were all saddened by the tragic events in Japan, but also inspired and in awe of Japan's ability to recover and rebuild. Part of the reason we held the hearing was to highlight the positive strides Japan was making in light of the tragic events. We need to continue to showcase the importance of the U.S.-Japan relationship. One other crucial lesson I learned was the important role constituents can play in calling, writing, and meeting with their Representatives of Congress to spur them to action. If you are concerned about an issue or policy, by all means contact your Member of Congress and get others to do the same. Members are there to serve their constituents and want to be reelected. You have more leverage and power than you think. Use it!

Palau Hearing

In a twist of fate I saw for the first time in four years the person scheduled to be my supervisor in Beijing appear to testify as one of four witnesses in a hearing we held on the Republic of Palau. Jim Loi, the former Chief of the External Unit in the Economic Section in Embassy Beijing became Deputy Assistant Secretary (DAS) for East Asian and Pacific Affairs. One of four DAS's in the State Department's Bureau of East Asian and Pacific Affairs, Jim was responsible for relations with Australia, New Zealand, and the Pacific Islands. Hence, he came to testify as the senior official from State Department on Palau. Japan colonized Palau during World War II and recognized its strategic significance.

It was ironic that the person scheduled to be my former supervisor was now called up to testify by the Subcommittee for which I worked. I had played a direct role in crafting questions for the Chairman and other Members to direct towards Jim and the three other witnesses at the hearing. Jim left Beijing for family reasons. His sudden rise within the Department was due to serving as chief of staff in the National Security Council to Kurt Campbell. When Kurt Campbell became Assistant Secretary, Jim Loi was rewarded and selected as DAS. State Department positions of authority are based on power and relationships to power. Jim had made the right connections while showcasing his ability to perform.

Palau, along with the Marshall Islands and the Federated States of Micronesia, has a unique relationship with the U.S. in which the U.S. provides guaranteed financial assistance to these Freely Associated States in exchange for U.S. presence. Palau entered a 50-year

Compact of Free Association with the U.S. after its independence in 1994 and has relied on U.S. economic assistance and defense for its economy and security. The U.S. provides economic assistance to Palau through the Department of Interior. Although a sovereign nation, the Republic of Palau is administered like a U.S. state and hence it is the Department of Interior that has the lead in coordinating programs, not the departments of state or defense.

The Senate introduced legislation in 2011 to approve the results of a 15-year review of the Compact to appropriate additional funds to Palau for fiscal years 2012 through 2024. The House held a hearing on November 30 in the Subcommittee on Asia and the Pacific to review Compact status and also ask for offsets to fund assistance to Palau through the departments of state and defense. Since both State and Defense view the importance of Palau strategically to U.S. national security interests, it was natural that Members would ask State and Defense rather than the Department of Interior to find funds within their budgets to offset the amounts requested and foot the bill.

OTHER CONGRESSIONAL HEARINGS

Besides hearings on Japan, China and rare earths, USAID climate change programs, and Palau, we also held hearings on expanded U.S.-South Korea relations. 2011 and the passage of the U.S.-Korea (KORUS) Free Trade Agreement (FTA) really set the stage for strengthened U.S.-South Korean relations. Our hearing on Korea focused on expanded U.S.-South Korea relations post-FTA. South Korean President, Lee Myung-bak, had earlier addressed both houses of Congress in a speech he made prior to the 112th Congress passing the FTA. I remember sitting in one of the Members seats six rows from the front podium where President Lee spoke, hearing his historic remarks in Korean and seeing him speak with such pride. Behind him was Vice President Joe Biden and House Speaker John Boehner.

What surprised me most was that there were so many Members that didn't show up. That was the reason why I was granted a ticket to sit so close to hear the President speak. The House Floor was packed, but mostly with visitors and congressional staff as opposed to the Members themselves. Congressman Manzullo showed up to his credit, but many others did not.

The passage of KORUS FTA caused many in Japan to worry that perhaps Japan was being left behind. The perception that Japan was overshadowed by South Korea was very real. Given expanded U.S.-South Korea trade ties and increased security cooperation against North Korean provocations, it was clear that U.S.-South Korea relations marked the dawn of a new era and Japan was scared. The Japanese government observed closely the remarks of senior U.S. officials and the media in proclaiming that U.S.-South Korea relations was the strongest ever and were showing signs of concern and jealousy. Japan's insecurity actually gave U.S. officials greater negotiating power over Japan in advancing the Trans Pacific Partnership Agreement and having Japan agree to terms favorable to the U.S.

Besides hearings, I had the opportunity to participate in a mark-up on U.S. and South Korean prisoners of war (POWs) and persons missing in action (MIAs) as well as to attend numerous meetings on China, North Korea, and more. The Pearson Fellowship serves as a great opportunity for State Department officers to gain an inside view of the workings of Congress. I was also fortunate to have face time with the Member. Not many Pearson Fellows are given the opportunity to plan and implement a hearing or even meet the Member as frequently as I was afforded the opportunity. I made full use of my time on the Hill.

While the benefits were many and I learned a great deal, I also must discuss the shortcomings of the Pearson Program. Officers are selected by a selection panel in Washington, DC and are chosen from a variety of backgrounds and areas of expertise or cones. The majority have at least eight years of Foreign Service experience and all must be tenured officers at the FS-03 or higher rank. Typically, those selected are FS-02 or FS-01s and are chosen because they have an interest in serving on Capitol Hill and are eager to take a non-traditional assignment outside Foggy Bottom. Pearson Fellows receive an evaluation during their one-year assignment and are paid by the Department of State. I was informed that the year I applied (2010 for a 2011 assignment) over 85 officers applied of which 12 were selected. To qualify, each of us had to submit a resumé and a statement of interest explaining our desire to serve on the Hill.

The biggest problem with the Pearson Fellowship is that it is not well organized or promoted effectively within or outside the Department. Moreover, once selected, candidates are left on their own to knock on doors and find their own placement in a congressional office. This can be a time consuming process. I remember it took me over two months to find a placement and for others, nearly six months. The Bureau of Legislative Affairs or "H" has a Senate and House liaison office on Capitol Hill, but neither was very helpful in securing my placement. Shockingly, during my entire year there, the liaison office organized only one event for the Pearson Fellows. Unlike the Charlie Rangel Fellows or other fellowship programs, there was very little support offered by the Department. One of the problems with State's reputation on the Hill is lack of outreach and communication.

The military and Department of Defense does a much better job reaching out to the Hill than State. Granted they have many more resources, but I find the Department lacking in cultivating stronger ties with the very Members that fund Department programs and budgets. The Department needs to support the Pearson Program better and also let officers engage the Hill more often. Unfortunately, H likes to control the process. I never could understand why everything had to go through H. Even U.S. Ambassadors are not allowed to go up to the Hill and talk about their subject matter expertise or engage Hill contacts without going through H first. I find that extremely disturbing. First, an Ambassador is the President's top representative abroad. They are given leeway to discuss matters of utmost importance with foreign dignitaries including foreign parliaments, and yet they are restricted from engaging their very own Congress. That makes no sense at all. There is a reason why Congress is cutting State's funding. Part of it is State's own doing.

To give an example, however, of the difference in resources the Department of Defense expends on Hill outreach versus State, take a look at the number of representatives from each department assigned there. The Air Force Liaison office with more than 70 officers on the Hill represents a number larger than the entire Bureau of Legislative Affairs including personnel assigned to the two Liaison offices. The majority of inquiries to the State Senate or House Liaison office is visa or consular related. The less than 10 individuals in both Liaison offices are comprised mostly of civil service and consular coned Foreign Service Officers. Neither has the type of positive reputation our military colleagues on the Hill enjoy. I realize Defense has more resources, but State doesn't utilize effectively the resources it does have and is guilty of keeping Hill engagement minimal to its own detriment.

It is difficult to justify asking Congress for more money to support State Department programs when the State Department is not fully utilizing the human resources it does have—its dual national assets. It's a waste of resources and there is absolutely no credible reason why the State Department cannot more fully utilize the background of dual nationals to achieve diplomatic victories not only in Japan but globally.

Country Desk Officer for Ghana/Guinea

After concluding my fellowship in Congress, my next assignment was Country Desk Officer for Ghana and Guinea in the Office of West African Affairs. The office director was a former Ambassador as were many of the other office directors in the Africa Bureau which was reassuring. We had a good team and good management. This would be my first experience serving as a Country Desk Officer responsible for two countries, not just one. Many of my colleagues also covered two or more countries, a great way to learn the various functions and responsibilities of a desk officer. In essence, our job was to be the main link between the State Department, the U.S. embassy, and host country government to promote bilateral relations. From assisting officials and American citizens to obtain visas to Ghana and Guinea, preparing incoming ambassadors and senior Department officials for their congressional hearings, responding to congressional inquiries, and working with the interagency to promote various U.S. government initiatives, a desk job kept one busy.

My job also was to clear the various memos, reports, and materials presented to me on a daily basis. We would work with the embassy to deliver demarches or messages to the host government, warn mission personnel of upcoming visits, remind the embassy of overdue or required deadlines for reporting, and serve as the overall go-to person on everything related to the country in question. If someone had a question about Ghana or Guinea, they typically would start off by asking me. I would then answer the question when possible or help connect the inquiring person or entity to the right person.

During my first week on the job, I was tasked with scheduling consultation meetings for the incoming ambassador to Ghana, Gene Cretz. Ambassador Cretz had previously served as Ambassador to Libya but was kicked out by Mohamed Qadaffi after a WikiLeaks cable upset the host government. Since he'd been a Middle East expert for much of his entire career, Ghana was new territory. As such, I set up meetings for him within the U.S. government from State, USAID, Defense, Justice, Commerce, as well as Peace Corps, Millennium Challenge Corporation, OPIC, EXIM, and others.

Before the U.S. Senate confirms an ambassadorial nominee there are strict regulations over whom he or she can consult. As such, meetings with private companies or lobbying organizations were out of the question. If the Ambassador wanted to meet with these groups privately he was on his own and would have to bear any consequences if discovered.

At the same time as I was dealing with an incoming ambassador to Ghana and preparing him for his confirmation hearing, his meetings, and briefing him on the latest news on Ghana, I had to do the same for the incoming ambassador to Guinea. Alexander Mark Laskaris was serving a tour as Consul General in Erbil, Iraq and was one of few Kurdish speakers in the Department. He was nominated as U.S. Ambassador to Guinea and I also had the responsibility of preparing his testimony, potential questions and answers expected at his hearing in front of Congress, and briefing him for his next assignment.

Within one month of assuming my job as Desk Officer on 5/14/2012, I was also pulled to assist with the Africa Growth and Opportunity Act (AGOA) Trade Ministerial Forum from 6/14-6/15 held in Washington, DC. My role was to serve as State Department Control Officer for United States Trade Representative Ambassador Ron Kirk. Ambassador Kirk was a political appointee, a two-time mayor of Dallas, and in his last six months, a U.S. Trade Representative. He had received a lot of criticism for not doing enough in terms of improving trade conditions for U.S. companies in China and overseas, but trade was never really his forté. He was and is a career politician. He came late to the opening session of the AGOA meeting which was quite embarrassing. He also appeared late to a bilateral trade meeting with the Angolans, clearly indicating not only with his body language but also with his words that he wasn't interested in engaging the Angolans. One wonders why individuals assume such responsibility when not willing to tackle the tough challenges that await. Some of the staff who represent political appointees themselves can be very demanding which can make for some unpleasant encounters in accommodating requests. Beware of politicians showing one face in public while another in private. It is important to treat aides and staff outside of your institution well, as you never know when the tables are turned and you may need their assistance.

Most disappointing is when you discover how personal interest trumps effective consideration of taxpayer monies and sense of duty when certain appointed officials pursue their own individual agenda at the expense of the greater good. I witnessed that time and time again during my State Department career with a number of political appointees. Individuals that had no qualms wasting taxpayer monies to pursue their own side business and political agendas. Within three months of my assignment as country desk officer, I was also tasked to assist with Secretary Hillary Clinton's last official visit to Africa. This entailed an eight-night, ten-day stop to seven countries in Africa. The amount of paperwork and preparation needed for these visits is astounding. We were able to successfully get it done with a lot of individuals contributing to our success.

ORIENTATION TO GHANA/GUINEA

Any visit to Africa entails obtaining up-to-date vaccinations and often enough a supply of anti-malaria pills. Yellow fever vaccination is a requirement and one I did not need to repeat since mine remained current from my time in Nigeria. However, meningitis and typhoid were recommended and I did need to get those vaccinations prior to my orientation visit. Mefloquine, doxycycline, and malarone were the anti-malaria options provided. I chose malarone because I only needed to take it one day before departure to Africa and then seven days after my return to the U.S. to make sure I was protected. Ordinarily, one does orientation visits to the embassy or embassies one covers within the first six months. I did not have that luxury as I had two ambassador designates to prepare for Congress, a Secretary of State visit, a presidential election, and my wife was pregnant with our first born John. My wife and I decided I should wait until after the birth of our son to do my orientation visits to Embassy Accra and Embassy Conakry.

With no direct flights from DC to Accra, I flew to New York JFK Airport and then took a direct flight from NY to Kotoka International Airport in Accra departing DC on February 2, 2013. I arrived in Accra on Sunday, February 3, 2013 for five days of consultations. On Saturday February 9, I departed Accra for Conakry transiting Lome, Togo for four full days of consultations. Taking Asky Airlines, the plane made brief stops in Ouagadougou, Burkina Faso and Bamako, Mali before landing in Conakry. Traveling within Africa can be costly and logistically difficult. Upon landing in Conakry, the Ambassador was kind enough to put me up in a spare room in his residence, by far nicer than any hotel I could stay at and safer. In Accra, there were some world class hotels that fell within government per diem so I chose to stay at the Movenpick Ambassador Hotel during my time in Ghana. Freezing cold in DC and NY, the warm weather in Accra and Conakry was a welcome change.

In Conakry, the U.S. Ambassador's residence is next to the German and Japanese ambassadors' residences. The residence is significant in that the first U.S. Ambassador to Guinea, John H. Morrow, an African-American, lived there from 1959-1961 with his family. The compound has expanded since then to include a pool and deck area plus sauna (no need to have a sauna in a tropical place like Guinea) but the history of the place remains. Ambassador Morrow wrote a memoir of his time as the first American Ambassador to Guinea, which highlighted U.S. priorities at the time as well as his personal insights into the challenges confronting U.S.-Guinea relations. Much of what he wrote in terms of challenges remains relevant today.

Given the proximity to the Japanese Ambassador's residence, I paid a visit to the Japanese Ambassador to Guinea for tea. An Africa hand and French speaker, Ambassador Nakano welcomed me into his residence and offered his insights into Japan's interests in the region. He wasn't shy to discuss the presence of the North Koreans in Conakry, nor discuss why unlike the State Department, the Japanese Foreign Ministry does not require its officers to take malaria prophylaxis. The Japanese are recommended to take anti-malaria medicine when traveling to the interior of a country where it would take time to treat a malaria patient, but that also remains voluntary.

Birth of Our Son John – 9/10/2012

During my time as desk officer, I was fortunate to witness the birth of my son John Francis Reiman on 9/10/2012. John entered at 7lbs 5oz in Sibley Memorial Hospital in Washington, DC. He is three-fourths Japanese and has his parents eyes and mother's lips. A bundle of joy. In the area of pregnancy, childbirth, and infancy, there are differences between Japan and the U.S. Japanese mothers are not encouraged to take medicine during pregnancy to deal with morning sickness. Medicine is frowned upon as possibly causing adverse side effects to the development of the child. Morning sickness is viewed as natural and therefore, as much as it is unpleasant, most Japanese women and doctors discourage medicine to treat a natural process. Japanese mothers also prefer natural birth as opposed to use of an epidural during delivery. This is not because Japanese women want to show strength, but because they believe that birth pains are natural to the delivery process and do not want any side effects that may occur, no matter how slight, as a result of medicine. They would prefer to live with temporary pain than live with a lingering doubt that perhaps use of medicine hurt the child's development in some way.

My wife's Japanese friends did not take medicine or request

an epidural. I tried on several occasions to convince her that many women do take them and that she should leave the option open. She decided to take both morning sickness medicine and an epidural and we have no regrets. It was during this period, however, that I became keenly aware of the cultural differences involved in the pregnancy and childbirth process between the U.S. and Japan. One of the shocks to her was the fact that in the U.S., hospitals discharge you within 48 hours of a normal delivery. In Japan, the process is more relaxed where women can stay up to 7 days under the care of nurses and doctors. I'm not sure I would want to stay for days in a hospital, but it is nice to have such an option, especially since there is so much going on after delivery and it is difficult to retain all the information the nurses provide us jam-packed into two-days with very little sleep.

We were fortunate that Eriko's mother came to visit us for a week right after John's birth to help with the household chores and also look after John. Mother-in-laws everywhere would have their own system of house maintenance and ideas for child rearing and there was no exception in our case. However, in only one week my mother-in-law certainly seemed to have a million and one sugges-tions for home improvement based on a Japanese model. We made the necessary adjustments from using the appropriate towels for drying dishes to purchasing the right cleaning materials. For those of you not married to a Japanese the standard protocol when a Japanese family member or friend visits is to take him or her shopping for gifts to present to coworkers upon return to Japan. I took Eriko's mother to several places in town so she could purchase uniquely U.S. food items and souvenirs, spending at least a few hours in the process. I did not think a shopping visit for coworkers would apply after childbirth, boy was I wrong. I was also surprised that while swaddling is recommended by doctors in the U.S., I could tell that my mother-in-law felt the baby should have freedom of arm and leg movement. As much as possible, she kept John's arms and legs free when in the crib or bed. She also brought Japanese treats like rice cakes and *mochi* to celebrate his birth and the customary *otoshidama* or small allowance from various family members to put into John's savings or to use to buy toys for him.

On the topic of children, for decades now the Japanese government and people have been told of the implications for an aging population. Yet Japanese are not having more children. This is a phenomenon not just unique to Japan but seen also in Singapore and other parts of the world. As women delay marriage to pursue careers or delay giving birth to continue career ambitions, Japan is in need of adapting to this social reality. Japanese are not eager to import labor from outside. That then requires the Japanese to make a conscious effort to bear more children. The Japanese government must encourage this to ensure the preservation of Japanese language and culture. Creating a Japan that meets the expectations and demands of its citizenry is vital in tackling the tough road ahead. Eliciting the views and recommendations of the Japanese public to create an environment more amenable to raising children and building more childcare facilities to accommodate the aspirations of Japan's great resource—its women—becomes important. While politicians campaigning for the office of prime minister are placing employment, social welfare, and education as their top campaign items, number one should be increasing the Japanese population followed by addressing the psychological needs of the populace through a more well-rounded educational system that emphasizes Japanese values.

Additionally, now is the time for the Japanese government to allow dual nationality and utilize the strengths of dual nationals for the prosperity of Japan. Dual nationals often speak the language and have the cultural nuance to serve as effective interlocutors for trade, investment, and exchanges. By making Japan a dual national friendly country and attracting more dual nationals to live and work in Japan, Japan can help mitigate the aging population problem, create a more tolerant and diverse society, and encourage more dual nationals to give birth to more Japanese citizens. More and more children are born to

Japanese and foreign parents. These children and their parents should have the opportunity to have both throughout their life. Welcoming these new "dual citizens" with open arms can bring about the change needed in Japan as well as positively impact Japan's economy. A new education program and system is needed in Japan to foster greater tolerance, optimize foreign and domestic talent, improve quality of life for all citizens and residents, and prepare for an aging population.

Fear and prejudice on the side of the Japanese government also breeds policies that prevent the utilization of dual national talent. What does Japan have to lose in accepting dual nationals? Japan can gain the labor, the revenue, and global status by viewing dual nationals as assets. Japan has much to offer, in terms of culture, history, science, technology, environmental studies and more. But, it is plagued with a fear of foreigners, and at times, what observers call xenophobia. An individual who obtains a professional legal or medical degree in the U.S. will not be able to apply it in Japan. Only individuals who have passed the Japanese bar exams and graduated from Japanese medical schools can go into those highly specialized fields. This exclusion ensures that those markets and industries are for Japanese only. Despite the shortage of nurses and doctors and other professional occupations, Japan maintains a conservative posture towards hiring from the outside. Japan has hired Filipino nurses, but it has been a slow process. With an aging population and youth eager to explore opportunities abroad, it becomes increasingly necessary to find ways to optimize foreign talent. Hiring farmers from abroad would be one way, for example, to increase agricultural production and improve Japan's dismal agricultural self-sufficiency rate. Xenophobic attitudes and policies must change given shifts in demographic dynamics.

THE 1948 ABORTION LAW AND U.S. ROLE

The U.S. also bears responsibility in Japan's declining population problem. During the Meiji period (1868-1912), abortions were illegal and counter to the country's goal of creating a strong political and military nation with economic prowess on the international scene. After Japan's defeat in World War II, however, Japan was effectively under U.S. occupation from 1945-1952, when a law legalizing abortions was introduced in 1948. Japan was experiencing a population boom and the Japanese government was struggling to provide for the growing population. The U.S. government for its part supported legalizing abortions in Japan and encouraged it. The main reason was not out of respect towards the then Japanese government nor to support the will of the Japanese people, but out of prejudice and fear that a growing population of Japanese meant strengthening the defeated enemy. Unfortunately, Japan is no longer facing a booming population but faces a declining population. The abortion law introduced in 1948 and supported by the U.S. government has led to the declining population in Japan and weakened the Japanese nation-state.

Had the U.S. not allowed for the legalization of abortions to take place under its watch in 1948, Japan very well could be enjoying greater population growth and economic growth. An aging population also makes it less attractive for foreign companies to invest in Japan as companies follow the consumer trail. With a declining population, the market also shrinks as the number of consumers able to buy products and services dwindle. The greatest challenge Japan faces is a demographic one in which households are not having enough children to reverse the aging population trend. The U.S. occupation policy, particularly towards legalizing Japanese abortions, has forever changed Japan's landscape and negatively impacted its future.

Board of Examiners Assessor

After two years of pushing paper as a country desk officer, I finally came to the realization that I should pursue a job focused more on people than paper. My number one choice overseas was the Director of the Foreign Service Institute's Yokohama Language Program. In order to qualify I had to retake my Japanese language exam which I did in August 2013 and scored a 4/4+ (5/5 is native level). That score was higher than the one I took shortly after entering the Foreign Service in 2002. The job required a 3/3 in Japanese. It would allow me to live on the campus at Yokohama, supervise the Japanese language instructors, and assist students to reach their required 3/3 in Japanese. It would also mean I could serve as de facto Consul General of Yokohama, an added bonus. Given my background in teaching, love for Japanese, and family situation with a young son and Japanese wife eager to live in a place like Yokohama, I eagerly applied. I asked for references and bid on the job, personally meeting with, and expressing my interest in the job to the Foreign Service Institute Dean of the Language School, William Haugh, and Deputy Assistant Secretary of State for Japan and Korea, Jim Zumwalt. Unfortunately, while I met the qualifications, it was advertised as a 01 job and as a 02 that meant I was not at-rank. This meant that if an 01 at-rank officer with 3/3 Japanese applied, he or she would be given the job. I could only hope that no 01s would apply. That didn't happen. At least four 01s applied for the job, cutting me out of the race.

My top choices domestically were to either work at the Foreign Service Institute (FSI) in Virginia or serve as an assessor at the Board of Examiners (BEX). I decided BEX made more sense. I had taught before, but never tested and recruited. I was eager to try something new. I also knew that the job would give me more time to spend with family, especially if my wife and I were to give birth to another child, something we had discussed and agreed upon. By signing up for a two year assignment at BEX, I could stay in DC, my wife could keep working, our son could continue going to his nanny, and there would be more opportunities for my parents to see their grandchild. Ultimately, it was the best choice we could make as a family at our particular stage in life. I could always apply for a job at FSI in DC or overseas in the future. BEX would also give me more time for work-life balance. While there were other jobs I was competitive for, I liked the idea of assessing the next generation of Foreign Service talent.

I began my seventh assignment in the Foreign Service as an Assessor in the Board of Examiners (BEX) in 2014. BEX is part of the Office of Recruitment, Examination, and Employment. While our primary job is to assess candidates for entry into the Foreign Service either as generalists or specialists, we also have ancillary duties. Mine were as Chair of the Mustang Program (a career mobility program for Civil Service and Foreign Service Specialists to enter the State Department as Foreign Service generalists) and the Conversion Program (aimed at allowing middle and senior level Civil Service and Foreign Service Specialists to convert to become Foreign Service generalists or specialists). The main difference between these two alternate entry programs is one was aimed at recruitment at the entry level and the other allowed individuals at higher grades to convert to the Foreign Service at the same grade and pay as their current position. Both had provisions that allowed candidates who failed to obtain tenure to return to their previous positions with step or salary increases that one would have accrued had conversion not taken place.

I enjoyed having the responsibility and ownership over these programs and finding ways to make them more effective. As Mustang Program Chair I led a Committee of 12 (half Senior Foreign Service Officers) to review the applications for Mustang candidates through a Qualifications Evaluation Panel (QEP). A three-member BEX QEP would review each Mustang application. Mustang applicants would apply for one of the five career tracks in the Foreign Service for generalists—political, public diplomacy, economic, management, and consular. The vast majority applied for political and management with the least amount applying for the economic career track.

Without these alternate entry programs, the vast majority would not qualify for entry into the Foreign Service. Their scores fall significantly short of those who passed the Foreign Service Oral Assessment (FSOA) through normal channels. In fact, both Mustang and Conversion candidates do not have to take the Foreign Service Written Examination which is an advantage for these candidates. Moreover, Mustang candidates can enter the first available A-100 or orientation class after passing the FSOA without having to wait on a candidate register like regular candidates. A distinctly unfair advantage. Essentially, a Mustang who just barely passed the FSOA with a cut-off score of 5.25 (a score that will not allow any candidate for any of the five career tracks to receive an offer from the registrar) can receive an offer for entry ahead of a regular candidate who performed much higher on the FSOA.

These alternate entry programs, while well intentioned, end up weakening, not strengthening the Foreign Service. The demand for Foreign Service Officer jobs is so high that we do not need to lower Foreign Service entry standards just because Civil Servants are not satisfied with being Civil Service employees within the State Department. The Civil Service needs to address weaknesses within the Civil Service employment and promotion system by focusing on improving the Civil Service, not bringing its problems over to the Foreign Service. Granted there are qualified and talented Civil Servants within the State Department. Given their work experience and institutional knowledge, they already have an advantage over the regular applicant pool with little to no work experience at the State Department. Let them take the Foreign Service Written

Exam like every other candidate and have them compete equally with the regular candidate pool, i.e. a job offer would be contingent upon how high you score on the Foreign Service Oral Assessment.

Unfortunately, once these alternate programs are created there are too many developing vested political interests that make them difficult to reform or end. Many Senior Foreign Service Officers have told me that their worst employees were Conversion candidates or Mustangs who entered through the back door. It makes sense, since these same candidates would never have received a job offer without these alternate programs, which end up taking away jobs from more qualified applicants.

Birth of Our Son Max – 5/18/2015

While serving in the Board of Examiners we welcomed our second son, Max Joseph Reiman, at 10:52 pm on May 18, 2015. Unlike his older brother John, born in DC at Sibley Hospital, Max was born in Virginia at INOVA Hospital. My wife Eriko had to be induced for nine hours. Every birth is a miracle, but Max's birth was unique in that his mother felt no pain and he came out with no need for his mother to push and while medical staff were outside the delivery room. As soon as Max came out, five medical staff rushed in to assist. It was quite a comical and yet dramatic entrance into the world. We named him Max after Polish Saint Maximilian Kolbe and Joseph after Jesus's father. It took more time for us to name Max than it did to name John, our first son. Our goal was to choose a simple yet historically powerful name that embodied the values and ideals we want Max to inherit, namely, humility, hard work, faith, and loyalty.

Now that I had two children, I decided to take practically all of my accumulated annual and sick leave to be with them. My wife was fortunate also to receive nearly three months of maternity leave. One Polish babysitter we found to help us temporarily re-marked that in Poland and in other countries in Europe it is not uncommon for women to receive up to one year of maternity leave. I can see why. I think both of us would like to have had more leave to fulfill the most important jobs we both have as mother and father—but we have bills to pay and college tuition to fund. We were extremely fortunate that Max was a healthy child. We were also fortunate that my parents could come and help us for two weeks after Max was born.

We were initially concerned about how John would react to his younger brother. Those fears were quickly allayed as John welcomed the new family addition and even started bragging to his nanny that he had a cute younger brother. It will be interesting to see how their relationship grows five, ten, twenty years from now. As parents, we hope they will both love one another even after we are gone. We also have two great reasons to work harder—John and Max.

BACK FROM PATERNITY LEAVE

I returned back to the Board of Examiners to work on August 3, 2015. The sleepless nights and adjustments necessary to attend to our newborn and arrange for our eldest to attend a new daycare plus go back to work required extra energy, already in short supply. It took about a month before I felt comfortable back at work again after being away for nearly two months, but I am thankful that I was able to take extended leave and had welcoming colleagues. One colleague, who took over the Mustang portfolio during my absence, did a particularly great job in advancing forward the reforms I had recommended earlier via a memo to the Director General. Surprisingly, the new Director General, Arnold Chacon, approved our recommendations to place Mustang candidates who pass the Oral Assessment on a rank ordered register of candidates based on career track. He also agreed to prevent Mustang candidates from using the Program to switch career tracks into already over-subscribed career tracks such as the political and public diplomacy career tracks.

It would take a year before those reforms were implemented, but I left the portfolio knowing that at a bare minimum, it helped pave the way to close some loopholes and strengthen the Program in line with other generalist programs, preventing the Program from disproportionately benefitting Presidential Management Fellows, and adhering more closely to the 1980 Foreign Service Act in not discriminating against the regular candidate pool. Another benefit of convincing the Director General to support reforms was that it spurred discussion on what the Department of State needed to do to reform the Civil Service. The discontent among Civil Service led so many to try to become Foreign Service Officers via alternate entry programs such as the Mustang Program. Some definitely merited entry, but the majority, as proven by their Oral Assessment scores, would never have received an offer for entry into the Foreign Service because their scores on the Oral Assessment were not high enough to compete with regular candidates who did not take the back door to enter.

I am extremely proud of making an impact at the institutional level per hiring, and consider it a significant accomplishment. It is not, unfortunately, strong enough to merit promotion, but I left feeling positive knowing I had made a difference as I handed off the portfolio to my colleague. Having done the Mustang and Conversion Programs for a year, I decided to take on a different portfolio for my second year, namely, assisting in drafting new test materials, conducting assessments of medical specialists such as regional medical officers and regional psychiatrists, and serving as the coordinator presenting briefings on the Foreign Service Oral Assessment to other agencies.

There is no shame in taking positions that allow you to have more time with family. Yes, you may face slower promotions at certain stages of your career, but you gain something far greater, time with family and renewed health as a result of greater balance in your life. Invest in your relationships because they will be there for you when your career ends.

Chapter Twelve

DISCOVER MY TRIBE: VARIED REFLECTIONS
ON JAPANESE ROOTS

Had I not faced so much discrimination as a dual national I would not have sought Asian American support groups and outside mentors and role models to help me fight for justice and champion diversity. I never thought the country that preached diversity and the organization that recruited me for my diversity would hold my diversity against me. One other reason for why I took an assignment in BEX was because of the discrimination I faced my second year as Country Desk Officer in the Office of West African Affairs depleted my emotional energy and spirits to the point that I needed an environment to work and think about potential opportunities outside State Department. It was hard enough raising a newborn let alone facing prejudice at work.

My first year was a joy with supervisors that championed diversity and treated me well. Unfortunately, the second group of incoming bosses came with their own set of insecurities and prejudices, making frequent offensive and inappropriate comments worthy of an Equal Employment Opportunity grievance, which many people choose not to file because of fear of retribution. I will never forget my new Office Director coming into my office on September 30, 2013, inquiring about my onward assignment plans. I mentioned I was applying for a Foreign Service job in Japan and discussed a Washington Post article on Japanese Americans being precluded from serving in Japan, expressing my disappointment. I then informed him that the job as Director of the Foreign Service Institute Yokohama language school to which I was applying required a test score of 3/3 Japanese and that I had worked hard to score an even higher score of 4/4+ in speaking and reading.

To my shock, he responded, "that's better than your English," followed by "I'm just teasing." Did he realize that my mother, an immigrant from Japan struggled with English all her life? Did he even think once to understand that in the context of the conversation he was belittling my background, and me as well? Obviously he did not. I was so shocked that a senior member of the Foreign Service would say such harmful, inappropriate, and offensive comments. All I could do then was look down and laugh it off as a defense mechanism. But I was hurt and his subsequent behaviors created a hostile work environment for me.

The following day, I sent him the article I was referring to on "*How Diversity Can Count Against You at the State Department,*" mentioning the negative impact preclusions on Asian Americans were having on morale. I emailed him stating, "not trying to dampen your spirits, but this certainly dampens mine," to which he never replied. It was my way, however, of showing him that these issues matter to me. I thought he would have gotten the picture. Boy, was I wrong.

He would continue inappropriate behavior such as passing by my desk throwing a penny at me saying "don't ever say I didn't do anything for you." Less than four months after his offensive comments on my English he made another, this time on January 14, 2014. I was in his office briefing him on my portfolio countries when again the topic of Japan came up. I had told him that no Japanese American had ever served as U.S. Ambassador to Japan and that many qualified Japanese Americans have not had the opportunity to serve in high profile policy positions related to Japan within the State Department. He said, "maybe they are just not good enough," followed by "did I just say that?"

I reminded him that we had an Acting Assistant Secretary of State for African Affairs as well as a Deputy Assistant Secretary of State for African Affairs who were of Japanese American descent. Not the best way to start the New Year. I was so offended that I spoke to the Africa Bureau's Equal Employment Opportunity (EEO) Counselor concerning the inappropriate comments. I told her I would not be filing an EEO complaint just yet, but wanted to know my rights and alert her of what may come if such behavior continued.

On January 17, 2014, I scheduled a private meeting with the Director in his office to go over personnel issues. I told him to stop making inappropriate comments/jokes about Japanese Americans and went over the comments he had made previously. He apologized, acknowledged that his comments were inappropriate and pledged not to repeat them. It took courage to confront him. I would be leaving in five months. Several of my colleagues who were civil service or recently arrived Foreign Service would not have that option. Many had reported to me of inappropriate behavior and comments they too had endured at the hands of this man. This Director was all about himself, his promotions, and criticizing others as a means to hide his own insecurities. It was obviously clear to all of us that his people and leadership skills were wanting. He had previously served as a Deputy Chief of Mission in two different locations. It baffles me that such individuals are promoted, much less given the opportunity to lead an office or mission. What a pity. What a shame. What a sham.

CHIEF DIVERSITY OFFICER MEETING

The gentleman that ran the Office of Civil Rights within the State Department was an African American political appointee who frequently attended meetings held by various minority organizations, including the Asian American Foreign Affairs Association (AAFAA). John Robinson was not only the Director of the Office of Civil Rights but also the Chief Diversity Officer, a position he assumed in 2008. John offered me his card and provided some advice. He told me that it would be better to schedule an appointment with the incoming Director General under the umbrella of an organization like AAFAA or with other Japanese Americans to hit home the point about discrimination more strongly. He also was eager to exchange views and suggest various Asian American organizations I could join. I appreciated his time and eagerness to assist. He kindly introduced me to attorneys in the office.

I decided not to let the racist remarks of my supervisor slide. I was willing to see how the Office of Civil Rights within the State Department could assist. I met a very friendly attorney of Asian American descent who was sympathetic to my concerns. She recommended we keep in touch and that I provide her with documentation on the types of comments and behaviors that were leading to a hostile work environment. I agreed. She also said that she would report my comments to the Bureau of Human Resources as part of a harassment case and that this could lead to an investigation. I was happy to provide her with names of other individuals who had been on the receiving end of inappropriate remarks throughout the time this supervisor, a member of the Senior Foreign Service, served as Office Director.

More Discrimination

The same Office Director who made racist remarks increased my workload threefold and would not recommend me for promotion when I performed my duties. He was using my evaluation to get back at me. He also would not promote others in the office. I could not believe that someone would ask his subordinates to do so much for him while ignoring them and refusing to promote them or putting them in positions for promotion.

Who wants to work for a person who will not promote his employees but is only concerned with himself? Not me. Not only did I decide to inform the Office of Civil Rights, I also notified the Principal Deputy Assistant Secretary for African Affairs that I would formerly file an equal employment opportunity (EEO) complaint against the individual. He apologized and said he was sorry I had to encounter such discrimination and asked if it would be acceptable for him to notify the Assistant Secretary accordingly. I told him go right ahead.

We do not need leaders, especially at the Senior Foreign Service level, to be leading embassies if they are incapable of managing a diverse workforce and cannot vigorously support merit and EEO principles. Knowing that formally filing an EEO may take two years to do, I was willing to go through the process to gain justice not only for myself but for everyone else he offended.

By raising an EEO issue, the person in question was denied an ambassadorship in a post in Africa initially. Sadly, after he had used his personal connections to serve as an Office Director in the Office of East Asian and Pacific Affairs, he received a nomination to become the next U.S. Ambassador to Somalia. I question this decision and believe the individual will use his nomination for ambassador to validate his approach to diversity as the right approach. This would be another sad happening in the State Department. The American taxpayer deserves better.

In the summer of 2017, my former boss who became U.S. Ambassador to Somalia resigned while serving as U.S. Ambassador. I heard that he decided to resign rather than be fired as a result of numerous reports citing his inappropriate sexual misconduct. Allegedly, his extramarital affairs had involved even members of the Diplomatic Corps outside the U.S. Embassy. It seems his years of misbehavior and misconduct finally caught up with him, but not after so many lives were negatively affected. This person never should have received positions of authority where he could abuse his power and harm others. Speaking up is always the right thing when it comes to discrimination or any kind of harassment. If you do not do so, chances are such behavior will continue and harm others.

Tokyo Jobs on the Bid List – Maybe This Time?

On the summer 2015 bid list I saw only one Tokyo political officer job at the 02 level. The job would cover historical issues, the two Koreas, and trafficking in persons. The officer selected would be required to draft cables on Japan's relations with the Koreas, historical animosities, draft the annual trafficking in person's report and serve as control officer for the various delegations and VIPs that routinely pass through Tokyo. Knowing that Tokyo is a popular destination for many officers, I lobbied early for the job, contacted the incumbent, expressed my interest to the Deputy Director of the Japan Desk, sought out people I knew on the Japan Desk to put in a good word to leadership, emailed the Office Director, emailed the Political Counselor in Tokyo, and visited the Deputy Assistant Secretary of State responsible for Korea and Japan Ambassador, Sung Kim, to express my desire to serve in Tokyo. I also had friends and colleagues I knew send an email on my behalf to the Deputy Chief of Mission in Tokyo, Jason Hyland, to make sure I would at least be considered.

There were no consulate jobs at the 02 level in my desired career track, leaving Tokyo the only option per jobs in Japan. I also subsequently sent an email to the Economic Minister Counselor in Tokyo expressing my interest in two economic officer jobs in Tokyo also starting in 2018 at the 02 level. With 4/4+ Japanese tested in 2013, my language score was still valid. All three jobs at Embassy Tokyo (one political and two economic) required 3/3 Japanese and candidates with no language would be given 2 years to attain that proficiency level. Someone like me who already had the language, however, would not receive any language training and therefore must somehow find a way to fill the two year gap before the State Department's Career Development and Assignments folks would panel me into the three year Tokyo jobs covering 2018-2021.

In order to fill one year, I found a one-year exchange program which allows officers with 3/3 Japanese or higher at the 02 level to spend one year working at Japan's Ministry of Foreign Affairs as part of the Baker-Kato Ministry Exchange Program. The Baker-Kato Diplomatic Exchange was named after U.S. Ambassador, Howard Baker, and Japanese Ambassador, Ryozo Kato, in an attempt to deepen knowledge of each other's ministries and strengthen U.S.-Japan relations in the process. The first American to participate in the Exchange was Raymond Greene, former Consul General in Naha, Okinawa and Deputy Political Chief at the American Institute in Taipei. I met Ray during my first tour in Taiwan.

Although I had applied for the Baker-Kato and was not accepted several years ago as a 03 officer, I decided to try again as a 02. Previously, all that was required was a statement of interest. The catch then as it is now, however, is that one must first secure a three-year onward assignment in Japan or else one cannot participate in the Baker-Kato Exchange. One new change in the application process, however, was a requirement that one also submit two letters of recommendations, one at the Office Director level and one at the Ambassador level if overseas. I secured both and submitted along with my resumé, statement of interest, and application to the training and details person within the Career Development and Assignments (CDA) responsible for the program. When I asked who would evaluate, she said five people would determine who to accept with one senior Department official from the East Asia and Pacific Affairs Bureau weighing in.

I know there are very few 4/4+ Japanese speakers in the Department at the 02 level willing to work at the Ministry of Foreign Affairs for a year so I knew I would have some chance and be competitive. Unlike promotion boards, however, the names of the committee members making the decisions in the selection process for the Baker-Kato are not revealed. I found that not to be a transparent process. One should be able to know who the committee members are as well as have members who know you recuse themselves as well to ensure integrity in the process.

If I were able to get both the three-year onward assignment in Tokyo and the Baker-Kato, I would only need to fill the one-year gap in DC. I was confident I could do so either by doing a 1-year detail, a short y-tour or remain for a third year at the Board of Examiners. A third year at BEX would not be ideal for the career, but for Japan and the family and fulfilling my dreams, it was well worth considering as a last resort.

Having spoken with various decision makers I also spoke with the Bureau's Assignments Officer in EAP/EX per bidding on Tokyo. He told me that so many officers who did one year assignments in Priority Staffing Posts (PSP), i.e. war zones or high danger posts such as in Iraq, Afghanistan, Yemen, and Pakistan, were attempting to take advantage of linked assignments to go to Tokyo. He said the most popular destinations for PSP bidders who received preferential treatment to gain assignments in East Asia were Tokyo and Bangkok. The linked assignments system has created tremendous amounts of chaos in the Foreign Service and ensured that people who are not qualified to serve in certain locations receive assignments over more qualified officers. Tokyo, I was told, was receiving bids from 03 officers at PSP locations attempting to obtain stretch positions at the 02 or double stretch positions at the 01 levels in Japan who were clearly not qualified to serve there.

I was not selected not because I was not qualified, but because the system failed to uphold the integrity of the process in allowing Japanese American dual nationals with language, background, and expertise, an opportunity to serve. Repeatedly, the Foreign Service assigns people based on networks, "who you know," and political factors as opposed to true qualifications. Sending yet another officer to Japan who is not the most qualified only leads to the type of damning Office of Inspector General Reports like the one in 2015 bashing Embassy Tokyo leadership. Try and try as I may, no door would budge to let me into the Japan club.

SYSTEMIC DISCRIMINATION

Despite the rules regarding bidding that decision makers should not inform candidates in advance if they are the top candidate or not, we see this rule broken all the time. I received an email from the Acting Minister Counselor for Political Affairs in Tokyo several weeks before bids were due that there were many qualified candidates and that I should look elsewhere without even giving me an opportunity for an interview. I responded back asking her for advice and guidance on how I could be more competitive next time. She never responded.

When I had paid a courtesy call to the Deputy Director of the Japan Desk, a 02 Officer in a 01 stretch position, he asked about my origin as opposed to focusing on my qualifications. He asked questions about how I was able to increase my language score in Japanese significantly without taking a Foreign Service Institute course. That is irrelevant. What is relevant is that I have 4/4+ Japanese and worked hard to attain that score and have competent skills for the job. Yet, people focus on national origin. When I mentioned I would be interested in filling a one year gap by applying to the Baker-Kato Exchange and that I bring necessary skills such as fluency in the language, he mentioned that I would fit in well with the Japanese Ministry of Foreign Affairs because "you look like them." These statements are not only violations of EEO laws and regulations based on national origin, but also a clear sign that the Department's discriminatory policies are ever present. Unfortunately, unless some-one raises these issues or a lawsuit is filed, the Department takes the "no harm, no foul" approach to diversity.

Bidding on Principal Officer Jobs in Japan

During my second year at the Board of Examiners I applied as well for positions as Principal Officer in both the U.S. consulates in Fu-kuoka and Sapporo, Japan. I lobbied the appropriate Deputy Assistant Secretary (DAS) in the Bureau of East Asian and Pacific Affairs, at the time, Ambassador Sung Kim. We had a pleasant conversation and I expressed my interest. He asked if I had notified my interest to the Director of the Japan Desk, Joseph Young. I mentioned that I did. Joseph Young, however, never responded to my requests for a meeting. Again, another lost opportunity for the Department and reflection of poor leadership on the part of the Director. A 15-minute meeting would not have been a terribly difficult session to hold, espe-cially when the DAS was able to take 30-minutes out of his schedule to meet with me. I could never understand why individuals like Joseph Young could not see the value in encouraging Japanese American of-ficers with fluent Japanese to work on Japan affairs and leverage their skills to represent the American people. The situation was very disap-pointing, and it reiterated for me the exclusive, almost racist approach to keeping Japanese Americans out of the U.S.-Japan policy circuit.

Despite these setbacks, and despite knowing that I had a slim chance of obtaining one of two principal officer jobs in Japan, I applied nonetheless. I wasn't going to let racism discourage me from pursuing my dreams. I was encouraged when I bumped into Ambassador Kim at the Foreign Service Institute and asked him about my chances. He said there were a lot more bidders on these jobs than he had expected but that he would strongly consider my candidacy. I never made the short list of names for the two jobs. But I had tried, and I did not give up. I had written my statement of interest for the Deputies Committee or "D" Committee for short which determines who will go out as Principal Officer after vetting the initial list by the regional bureaus. In my case, the Bureau did not even submit my name so the D Committee would never have even known of my qualifications or interest. As the door kept slamming in my face, I kept looking for other options. In the end, I suffered from discrimination for 16 years and the American taxpayers who paid my salary never received a proper return on their investment.

Burkina Faso or Saudi Arabia

With jobs in Japan off the table of possibilities, I had to bid on other overseas jobs. Burkina Faso and Saudi Arabia were two options, both requiring language training and affording me greater management responsibilities. I opted for Burkina Faso to learn French and position myself for future leadership positions within the Africa Bureau. I opted against the Saudi Arabia job for a number of reasons. First, I had reservations about our U.S. policy toward Saudi Arabia. I found it contradictory to call Saudi Arabia one of our closest allies in the fight against terrorism when the Saudis were involved in inciting violence between Sunnis and Shia, exacerbating tensions with Iran, and creating a humanitarian crisis in Yemen. Osama bin Laden was a Saudi. The Saudis financed terrorist groups and I felt our policies gave too much preferential treatment toward the Saudis on account of their oil wealth while giving them a pass on human rights, democracy, and religious liberty. Women could still not drive in Saudi Arabia, surveillance of Americans was common, and I did not believe it would be an ideal location for my family.

INTERVIEW WITH PRINCIPAL
DEPUTY ASSISTANT SECRETARY FOR EAP

During my 28 weeks of French language training at the Foreign Service Institute in preparation for my assignment to Burkina Faso, the former U.S. Ambassador to Burkina Faso Tulinabo Mushingi met with me and encouraged me to contact his friend, former U.S. Ambassador to Malaysia and then Acting Principal Deputy Assistant Secretary of State (PDAS) for East Asian and Pacific Affairs to express my interest in jobs in Japan. This same PDAS I had met as a Pearson Fellow during my time on Capitol Hill and he had struck me as a modest, kind person. But my meeting with him changed my views of him entirely. When I told him I would be going to Burkina Faso as Public Affairs Officer, the first question he asked me was, with how many children? I replied two. He then said, "What kind of parent are you?" implying that only a bad father would consider taking his children there. I was offended and shocked that this man would question our parenting decisions. We happen to be two very loving parents who care deeply about the welfare of our two young children. I did not take his off-the-cuff remarks humorously. In his presence I laughed it off, but thought that was an extremely inappropriate comment for a Member of the Senior Foreign Service to say.

He then asked me why I had not been able to obtain a posting in Japan despite my fluency in Japanese. He used the "F" word several times and asked if I had "f'---ed" up during one of my EAP tours earlier and if that accounts for why I could not get a Japan job. I said no. He asked if I was on an EAP "blacklist." I did not even know that such a list existed but it made me wonder about what kind of internal, non-transparent selection process secrets leaders like him were holding.

Finally, he asked me if I would be willing to do a Desk job in EAP. I told him if it would guarantee a placement in Japan, yes. He said there were no such guarantees. I then responded, in that case, having served as a Desk Officer for two years in the Africa Bureau, I would not be interested in repeating the same job in EAP.

He told me that having served in the Africa Bureau I would have a better chance of becoming a future U.S. Ambassador in West Africa than East Asia. I kindly responded that my Foreign Service dream job is not to become an ambassador, but to be the Director of the State Department Japanese Language School in Yokohama and concurrently the Consul General in Yokohama. He said that is a "stupid" job and that I should not pursue it as a Political-coned officer. I had had enough. First, this person whom I am expressing interest in serving insults my parenting decisions and then tries to crush my dreams by stating that my dream is stupid. Had he never thought that I had taken time to reflect upon what I would like for my life and career and that perhaps not everyone views becoming an ambassador as the be all end all? Obviously he did not. He made several false assumptions about me.

In sum, I thought his comments were highly inappropriate, undignified, and disgraceful. I walked away highly disappointed and discouraged, thinking, "I do not want to work for you nor your Bureau." This was the last straw after years of repeatedly trying to make my case to allow me to serve in the one country where I had fluency and expertise to add immediate value, as well as honor my parents. The PDAS's remarks confirmed in me that none of this mattered to the State Department. When one of the most senior ranking officers in the Bureau of East Asian and Pacific Affairs exhibits such poor behavior it wreaks havoc on morale. Does trying to serve America overseas in the one country you have language skills and expertise have to be this difficult? Unfortunately, I have found after repeated tries over the course of 16 years, the answer to be yes.

After 16 Years No Change

Three times I attempted to meet with the former Director General to discuss the dismal state of recruitment, retention, and promotion of Japanese Americans within the Department ranks and discuss concerns I have over discrimination towards Asian Americans in general. So many colleagues in the Asian American Foreign Affairs Association complained to me about preclusions they received from Diplomatic Security and disproportionate amount of hurdles each had to face to fight preclusions. Many Chinese Americans with fluent Mandarin are precluded from serving simply because a father or grandfather came from Mainland China. The Department recruited me because they said they wanted someone with Japanese language skills. They knew my background before I applied. Yet, when I entered the Foreign Service the very background they claimed was an asset turned out to be a liability and I was precluded from serving. If the Department had no intention of allowing me to serve in the first place it should not have recruited me.

It took me three years to fight Diplomatic Security to lift the preclusion, and my mother had to obtain U.S. citizenship even though she was a green card holder in the U.S. for over half her life and never once worked for the Japanese government to convince Diplomatic Security that we posed no threat. Why do we still need to prove we are American?

A mother who is a citizen of a country that we claim is one of our most important allies and who spent her entire life devoted to teaching Japanese to U.S. college students is now considered a threat to U.S. national security. This logic never made sense to me. Then again, the longer I've stayed with State, the more I discovered how so much of what we do goes against reason, such as trying to spend instead of save money out of fear that we will lose funding requests for the following year. We need to apologize to the American people.

Needless to say, I never did get to discuss the matter of discrimination towards Japanese Americans and Department culture precluding Japanese Americans from positions of influence on Japan policy. The Director General was too busy to spend 15 minutes to hear the concerns of people like me. After 16 years, I'm convinced that the Department of State will never work to improve the situation and enact real change without external pressure. Until the State Department is forced by Congress to institutionalize a program to nurture Japanese American talent and provide an avenue for Japanese Americans to serve at the highest levels working on Japan policy, I don't see change happening. Preaching a good game is not the same as practicing it.

I distinctly recall the former Deputy Director General who had served in Japan come to speak on diversity to members of the Asian Americans in Foreign Affairs group in the Delegates Lounge at Main State and began his introduction by talking about "your people" in referring to Asian Americans. He then tried to claim some connection to us by stating his wife is Asian. His entire talk, which was videotaped, was all lip service and not once did he mention a program or initiative that he advanced that led to improvements for the Asian American community. He said the right buzzwords such as "promoting diversity" but had little evidence to back them up. The man later received his ambassadorship to Romania after serving as ambassador to East Timor five years earlier. I've been disappointed that the Department has not met expectations of the American people—specifically that of Japanese Americans. I've served under three different U.S. Presidents and nine different Secretaries of State and the results are the same.

Since no audience was granted with the former Director General, I was encouraged to forget about meeting the Secretary. I'm not sure he nor Secretaries before him were duly aware of how much discrimination exists in the assignment process per Japanese Americans and Chinese Americans and other loyal Asian Americans wanting to use their language skills and cultural background to serve in Japan, China, or other Asian posts. Had the late Senator Daniel Inouye known, I'm sure he would have pushed to institutionalize a program within State to help Japanese Americans succeed.

Chapter Thirteen

COMING FULL CIRCLE:

MAKING UP FOR LOST TIME

Every heartbreak and setback happens for a reason. We can let that crush us or use that as motivation to make a positive difference in the life of others. I chose to write this memoir to give hope to other dual nationals to have the courage to keep both their nationalities and heritages intact. I also wanted to raise awareness among policymakers and government officials in both the United States and Japan that dual nationality is a positive asset that can be of immense benefit to both economies. In order to move forward, we need to acknowledge the negative aspects that are hindering the U.S. and Japan alliance from becoming stronger—the human capital aspect. Fear, ignorance, and prejudice remain the greatest obstacles to progress. There is no reason why the U.S. and Japan cannot embrace each other more fully. Allowing dual nationals to keep both nationalities and serve both countries is a win-win that demonstrates a positive evolution in the alliance and needs to occur given the changing demographic dynamics. Until this happens, neither U.S. nor Japanese diplomacy will meet its full potential.

If we let prejudice and fear divide us, no one wins. If we let love, tolerance, diversity, and inclusion reign, each Pacific power becomes stronger. I believe in the power of America. I also believe in the power of Japan. I believe both the U.S. and Japan can learn from each other. But we need to start with an honest conversation about the biases that hinder strengthening the U.S.-Japan alliance further. History matters. So do policies that prevent each side from reaching its full potential. The Japanese cannot delude themselves into believing that Article 9 of the Japanese Peace Constitution, which renounces war and prohibits Japan from developing offensive weapons, is what keeps Japan safe. Not at all. What keeps Japan safe are U.S. military troops stationed in Japan and the U.S. nuclear umbrella, which allows Japan to leave defense to the Americans and focus on other aspects such as its economy. The U.S., on the other hand, cannot ask Japan to shoulder greater defense burdens while at the same time supporting institutional barriers that prevent a transfer of power from the U.S. to Japan in defense matters. For so long, for example, Japan could not build its own fighter jets manufactured in Japan. Instead, the unspoken rule was that Japanese companies were allowed to build parts that go into the building of U.S. planes or missiles defense, but not independently on their own. If the U.S. is creating institutional barriers that prevent a transfer of power from the U.S. to Japan in defense matters, then the U.S. cannot ask Japan to shoulder greater responsibility when the institutional framework inevitably biases in favor of U.S. interests before Japanese. Similarly, the U.S. has to listen more to the needs of the Japanese public, not just Japanese politicians.

One thing is certain; the U.S. is not in Japan to serve the Japanese people. The U.S. presence is there to maintain U.S. military, economic, and political dominance in the Asia Pacific region and beyond. There is a strategic reason for the U.S. to be in Japan which gives the U.S. several advantages in projecting military might. Too often people forget that Japan had lived and governed independently for thousands of years until the U.S. forcefully opened up Japan in 1853 with the arrival of U.S. Commodore Matthew Perry and his black ships, guns loaded. Through naval military threats, the U.S. ended Japan's 200 year isolationist policy. Perry's intimidation tactics were a "wake up" call for Japan to unify and modernize its military, political structure, and economy or else face the threat of foreign invasion. Perry and the Americans came to Japan not in friendship, but with rocket shells, military threats, and intimidation. While trade was one reason why Perry came, the primary reason was military. The U.S. wanted to use Japan as a base where naval steamships could restock their coal supply. The U.S. Navy could use Japan as a port for its steamships in the east. The Meiji Reformation (1868) occurred as a direct result of Perry's ships and the realization by the Japanese ruling elite that Japan needed to modernize in order to defend itself against foreign invasion.

Japan one day may consider relying less on the U.S. military shield and demand greater independence and autonomy. For now, Japan's future is very much tied to the U.S. militarily, economically, diplomatically, and agriculturally. We can deceive ourselves into believing that Japan is an equal partner of the U.S. and that Japan can call its own shots. We can even write nice sounding "talking points" and briefing memos to convince ourselves, and our Japanese counterparts that our initiatives benefit Japan. Diplomatically, that sounds nice. Practically, we are using diplomatic lingo to embellish the truth.

If we really want to help Japan, perhaps sending American farmers raise Japan's agricultural self-sufficiency rate is one solution. Pre-WWII and immediately after 1945, Japan's food self-sufficiency rate was over 70 percent. After the Agricultural Basic Law came into effect from 1961 onward, you saw a perilous decline in Japan's agriculture sector resulting in loss of farmland, loss of employment in agriculture, and consequently loss of food production. Today, Japan's agricultural self-sufficiency rate is well under 40 percent, a dramatic decline from pre-WWII levels and it is the lowest among developed countries. Even developed countries like the U.S., France, Germany, and UK have experienced declines in agricultural production, employment and so forth, but it is the rate in which Japan's agricultural sector has declined that is most alarming. Japan can't feed its own people growing its own food. It has to rely on imports. Many of these imports come from the U.S. So Japan not only is dependent on the U.S. for defense and security, it also relies on the U.S. for food.

The decline in agriculture also means a change in diet. As farmers reach retirement and face economic challenges to continue to plow the land, Japanese consumers face the consequences. Certain vegetables and plants unique to various regions of Japan are no longer grown. Farmers, faced with competition from imports are unable to maintain their livelihoods. Land once used for agricultural production is now used for other purposes or lying idle. Too often we ask the wrong questions. We ask what we need from Japan and what we need to do to get our demands met rather than sincerely asking the Japanese what they want and how we can help meet their objectives in a mutually beneficial manner. Active listening is needed more than ever.

There is a real need for Japan to create its own blueprint for the future, including in the area of defense, and demand greater autonomy, flexibility, and authority if the U.S. is really serious about having Japan shoulder more of the military burden and Japan is committed to this end. Relying exclusively on the U.S. for decades has had both positive and negative consequences. The positive includes becoming one of the world's leading economies, a technological powerhouse, and a peaceful nation. The negative includes losing sight of independence, declining agricultural production, population decline, and taking decisions that do not advance the soul of the Japanese nation. Losing the war does not mean hanging one's head in shame and saying, "Well, everything in the past is wrong." There is much beauty and richness in Japanese history, culture, and tradition that Japanese and non-Japanese can appreciate. It's time for Japan to share more of that with the rest of the world. The U.S. can learn from Japan's environmental prowess and technological advances, team oriented spirit, and family business structure where CEOs do not take disproportionately large compensation packages at the expense of layoffs and shareholder profits while the very companies they run go bankrupt.

Japan cannot rely on any other country but its own to devise a blueprint for a bright future. This must include contingency plans on how Japan would govern its polity, military, and economy post-U.S. presence. During peacetime is when this planning should take place prior to the outbreak of an emergency or crisis. More transparency and communication involving the support, active participation, and feedback from the Japanese public is necessary. School children, young adults, and workers should all be encouraged to voice their opinions and feel as though the government does indeed value their thoughts. Too often, their voices are ignored. Japan has the opportunity to rebuild itself through developing democracy from the ground-up as opposed to imposed from above, a legacy of the U.S. occupation. Now is the time for Japan to take its gains and make the country even more prosperous. Attracting dual nationals is a crucial step in the right direction.

Creating a blueprint for the future does not mean abandoning its relations with the U.S. nor severing military or trade tries. This is where diplomacy comes into play. Japan can and should reconcile with its neighbors and use an independent diplomacy to seek its own interests vis-a-vis all countries in the region. The scenarios in which Japan can do so I leave in the capable hands of the Japanese themselves to devise and discover. I want to be a part of a stronger, healthier, and more prosperous U.S.-Japan alliance. More than any military alliance, I firmly believe the future of the relationship rests upon utilizing the greatest asset both sides have—their growing dual national citizenry.

Am I willing to die for America? Absolutely. Am I willing to die for Japan? Absolutely. I make no apologies for loving both countries and both people. They are both part of my family. Neither should you if duality and diversity matter to you. When I look back at my life or want people to remember me, here's what I will have carved on my tombstone in English and Japanese:

KEN OBATA REIMAN
AN AMBASSADOR TO TWO NATIONS
100% LOYAL TO BOTH

What will your legacy be? Think about what you want written on your tombstone, and let that define the path you take. Even if your dreams do not come true, meaning lies in pursuing them. Having dreams enriches your life and you create meaning for yourself and others. If I can imagine a more loving, tolerant world, a world where dual nationals can be authentically both without facing prejudice and discrimination, then there is hope in human evolution.

Chapter Fourteen

How the Acronym of D.U.A.L.I.T.Y. Reveals the ANSWER

Duality is a gift from God and a gift from my parents. In honoring my duality I am honoring my creator, my parents, and my grandparents. I am grateful to receive this gift. And I choose to keep both nationalities out of love and respect for both the U.S. and Japan. How deeply I wish my duality could be used to serve U.S.-Japan relations and strengthen the human bonds between these two great nations. Family ties run thicker than friendship. Dual nationals like myself have a greater stake in ensuring the prosperity, safety, and security of this relationship precisely because we have family on both sides of the Pacific. Let us serve. Let us employ our gifts for the benefit of both the American and Japanese taxpayer. Let us champion your interests. Let us prove our worth. I am not an enemy of either country. Stop treating me like one. So many individuals invested in my dual upbringing and education that I want to pay them back by making a meaningful contribution to both countries. Writing is one way I hope to spur positive change. The American and Japanese taxpayers deserve better. The U.S. and Japanese governments are capable of replacing fear with love.

I cannot get rid of Japan even if I tried. I cannot get rid of America even if I tried. I do not want to lose either country just as I do not want to lose either parent. Through my sacrifice and publication of my memoir, I want both governments to embrace dual nationals as assets, allow them to serve in their country of national origin, and enact policies and legislation to provide them with the same opportunities to thrive like other citizens.

I learned a lot and carried a lot of stress on my shoulders as a dual national U.S. diplomat trying to simply be true to myself when others attempted to make me choose sides. I do not have divided loyalties as some would try to argue, I have united loyalties. Two is greater than one. My grandmother and those who invested in me taught me to see God in others. I see God's face present in a Japanese face as I do in an American, Nigerian, Guyanese, or any other nationality. And in the first letter of the acronym of DUALITY lies the first truth. That *Deus* or Latin for God is in charge. We cannot think we can outsmart the Creator. Ultimately, His will wins out. Let's examine each letter of the acronym DUALITY to see what treasure lies within each of us. The answer to living a life worth living, an authentic, meaningful one lies in following the truths behind each letter and applying them in your life.

D is for Deus

The first letter D stands for *Deus,* Latin for God. Everything begins with God. There is a saying in the Analects of Confucius or Lunyu that captures the concept well: 生死有命, 富貴在天 "Life and death have pre-determined appointments; riches and honor are from heaven." Living right by doing right is all we can do. The rest is in Heaven or God's hands.

Duality can be turned into a gift of the most divine kind when one has faith in something bigger than oneself. *Deus* is the source for all inspiration and diversity. I could not achieve what I did without the hand of God guiding my steps.

The difficulties and struggles I faced and the suffering I saw as a result of humans not following the will of God, actually increased my faith in God. I realized that I relied on and depended on God for everything. My will was nothing if it was not in some way connected to God's plans. Going against God is like swimming against a current with no lifeline and no hope for rescue. I know of diplomats who lost faith in God or decided not to practice their faith out of convenience or simply because the human suffering they witnessed made them question God's existence. For me, the opposite occurred. When I finally embraced God, I gained my freedom and courage to speak out against injustice.

U is for Understanding

The second letter U stands for understanding. When we understand who we are, and increase our own self-awareness through a relationship with our divine Creator, we create opportunities for success. Understanding is not independent of Deus. The two are intimately linked together. Cardinal Robert Sarah is right when he states in his book *God or Nothing*: "Without God man neither knows which way to go, nor even understands who he is."

It is important to understand that each one of us was formed divinely in the image of God. We can put fear behind us if we understand that God has incredible plans for us, that what matters is making the most of today, and to create time for prayer and interior reflection.

Fear cripples us and prevents us from taking important steps need-ed to achieve our full potential, understand who we are in relation to others, and move forward in a positive direction. Understanding our value through God's eyes allows us to see beyond our imperfections and see the light needed to penetrate our hearts and make us into the men or women we were meant to become. I am the man I am today because God gave me understanding. He let me know that I am loved and I am valued and that my job is to spread that message to others.

A is for Authenticity

The third letter A is for authenticity. When facing threats to our human dignity, we need to *increase* and *expand* ourselves and our world, not hide from it. We need to powerfully assert our authenticity. When you speak and act with authenticity, you increase and expand yourself and your world—your whole life changes. Increase your authenticity and you increase not only your belief in yourself, but help others believe in you too.

Authenticity does not mean you are always in control. It means understanding your strengths and weaknesses through increasing your self-awareness and applying your gifts to benefit others. It requires humility. You are created uniquely, but you are no better than someone else. Through understanding and prayer you find your authentic voice. This may take time, even years, and you may find yourself wandering in the desert. But the process of becoming your authentic self is a lifelong journey; embrace that ride. The answers are within you. Take the time to probe deeper.

L is for Lead

The fourth letter L is for lead. Become the leader of your own life, the determiner of your destiny, and learn from each success and each failure. You set the terms and schedule and timeline of your own success. You own the rights to your success. You are your own brand. You call the shots and take the credit or blame for what you can control in your life.

When you're the leader of your own life, you own your successes, you own your mistakes, and you move forward with all the drive of a leader. It all starts with you and is an integral part of the success process. Seek role models who can teach you, learn from them, and read history to find examples of how individuals can triumph even in the face of overwhelming adversity.

I is for Ikigai

The fifth letter I is for *Ikigai* or "reason for being" which is a Japanese concept for finding your passion in life. When we have our *ikigai* we have to live that out. When we move toward letting our *ikigai* determine our career, we embrace our authenticity and fully become who we are meant to be. Think about what you enjoyed as a child or what motivates you, what you would do even if you were not paid for it. Move toward achieving what gives you meaning and value, the money will follow. Through time with God, understanding your strengths, being authentic, and being the leader of your own life, you find your *ikigai*. Pursue it with all your heart.

Each person has a different path to take in life. Sometimes your choices are not always obvious nor do they match your ideals. But you have to play with the cards you are dealt. Find meaning in what you are doing, assess your priorities outside of work, and search for outlets to pursue your passion outside of work hours. You may be able to find internships or opportunities in a career field closely linked to your dream job. Whatever your situation, never give up on your *ikigai*.

T is for Together

The sixth letter T is for together. Together with like-minded individuals who are achieving their dreams and goals—others you respect and admire, you can achieve even more. Success is contagious. Uniting with successful, positive people will bring out the best in you. Together you will accomplish more than you ever imagined. Surround yourself with talented people who have their *ikigai* and live it out daily.

Seek mentors and join affinity groups or create your own, as there is power in numbers. Together your collective voice and therefore influence is greater when you have a whole group of people championing your cause. In difficult times, find allies that can encourage you to pursue your *ikigai* and inspire you to live the life you were meant to lead in spite of adversity.

Y is for Yearning

The final letter Y is for yearning. Once we have determined our *ikigai*, found allies, and united with positive people, we need to avoid becoming complacent. We need to yearn to increase our authenticity, yearn to start talking to God with more frequency, and yearn to increase our desire to help others around us succeed. When we do so, we transform ourselves, and our world. Extraordinary becomes the ordinary.

When we yearn for more positive production out of ourselves and our communities and our governments, we create a better world for everyone to live in. Setting goals daily, weekly, monthly, and annually helps us keep on track to constantly become the best version of ourselves.

If you ever felt you did not fit in for whatever reason I can empathize with you. I felt that all the time I was in the Foreign Service I was asked to be half of who I am as a U.S. diplomat. It was only until I embraced all of me, in spite of fear and retribution that I started regaining my authentic self. Perhaps you are contemplating a career in diplomacy or are a dual or triple national seeking comfort in knowing that there are others like you, but wondering where you fit in. Take comfort knowing that you are not alone. We can create our own community of dual or multiple nationalities. Together, we can lobby governments to acknowledge and embrace us. And, if you never knew how complicated being a dual or triple citizen might be, maybe now you can empathize. We bleed just like you. Our blood is marked in more than one country's flag.

There is no end to finding your true self, but be open to change. I'm constantly struggling to define my identity more clearly. Just when I thought I found an answer, some event, person, or idea would take me back to square one. And I start questioning what it all means. Be yourself. Accept your uniqueness. But bear in mind, the journey to feel comfortable with yourself in a society and world that just doesn't quite know what to make of you, or opposes you will take time. Expect that your "self" may change and evolve with time too. And all you can do is find that place in your heart you call your spiritual home. You'll know it because it always calls you back. And your home may be in two or more vastly different locations. Keep all of them. I did and I have no regrets.

My high school graduation with my mother and father in 1996 at Brophy College Preparatory in Phoenix, Arizona. The beginning of my Jesuit education where we were taught to be men and women for others. Go Broncos!

Receiving an award in 2014 from Assistant Secretary of State for African Affairs Jonnie Carson. I served as Desk Officer in the Bureau of African Affairs from 2012-2014 covering Ghana and Guinea.

With Secretary of State Hillary Clinton and other Department colleagues. I am standing in the far left, second row. This photo was taken during my time as a Pearson Congressional Fellow in 2012. I served later as the Africa Bureau's paper coordinator for Secretary Clinton's final nine-country visit to Africa in 2014 as Desk Officer for Ghana/Guinea.

A wedding photo of my parents in Tokyo with my mother's extended relatives. My grandfather is seated in the first row in a wheel chair, next to him is my grandmother.

Here with my American grandmother, when I was two and a half years old.

I'm 5 years old standing in the front row near the drum with Japanese classmates during a music class in 1983 at Tanaka Elementary School and kindergarten in Tokyo, Japan.

Me and my Japanese grandmother. She was a devout Buddhist. The photo was taken in Japan where I would spend my summers with her.

My two boys - John Francis Reiman and Max Joseph Reiman resting on our bed in Alexandria, Virginia.

I served my Pearson Fellowship in the U.S. House of Representatives for Congressman Donald Manzullo from 2011 - 2012. He was the Chairman of the House Foreign Affairs Subcommittee on Asia and the Pacific during this time.

A family photo of my Japanese mother's family taken during WWII. My grandfather seated was 54, my grandmother seated with boy on her lap was 24 and the little girl seated next to my grandfather was my mother at age 4. The Obata family photo depicts the war time era.

My father Carl Walden Reiman and mother Etsuko Obata married in 1975 in Tokyo in a traditional Japanese wedding ceremony. The two met as graduate students at the University of Wisconsin.

ACTIVITY

This activity allows you, the reader, to create a Bill of Rights found within the context of a diplomatic bilateral treaty to make a positive political statement and affirmation that dual nationals must be respected, valued, protected, and promoted as assets to both countries. Feel free to comment on my website to add to this short list. Together, we will create diplomatic history. Two is always better than one. But in this activity, a million voices heard can turn this from an imaginary exercise into a political movement and finally an acceptance by both the United States and Japanese governments that they too must do more to employ, embrace, empower, educate, and promote dual nationals to take the U.S.-Japan alliance to the next level of friendship, trust, and economic success. Diplomacy is useless unless it represents the values of its citizenry and responds to the demands of its local constituency.

U.S. and Japan
Bilateral Treaty on Dual Nationality

The United States Government and the Government of Japan agree to and affirm the following principles in regards to dual citizens of the United States and Japan:

1. The U.S. and Japanese Foreign Ministries will accept dual nationals to serve in a diplomatic capacity while maintaining both nationalities without prejudice, preclusions, or threats of renunciation.

2. Dual nationals will be viewed as assets rather than liabilities.

3. Dual nationals can retain their citizenships and serve in either country without any questions to their loyalty.

4. Japan will allow dual nationals to keep dual citizenship, preserve Japanese values, and promote greater inclusion and diversity among its citizenry.

5. Legislation will be introduced through the Japanese Diet to allow dual nationals to keep dual citizenship and protect their right to keep both.

6. Japanese American voices will be valued more by both U.S. and Japanese government authorities as critical to the future of U.S.-Japan relations and both governments will make a joint statement affirming their commitment to protecting dual national lives.

7. A U.S.-Japan Committee on Dual Nationality will be formed to examine the best way to legally protect dual

nationals of the U.S. and Japan and allow their talents to be fully maximized for the benefit of both countries.

8. Any Committee on Dual Nationality shall include dual national members on the Committee and provide ample opportunities for soliciting public feedback from dual nationals regarding policies that directly impact them.

Feel free to endorse as is or comment and add points to this treaty via Ken Reiman's website at: www.KenReiman.com. To our dual success! Together let's change the way governments do business and the way societies understand and view dual nationals to create a more tolerant and diverse world. One that reflects changing demographic dynamics.

 Ken Reiman

ACKNOWLEDGEMENTS

There are many people I would like to thank for their support in making this book project possible. First, my family, particularly my wife who steadfastly encouraged me to tell my story with candor. My two children for inspiring me to create a better world for them. The editors and team at Indigo Publishing for believing in me and the message of duality. The coaches and teammates who shared their time and contacts to connect me with the right publisher. Finally, the State Department for allowing me to experience life as a U.S. diplomat and sharing that experience with others through the publication of this book. May we continue to raise the bar higher in meeting the expectations of the American people and the world we serve.

About the Author

Ken O. Reiman

Ken Reiman is a current United States Foreign Service Officer for the United States Department of State. Ken has served for over 16 years in the diplomatic corps as a U.S. diplomat faithfully serving the United States in every cone of expertise: political, economic, consular, public affairs, and management. From his entry into the Foreign Service in 2002, and subsequent first diplomatic assignment in Taiwan, Ken's career of service has spanned four geographic regions from Asia to Africa to South America and the Caribbean.

Eager to contribute to the success of U.S. diplomacy, Ken has coached U.S. ambassadors and senior State Department officials, selected the future of the Foreign Service, advised Members of Congress, liaised with foreign ministers and heads of state, mentored diplomats, and trained foreign affairs professionals for overseas assignments in Asia and Africa. He speaks Mandarin, Japanese, and French.

Ken is the recipient of numerous Department of State Medals of Honor and Letters of Commendation for his diplomatic service in advancing United States political, economic and commercial interests, managing crises, and protecting United States citizens overseas. He is the proud parent of two Japanese American boys: John and Max to whom this book is dedicated.

CPSIA information can be obtained
at www.ICGtesting.com
Printed in the USA
LVHW012054120720
660475LV00011B/455

9 781950 906055